FIRST LOGIC

THIRD EDITION

Michael F. Goodman

University Press of America,® Inc.
Lanham · Boulder · New York · Toronto · Plymouth, UK

Copyright © 2012 by
University Press of America,® Inc.
4501 Forbes Boulevard
Suite 200
Lanham, Maryland 20706
UPA Acquisitions Department (301) 459-3366

10 Thornbury Road
Plymouth PL6 7PP
United Kingdom

Library of Congress Control Number: 2012946949
ISBN: 978-0-7618-6007-5 (paperback : alk. paper)
eISBN: 978-0-7618-6008-2

This book is dedicated to

Jay and Moira

Table of Contents

Preface to the Third Edition

The usual reasons for a subsequent edition of a textbook being issued are, one, to correct significant errors, typographical and otherwise, and two, to incorporate new as well as revised materials. These reasons apply here. The exercises in most chapters have been both revised and expanded, sometimes largely. A number of significant changes (read "improvements") have taken place. As a result of the lack of use of the two chapters on Aristotelian Logic, they have been entirely deleted from this edition. This is *not* by any means for a lack of appreciation of the Aristotelian system. What is wanted is a text which does not contain chapters not studied in the classes for which this book was written. The Aristotelian chapters were simply not being used.

I remain convinced that presentation is *the* crucial element in teaching and learning and I am continually on the hunt for the better way of tendering the discipline of logic. The probability is high that some errors still exist within, both in the simple aspect of the typography as well as in the substantive areas of logic itself. Whatever errors there may be are my responsibility alone.

I wish to thank my friends, teachers and colleagues at Michigan State University, San Diego State University and Humboldt State University for helping to make clearer to me ideas surrounding the concepts and techniques of logic. Counted here are Herb Hendry, Jim Derden, Stan Weissman, Bob Snyder, Loren Cannon, Tom Weston, Joe Hanna, Stan Mortel, and Rich Hall. Also, many thanks are due to the numerous students in *all* of my logic courses over the years for helping this sometimes backward teacher. Special thanks are due to my wife Hollie for her unfailing patience with me during this rewrite.

MFG
Arcata, CA

Key to Symbols:

R,S	predicate letters (A – T, 'Rx' = 'x is an R')
p,q	sentence letters (also, 'r' / 's' / 't' / 'u')
x,y	individual variables (also 'w' / 'z')
•	conjunction ('and' / 'both')
v	disjunction ('or' / 'unless')
→	material implication ('if...then' / 'only if' / 'implies that')
↔	material equivalence ('if and only if' / 'necessary and sufficient')
⇔	logical equivalence
-	negation ('not' / 'it is false that' / 'it is not the case that')
⊢	conclusion indicator
(∃)	existential quantifier ('(∃x),' 'there exists an x such that')
(Φ)	universal quantifier ('(x),' 'for any x')
=	identity ('x = y' = 'x is identical with y')
( )	groupers (e.g., (r → s)), also, brackets ('[ ]') and braces ('{ }')

1. Core Concepts

1.1. Preliminaries

It is impossible to define the term *logic* in one sentence, unless you are willing to overlook detail. It is the study of the nature of argumentation, good and bad reasoning, language, statements and assertions, inference, induction and deduction, soundness, consistency and a great deal more. Essentially, the logician (one who studies logic) begins with the search for the distinguishing features of correct and incorrect arguments. And since some of the features of arguments in general are soundness and validity, it follows that the logician will also be interested in these concepts.

The study of logic has a practical as well as a theoretical side; it is simple and complex, even in a first course. On the practical side we might ask, "How is the study of logic to be of help in my everyday activities?" Part of the answer to this question is that since we already know how to reason pretty well already, without having studied logic formally, and since we use this knowledge every day, and since studying logic can only heighten this ability, it follows that studying logic will help us to reason better in the everyday, ordinary world. For instance, let's say you have a friend who feels quite strongly about which Senatorial candidate should be elected. Your friend says, "My candidate is for strong but fair measures in timber harvesting, while the other candidate has expressed no interest in environmental concerns whatsoever." You're friend has just given a reason for voting a certain way. Behind that reason is an argument. And, though it is unstated, you understand the argument well enough not to ask your friend to make it explicit. The argument might be:

> Whichever candidate expresses environmental concern is the candidate for which we should vote. My candidate expresses environmental concern; the other candidate doesn't. You are concerned with the environment. Hence, you should vote for my candidate.

There are argument that are not straightforward in the least, however, arguments we cannot be quite so confident about accepting. Consider:

> The Christian God commands people to love one another. This God

1

would never command people to do something which is impossible for them to do. It is impossible for people to control their emotions. Hence, love is not an emotion.

Analyzing these arguments from a logical point of view is but one way we have of determining whether or not they are acceptable. We will be outlining various techniques used by logicians in the chapters that follow.

There is a way of testing the acceptability of an argument that is not within the purview of the logician *qua* logician. Simply put, if one or more of the sentences supporting the conclusion in an argument is false, the argument is unacceptable. And of course you don't have to be a logician to tell when some sentence is true or false. Consider the following two arguments:

(A)	(B)
All bricks are toys.	All dolphins are mammals
All toys are blue.	All mammals are warm-blooded.
So, all bricks are blue.	So, all dolphins are warm-blooded.

Both (A) and (B) are acceptable from the logician's perspective. This is to say that *if* each of the first two sentences of each argument is true, then the last sentence of each argument will also be true. The operative word here is "if." We note, however, that each of the sentences in (A) is false. Hence, we would never find ourselves being convinced by this argument. That is, we would never come to believe that bricks are blue based on the sentences that all bricks are toys and all toys are blue.

Argument (B), on the other hand, is a different matter. It has the same form or structure as (A), but the sentences are different. If you believe that the first two sentences in (B) are true, then presumably you also believe the last is true. But what if you aren't sure about the truth of, say, the second sentence in (B)? If you want to know whether it *is* true, you might find a marine biologist and ask. It wouldn't be a good idea to ask a logician because matters of marine biology are not the kinds of things most logicians are formally trained to know about. In fact, the study of logic itself is not designed to give a person increased knowledge about what is and what is not true about the world, as far as factual information is concerned. One must go outside one's study of logic to obtain this sort of knowledge.

Back to argument (B). If we were to discover that the first two sentences are true, then it seems we would be compelled to believe that the third sentence is also true. If we failed to accept the third sentence as true while at the same time believing that the first two are true, we would be guilty of faulty reasoning, of committing an implicit contradiction (more on contradictions further along).

An important fact to remember about logic is that it is a tool. Aristotle, the ancient Greek philosopher, wrote the first treatise on logic that we know of. He called it "Organon" (organ or instrument). Some people find the study of logic fun, simply learning about it. Nonetheless, we *use* logic, every day. We are constantly bombarded with arguments attempting to persuade us to buy this product, vote for that person, accept this proposal, arrive on time for that meeting, and so on. One of the most effective methods that has been devised for deciding whether to accept or reject any given argument is logical analysis of arguments themselves. And this logical analysis is what much of this book explores; its concepts, content, and techniques.

1.2. Basic Terms and Concepts

An *argument* is a series of assertions (two or more) about the world, one of which is intended to follow from the other(s). Example:

(1) If infanticide is morally permissible, killing is not wrong.
(2) If killing is not wrong, then suicide is not wrong.
(3) So, if infanticide is morally permissible, suicide is too.

Sentences (1) and (2) above are called the *premises*. They are supposed to provide a certain amount of support for the *conclusion* (3). When the premises provide complete or conclusive support, the conclusion is said to follow from the premises with logical necessity. This is to say that, necessarily, if the premises are true, the conclusion is true, or, if one accepts the premises (as true), then one is bound to, or *must*, accept the conclusion (as true). When premises provide less than full support for a conclusion, but do provide *some* support, the conclusion is said to follow from the premises with some degree of probability. For example,

(1) When Butch goes camping, he takes an axe.
(2) Butch has an axe with him now.
(3) It follows that Butch is going camping now.

In the above argument, the conclusion does not follow with necessity from the premises. Even if the premises are true, Butch may not be going camping at all, but perhaps taking the axe to get it sharpened or perhaps taking it home after just having purchased it. Butch might be intending to do many other things by having the axe with him, none of which involve going camping at that moment. However, we say it is *probable* that Butch is going camping, because *usually* when he is carrying his axe around, he is indeed going camping.

Part of the specific vocabulary of logic, as a discipline, is the meaning of the term *valid*. It applies to arguments only. An argument is said to be *valid* if it is impossible for the premises to be true while the conclusion is false. This is the definition of 'valid argument' that will be used throughout this book. It is *the* definition of 'valid argument' used by all logicians working in a system such as this. Any argument that is not valid is termed *invalid*. The following arguments are valid and invalid, respectively.

(A)
Some nurses are trained in surgical techniques.
All those trained as such can perform surgery.
Hence, some nurses can perform surgery.

(B)
All oil paints are slow to dry.
Some things that are slow to dry are made of concrete.
So, some oil paints are made of concrete.

It can be seen that if the premises in (A) are true, then the conclusion cannot be false, while in (B) it is quite possible that even if the premises were true, the conclusion could be false. As it turns out, the conclusion in (B) is, indeed, false.

As will become increasingly apparent, the concept of truth is extremely important for much of the logician's work. Recall, however, the earlier remark that it is not the logician's job to determine which sentences in arguments are in fact true and which are false. The basic question that concerns the logician at this level is this: *Is the argument valid or invalid?* But on our definition of validity, we appeal to the notion of truth. The closest the logician comes to talking about the actual truth of sentences is when a certain kind of argument is referred to, namely, a *sound argument. A sound argument is an argument that is valid and has true premises.* For example, consider the following two arguments:

Christian Huygens was either a scientist or a poet, but not both.
Huygens lived between 1629 and 1693 and wasn't a poet.
It is shown, hence, that Christian Huygens was a scientist.

Christian Huygens was either a scientist or a poet, but not both.
Huygens lived between 1625 and 1695 and wasn't a scientist.
Hence, Christian Huygens was a poet.

The first is sound because a) it is valid and b) both premises are true. The second argument is unsound, however, because Huygens did not live between 1625 and 1695, which fact renders the second premise of the second argument false. The second argument *is* valid, however. This is so because *if* the premises of the second argument *were* true, the conclusion would also have to be true. Given the definition of 'sound argument,' the only way valid unsound arguments differ from valid sound arguments is that the former have one or more false premises.

1.3. Validity and Acceptability

It may sound odd that a valid argument may be unacceptable and that an invalid argument may be acceptable. But on the definition of validity we have adopted both of these oddities are quite possible. Consider the following argument.

If Yuma is 20 miles east of San Diego, Yuma is in California.
Yuma is 20 miles east of San Diego.
Therefore, Yuma is in California.

This is a valid argument because if the premises were true, it would be impossible for the conclusion to be false. However, since the second premise *is* false, and would be rejected by anyone who knows this fact, the argument itself is also to be rejected. In other words, where one or more of the premises in any argument is/are unacceptable, the entire argument is unacceptable. If this argument were presented to a person who knows that Yuma is not 20 miles from San Diego, but does not know whether Yuma is in California, this person would not come to believe that Yuma is in California on the basis of the premises alone. This is not meant to imply that the person would come to believe that Yuma is not in California simply because the second premise is false, however. Consider the following argument:

Earp is the easternmost town in California.
Reno is west of Earp.
Therefore, Reno is in California.

Each of the premises of the argument above is true. But the conclusion is not true. These facts show that the argument is invalid. Owing to the particular geographical shape of California, some towns outside of California are west of the easternmost town in California. A person could, however, come to believe that Reno is in California on the basis of the premises above. But this could only be so if the person failed to consider, or was perhaps incorrect about, the shape of California. A crucial point here is that since the conclusion is false, the argument is unacceptable, which should make it clear that any argument containing one or more false sentences (whether as a premise or as a conclusion) is unacceptable.

As can be seen from the examples above, arguments can have premises with varied *truth values* and still be valid ('truth value' is a term used to name a certain characteristic of sentences; the truth value of a true sentence is truth and the truth value of a false sentence is falsehood). That is, a valid argument can have all true premises and a true conclusion, or all false premises and a false conclusion, or all false premises and a true conclusion, or one or more false premises and a true conclusion, or one or more (but not all) true premises and a false conclusion. What a valid argument *cannot* have is all true premises and a false conclusion. Each of the following four arguments is valid.

John F. Kennedy was the 35th U.S. President.	True
Kennedy was born in Massachusetts.	True
So, the 35th President was born in Massachusetts.	True

Cantinflas starred in the movie "Key Witness."	False
"Key Witness" was a biography of Einstein.	False

Hence, Cantinflas starred in a biography of Einstein.	False

The cane toad's paratoid gland produces toxic secretions.	True
If this is true, then only the cane snake is its predator.	False
So, only the cane snake is a predator of the cane toad.	False

Abraham Lincoln was born in 1808..	False
Edgar Allen Poe was born in 1808..	False
Charles Darwin was born in 1808.	False
Hence, Lincoln, Poe and Darwin were born in the same year.	True

Each of these arguments is valid because if the premises were all true, it would be impossible for the conclusions to be false. The last of the arguments is the most interesting of the group, as it is hard to believe that false premises could lead to a true conclusion. What is important is not that the premises are in fact false, but that *if* they were true, the conclusion would also have to be true. It turns out that Lincoln, Darwin and Poe were each born in 1809, rendering the premises false and the conclusion true.

What makes an argument valid or invalid has nothing to do with the content of the argument. Validity and invalidity are products of the form of arguments. *It is form that matters, not content.* For example, we can use the same form as in the third argument above, borrow some nonsense from Lewis Carroll and Dr. Seuss, and still get a valid argument:

Snarks are sneeches.
If snarks were sneeches, then oceans would be beaches.
Hence, oceans are beaches.

The important question regarding the validity of any argument is always, *Could the conclusion be false while the premises are true?* When one applies this question to any argument, if the answer is *yes*, then the argument is invalid. If the answer is *no*, the argument is valid. Consider another example where form clearly determines validity.

All comets are made primarily of dust and ice.
All comets release huge amounts of gas as they approach the sun.
Therefore, all comets are comets.

The first thing to notice here is that the conclusion is logically true, which is to say that there is no case in which the conclusion is false. On this consideration alone, we see that it would be impossible for the premises to be true while the conclusion is false because the conclusion cannot be false. So, the argument is valid. It is valid strictly by virtue of the definition of *valid argument* we have adopted. Even if the conclusion had nothing to do with the premises, say, if the conclusion were "All flutes are flutes," the argument would still be valid. *It's all form.*

Back to acceptability. To repeat, each of the arguments above is valid. However, with the exception of the first, each argument is to be rejected solely on the basis of there being at least one premise that is false. An important point to remember is that validity and acceptability are neither mutually inclusive nor mutually exclusive. The same point can also be made with respect to invalidity and unacceptability. From the strictly logical point of view, all invalid arguments are unacceptable because the premises do not fully establish the conclusion. However, in the lived world, i.e., the world of our everyday experience, we rarely, if ever, take the strictly logical point of view. There are always other factors to consider. This leads us to affirm that some invalid arguments are not to be rejected lightly. Consider:

> Bus 17 has passed Caleb's house at 2am for the last 15 years.
> The time is now 1:51am.
> Hence, Bus 17 will pass Caleb's house in 9 minutes.

The extreme regularity of Bus 17, as evidenced by the first premise above, would lead us to believe that it is highly probable that the bus will again come by at 2am. "Probable" is the key term here, for we realize that it is possible for a bus to be early or late on any given day for any given destination. Strictly speaking, it is possible for the premises to be true and the conclusion false in the above argument, that is, that the bus will pass Caleb's house in more or less than 9 minutes. But since the conclusion follows from the premises with (in this case) a high degree of probability, we would accept the argument. What this means in practical terms is that if Caleb is at all interested in catching the bus, then he will get to the bus stop a bit early just in case the bus arrives early.

In accepting the argument, we would by no means be affirming that the conclusion follows with any sort of logical necessity. We would simply be saying that, based on past evidence, it is highly likely that the train will pass in 9 minutes. A more difficult argument to assess is the following:

> On 43% of the days with weather patterns of kind R, it has rained.
> Today's weather pattern is of kind R.
> Hence, it will probably rain today.

Weather forecasting is notoriously difficult, and it comes as no surprise if we find ourselves undecided about accepting or rejecting the above argument, because 43% is not such a high percentage that we can be very confident that it will rain. Our first inclination might be to point out that even a 75-90% chance of rain only yields that much probability; and a probability it remains. However, that we are dealing in percentages here no one denies. What is important is the fact that as the probability that it will rain increases, it seems natural to say that the acceptability of the argument increases in due proportion.

This being so, we say there are degrees of acceptability of arguments. The imprecision we note of arguments with only probable conclusions bespeaks the difficulty students of logic typically recognize in assessing them. No attempt will be made here to treat these sorts of arguments in detail. The point in devoting space to them at all is that arguments of this kind frequently occur and it is well to be able to distinguish arguments whose conclusions follow with some degree of probability from those whose conclusions do not, and also to recognize that just because these arguments are formally invalid, that in itself is not a reason to dismiss them out of hand. Here is one further example. If you get up in the morning, check the local weather forecast on the television, and discover that there is a 93% chance of rain during the day, you are more than likely going to prepare by taking an umbrella, a raincoat and/or a hat when you go out (we assume that you trust, more or less, such forecasts). The argument being accepted here is something such as this:

> The meteorologist forecasts 93% chance of rain.
> The meteorologist is usually pretty close in her/his predictions.
> If it is going to rain, I will need an umbrella. . . .
> It is highly likely that it will rain.
> So, it is highly likely that I will need an umbrella. . . .

This is an acceptable argument, because if the premises are true, then it is highly likely that the conclusion is true as well. Might all the premises be true and the conclusion false? Yes. Hence, the argument is invalid. So, what we have here is an acceptable invalid argument.

One important conclusion of this section is that some valid arguments are not arguments we would accept, while some invalid arguments are arguments that we *would* accept.

An argument's acceptability is conditioned by the unique beliefs held by the judge of the argument. An argument will be acceptable to a person if the person has good reason to believe that the premises are true and if he/she judges that the conclusion follows with a somewhat high degree of probability (there is no clear answer as to what level of probability is itself acceptable). Consider, for example, the following argument about which horse in a race it would be good to place a bet on:

> Joy Ride has been out of the money in the last 5 races on turf.
> Joy Ride has been in the money in only 3 of the last turf races.
> Joy Ride's best time at 8½ furlongs on turf is 2:57.
> Yet Stay has been in the money in the last 8 races on turf.
> Yet Stay's best time at 8½ furlongs on turf is 2:54.
> Today's race is a turf race.
> Joy Ride and Yet Stay are in the race today.
> No other horse in the race has as good a time on turf as these two horses.

Hence, the best bet in this race is Yet Stay.

On the basis of this eight-premise argument alone, we might affirm that it would indeed be most prudent to bet on Yet Stay. But, what if you saw Joy Ride's workout on the morning of the race, were impressed, and came to believe that Joy Ride was "due for a win"? You might also note that the difference in turf times for Joy Ride and Yet Stay is only 3 seconds. "That's not much," you think. Now a friend points out that these two horses have been in seven races together, and that Joy Ride has never come in ahead of Yet Stay. But you reply that Yet Stay has just gotten over a cold and must be a bit weak from the illness. Your friend notes that Yet Stay is carrying two pounds less weight, including jockey and gear, than Joy Ride. You reply that this is the first time this jockey has ever ridden Yet Stay but that the jockey on Joy Ride has ridden Joy Ride three times previously, with one win and two places.

And so it goes, with seemingly good reasons for betting on either horse. It seems especially difficult to determine just what is to count as an overriding reason for choosing to bet on one horse rather than the other. The set of beliefs held by the person betting will surely lead that person to bet one way or the other. Hence, one set of premises will "move" the person betting in a way which the other set won't. Perhaps, for example, the person thinks it's much more important that Yet Stay had a cold than that it is carrying two pounds less than Joy Ride. Since the logic of psychology is not within the scope of this book, this is a good place to stop, the point having been made that some arguments are more difficult to analyze for acceptability than others.

As a general principle, we will say an argument is *acceptable* if there is sufficient reason to believe the premises to be true and if the conclusion follows from the premises with at least a high degree of probability.

1.4. Inductive Arguments

The name applied to any argument in which the conclusion follows with some degree of probability (but does not follow conclusively) is *inductive argument*. For example,

A large majority of Pavlov's dogs have been trained to salivate at the sound of a certain bell. Don recently acquired one of Pavlov's dogs. So, Don's dog will salivate at the sound of a certain bell.

Presuming that Don's dog was one of the majority that was trained to salivate at the sound of the bell, unless the dog was somehow "de-programmed," we can be confident that it will salivate when it hears the ring of the bell. Confidence, however, is not identical with knowledge. Many things may happen/have happened which might prevent Don's dog from salivating when it hears the bell, e.g., it may not have been trained as well as some of the other dogs, or it might, unknown to us, actually have been retrained. The point is that though it is *logi-*

cally possible that the conclusion is false while the premises are true, we have good reason to believe that the dog will indeed salivate on command, i.e., reason to believe that the conclusion is *not* false. This is especially so if there is no available evidence that the dog was in fact retrained, etc. Hence, since it is possible that the premises are true and the conclusion is false, we admit that the argument is formally invalid, but, for all that, that the argument is more or less acceptable.

Another example of an inductive argument is one that proceeds from premises that are either
particular or of limited scope to a conclusion that is a generalization. Consider:

> The raven I observed on Monday was black.
> The raven I observed on Wednesday was black.
> The raven I observed on Saturday was black.
> Hence, all ravens are black.

The premises in the above argument are all particular, specifying the observation of a certain bird (e.g., the one seen on Monday). The conclusion, however, is general, a generalization, universal in scope. In chapter 2, we will encounter a fallacy of reasoning known as Hasty Generalization. The above argument commits this fallacy because while there is some evidence that all ravens are black (that is, the three ravens that were observed), the number of observations of black ravens in this case is much too low to warrant the universal conclusion. The conclusion is drawn "hastily." Even if a very large number of observed ravens turned out to be black, all that one would be logically permitted to claim would be that "probably" all ravens are black. It is unclear what a sufficiently large number of observations would be in this sort of case.

Inductive arguments can also have particular conclusions. The argument below is a good example.

> Ninety-three percent of rock guitarists play guitars made either by Fender or Gibson.
> John Mayer and Stephen Stills are rock guitarists.
> Hence, it is likely that Mayer and Stills play guitars made either by Fender or Gibson.

Most people would say that this argument is acceptable even though the conclusion may be false while the premises are true. The reason for its acceptability would be that ninety-three percent is fairly large.

Here is another example of an inductive argument that has a conclusion that is particular.

> When Sue goes fishing, she takes her fishing rod along.
> She has her fishing rod with her now.
> Therefore, Sue is going fishing.

Notice that this argument doesn't say that there is a probability that Sue is going fishing. It says nothing about probabilities at all. The point is that even though the argument doesn't state as much, it is indeed probable (given the premises) that Sue is going fishing. The probability may be high or low, depending on whether the evidence is strong or weak. That is, perhaps Sue's having her rod with her really isn't very good evidence that she's going fishing. The argument, then, would be counted by us as less acceptable than the following argument:

> When Sue goes fishing, she takes her fishing rod along.
> She also takes her waders and her tackle box.
> She has her rod, her waders, and her tackle box with her now.
> Therefore, Sue is going fishing.

The more evidence we mount for a conclusion, the more acceptable the argument becomes, because an increase in evidence increases probability. However, the argument is still invalid just because the premises may all be true and, still, Sue may not be going fishing but rather, say, to a costume party.

Perhaps one of the most common of all inductive arguments is the one that proceeds from premises based on knowledge about the past to a conclusion that makes a claim about the future. It is called the predictive argument. A few examples are in order.

> Gene spilled honey on the counter last Thursday evening, failed clean it up, and ants gathered to eat it by Friday morning.
> Kathy spilled honey on the counter last Sunday evening, failed to clean it up, and ants gathered to eat it by Monday morning.
> Ty spilled honey on the counter last Tuesday evening, failed to clean it up, and ants gathered to eat it by Wednesday morning.
> We can conclude that the next time anyone spills honey on the counter and fails to clean it up, ants will gather to eat it.

> The sun has risen in the Eastern sky every morning for millions of years.
> Hence, the sun will rise in the Eastern sky tomorrow morning.

> Ever since Mrs. Hirsch moved into the neighborhood, when we hit a ball into her yard, she takes it into her house and won't give it back to us. So, if we hit another ball into her yard, she'll take it and not give it back.

Each one of these three arguments goes from premises that rely on some knowledge or reasonable belief about events in the past to conclusions that make predictions about the future. In each case, it is not difficult to imagine an alteration of events that would make the conclusions false while the premises remain true. The second argument is perhaps the most famous. At least two scenarios may come to mind here: a) Scientists assure us that the sun will eventually cease to exist. When that occurs, it will most definitely not rise in the Eastern sky. b) Imagine a situation in which the Earth suddenly begins to rotate on its axis in the opposite direction. In that case, the sun would rise in the Western sky, not the Eastern.

The ideas put forth in both (a) and (b) above are themselves products of inductive reasoning. This is so in the case of (a) because scientists base their predictions of the sun's demise in part on the probability that the laws of nature will remain the same as they are at present. It is the same with scenario (b); while it is not impossible for the Earth to change its rotation, it is highly unlikely, given what we know about past events having consequences for the stability of the Earth in its rotation. This reasoning is inductive.

1.5. Deductive Arguments

There is disparity between the way different logicians characterize *deductive arguments*. All seem to agree, however that deductive arguments are either valid or invalid. A *valid deductive argument* is an argument in which it is impossible for the premises to be true and the conclusion false at the same time. This is, essentially, the definition of a valid argument. Take two examples:

> All of Frank's books are clothbound.
> All clothbound books are more expensive than paperbacks.
> So, all of Frank's books are more expensive than paperbacks.

> If Monica is a professional, then she has responsibilities.
> If Monica has responsibilities, then she has an ethical code.
> So, if Monica is a professional, then she has an ethical code.

If the premises were true in each of these arguments, then the conclusions of the arguments could not be false. Hence, they are both valid arguments. Consider the following argument.

> No Republicans are Democrats.
> No college administrators are Democrats.
> Therefore, No Republicans are college administrators.

Pretend for a moment that all the premises in this argument are true. This argument contains no statement of probability, either in the premises or in the conclusion. In fact, it looks as though anyone who presented this argument might judge that the conclusion followed, not with mere probability, but with certainty, or, that the premises provided conclusive support for the conclusion. We know that this is not so, however, since the argument can be shown to be invalid, that is, that it is possible that the premises are true while the conclusion is false. Given that it would not be appropriate to call this argument *inductive*, since the conclusion does not seem to follow with *any* degree of probability whatsoever from the given set of premises, we can call this argument an *invalid deductive argument*. An invalid deductive argument is simply an invalid argument that is not inductive.

The duel concepts of deductive and inductive arguments will not be stressed in further chapters. While the discussion in the last two sections is important for understanding two forms in which arguments are presented, it is still the validity/invalidity of arguments that the logician has as a major object of concern. Hence, these concepts (validity and invalidity) will be crucial to much that follows.

1.6. Recognizing Arguments

As mentioned, the two major constituents of an argument are the premise(s) and the conclusion. When one is being careful in constructing an argument, one usually makes it explicit just what conclusion one has in mind. When we want to call anyone's attention to the conclusion of an argument, we mark it off from the premises by including a word or phrase intended to draw attention to the fact that the sentence coming up is the conclusion. We call such words and phrases *conclusion indicators*. Some conclusion indicators are:

Therefore	So	This proves that
Thus	In conclusion	It follows that
Consequently	We may conclude that	We may infer that
Hence	This entails that	This shows that

Similarly, to note that some sentence in an argument is a premise, rather than the conclusion, we use a *premise indicator*. Some premise indicators are:

Since	For	Inasmuch as
As	Because	For the reason that
Follows from	As indicated by	May be inferred from

In the examples that follow, it will be shown that the structures of arguments are as diverse as the subject matters themselves with which they deal. Consider the following argument, in which the conclusion is stated at the beginning.

A great uncertainty surrounds the concept of the nature of the mind, inasmuch as science explains it in physical terms, religion explains in spiritual terms, and some philosophers explain it in ways different from either of these.

There are a number of points to be made here. First, up until now I have presented most arguments in a quite linear fashion, stating premises first and conclusions last. Second, note that the argument above is presented as one sentence.

This should cause no concern because we can pick out at least four separate ideas being put forward. Each of these ideas can be seen as assertions about the world and can be translated into premises and conclusion. The premise indicator is "inasmuch as" and appears directly after the first complete thought in the argument. When we breakdown what follows the indicator phrase, we come up with the following three sentences, the premises of the argument:

Science explains the mind in physical terms.
Religion explains mind in spiritual terms.
Some philosophers explain mind in ways different from both science and religion.

Since these three sentences follow the premise indicator, these three sentences are the premises. Note how these three sentences are supporting, or presenting evidence in favor of, the conclusion. The next argument is different.

As mind can be explained in physical terms, it follows that mind is a physical entity, since it would be impossible for mind and body to interact if mind were spiritual.

Here, the conclusion appears as the middle sentence, bounded by sentences each of which contains a premise indicator. In general, an indicator word or phrase comes directly prior to the sentence it indicates as premise or conclusion. The next argument is again different.

For the reasons that John Locke and Baruch Spinoza were born in the same year, and that the year was 1632, and that they were both interested in the study of philosophy, we conclude that Locke and Spinoza were contemporary philosophers of the 17th century.

The above is a three-premise argument, with the (plural) premise indicator "for the reasons that" appearing at the beginning of the sentence itself and the conclusion indicator "we conclude that" appearing directly before the conclusion. Another way of representing the same argument would be:

Since Locke and Spinoza were born in the same year, and since they were born in 1632, and since they were both interested in philosophy, it follows that they were contemporary 17th century philosophers.

This shows that it is not so much how one expresses an argument that matters as long as the meaning of the sentences is uniform throughout. Premise and conclusion indicators are interchangeable whenever they occur. That is, 'as,' for example, is no less an indicator of a premise than 'since' or 'because' or 'inasmuch as.'

The occurrence of premise and conclusion indicators greatly increases one's chances of recognizing not only the premise(s) and conclusion in some argument but also that some set of sentences comprises an argument at all. The following two sentences are not arguments, even though they contain what may look like premise and conclusion indicators.

As you can see, WWII was preceded by economic instability and uncertainty.

With the decline in social status of the poor, so too an increase in crime follows.

Neither of these sentences is presenting support, or evidence, for any conclusion. They both simply state a fact, or opinion.

A crucial point to remember when attempting to pick out an argument is that an argument is intended to show (explicitly or implicitly) that one of the sentences follows from another, or some others. Consider the following argument, without indicators:

In Missouri and Alabama you can get yourself imprisoned for having one marijuana cigarette in your possession, while in Oregon you get a slap on the hand and in California you can make a few bucks. The Law sure is strange.

If you're not sure what to make of this argument, at least you're not alone, as it isn't very clear exactly what conclusion the arguer is putting forth. It could be that the arguer is just misinformed about the fact that various states have various laws regarding drug possession. Or, it could be that the arguer is making some claim about the concept of law itself. The conclusion is ambiguous and would need to be made explicit for purposes of analysis. For all that, there really does seem to be an argument here.

There is a certain sort of sentence that looks like an argument to many people, initially, but isn't. It is called a *conditional sentence*. The most common way of expressing a conditional is by using the "if . . . then" construction, like so:

If jobs decrease, then the number of welfare recipients will increase.

In a way, the first part of the sentence (called the *antecedent*) looks like a premise and the second part (the *consequent*) looks like a conclusion. However, there is no premise or conclusion here. The primary distinction we can point to between a conditional and an argument is that in an argument the premises are stated as assertions whereas in a conditional the antecedent is not stated as an assertion in its own right but is preceded by the term "if." The sentence above does not assert that jobs will decrease, but is saying that *if* jobs decrease, then welfare recipients will increase.

The following are each conditionals, with the "conditional indicators" in Italics:

> Frank will go sailing tomorrow *if* Eddie and John go.
> We'll go sailing *only if* the weather isn't stormy.
> Hoisting the jib is a *sufficient condition* for catching wind.
> Trimming sail is a *necessary condition* for losing wind.
> John will crew *on the condition that* the boat is sound.
> John's crewing *implies that* the boat is sound.

Much more is to be said about conditionals, as sentences, but will have to wait for Chapter 3.

1.7. Counterexamples

Thus far, the discussion has worked mainly around the concepts of validity and invalidity of arguments of various forms, but without indicating how one can determine whether any given argument is or is not valid. In this section, a method for showing the invalidity of arguments is presented. It is typically known as the *counterexample method* or as *refutation by analogy*. It is important to keep in mind that this method is designed to show invalid arguments to be invalid; it is not designed to show valid arguments to be valid. Showing validity will be introduced when we get to the method of Truth Tables, Chapter 4.

Let's say someone presents the following argument,

> Since no IQ tests are reliable intelligence indicators, it follows that some reliable intelligence indicators are culturally neutral, because some culturally neutral exams are not IQ tests.

It will help in analyzing the argument by putting it into a more simple form, clearly indicating the premises and the conclusion, like so,

> Some culturally neutral exams are not IQ tests.
> No IQ tests are reliable intelligence indicators.
> So, some reliable intelligence indicators are culturally neutral.

In terms of the acceptability of the argument, one might first try to show one or both premises to be false. The second premise might look especially vulnerable, since some people would argue that IQ tests are reliable for measuring intelligence. This is a highly debatable issue and it is unclear how it can be resolved so that all concerned are satisfied. But this sort of consideration, that is, whether or not the argument is acceptable, does not tell us much about the actual validity of the argument. For that, we need some way of determining whether it is possible for the premises to be true and the conclusion false.

To show that the above argument is invalid, it suffices to show that there exists a second argument, *which has exactly the same form as the first*, in which the premises definitely are true and the conclusion definitely is false. Such an argument is the following:

Some racquetball players are not teenagers.	True
No teenagers are penguins.	True
So, some penguins are racquetball players.	False

That this argument has the same *form* as the first is shown by noting that the only changes made are the replacements of 'culturally neutral exams' with 'racquetball players,' 'IQ tests' with 'teenagers,' and 'reliable intelligence indicators' with 'penguins.' The second argument is clearly invalid, since each of the premises is obviously true and the conclusion is obviously false. The second argument shows that any argument with the same form as the original is invalid. This is true no matter what the content of the counterexample argument may be, i.e., no matter what the counterexample argument is about in terms of subject matter. What the counterexample method shows is that the original argument has an analogous argument in which the conclusion is false while the premises are true, or, that the conclusion does not follow from the premises. Since it is the *form* of arguments that matter, in terms of their validity, rather than their content, if one can show that the form of some argument disallows the conclusion following from the premises, one will have refuted all arguments of the same form, regardless of content.

Consider now the following argument:

All people who appreciate a good pass like to win.
All hockey fans like to win.
So, all hockey fans appreciate a good pass.

It is important to recognize that just because the conclusion in an argument is true, that does not mean that the conclusion follows from the given premises. In the above example, it is likely that, taken in a certain way, the conclusion is indeed true. If we say that a hockey fan is a person who knows a fair amount about the game, has watched the game played more than just a few times, understands many of the nuances of the game, including offensive and defensive maneuvers, likes the game, etc., then it would seem that, given that passing is a special kind of maneuver in the game of hockey, the fan would appreciate a pass that is well executed. A counterexample to the above argument is,

All bees are social creatures.	True
All chimpanzees are social creatures.	True
So, all chimpanzees are bees.	False

Below is another example:

> Either a Democrat or a Republican will win the election.
> A Democrat will win the election.
> So, a Republican won't win the election.

Counterexample:

Either lions or antelopes live on the African savannah.	True
Lions live on the African savannah.	True
So, antelopes don't live on the African savannah.	False

The first argument here is kind of tricky because of the use of the phrase "either/or" in the first premise. It is easy to make the judgment that when someone uses "either/or," that person is using it in the exclusive sense, that is, to mean "either one or the other but not both." However, even if the person making the argument above were using it in the exclusive sense, that does not alter the invalidity of the argument. The counterexample argument clearly has the same form as the original and has true premises and a false conclusion. The sense of 'either/or' being used here is the inclusive sense, which means "either one or the other and perhaps both."

To use the counterexample method is to attempt to create an argument with the same form as the one presented, but which has true premises and a false conclusion. It is important that the counter-example argument contain sentences that are clearly true and false, i.e., try to make the premises trivially true, as in "All bees are social creatures," and the conclusion trivially false, as in "All bees are chimpanzees." Most people find that beginning with a trivially false conclusion is the easiest. Then, simply match the counterexample premises with the premises of the original argument. An example:

> No retired corporate lawyers are people who have contributed to the
> literature on Freudian psychology.
> All people who have contributed to the literature on Freudian
> psychology are famous Freudian psychiatrists.
> So, no retired corporate lawyers are famous Freudian psychiatrists.

The form of this argument is:

> No xxx are yyy.
> All yyy are zzz.
> So, no xxx are zzz.

Now we must choose the subject matter of the refuting argument. We can use the following classes: {lions} {tigers} {animals}. The first step is to create a trivially false conclusion. Let us replace 'xxx' with 'lions' and 'zzz' with 'animals,' and create the following conclusion:

No lions are animals.

We can do the same with the premises:

No lions are yyy.
All yyy are animals.

What remains is to "plug in" the remaining category to replace 'yyy.' Let's replace 'yyy' with 'tigers,' the result being the following argument, which, being a legitimate counterexample, refutes the original argument.

No lions are tigers.	True
All tigers are animals.	True
So, no lions are animals.	False

Until now, we have been considering arguments with quite simple forms. The counterexample method of proving invalidity can be used, in principle, on *any* invalid argument. The following is an example of a different kind:

If the U.S. Space Program would have landed a person on the moon in 1961, the conspirators in the Kennedy assassination would have had second thoughts about their intentions. Since the first person to land on the moon landed in 1969, we can conclude that the conspirators had no second thoughts about the assassination.

Setting out the argument with its premises and conclusion shown explicitly, we can rephrase it as follows:

If the U.S. Space Program would have landed a person on the moon in 1961, the conspirators in the Kennedy assassination would have had second thoughts about their intentions.
The first person to land on the moon landed in 1969.
Hence, the conspirators had no second thoughts about the assassination.

To begin our counterexample, we put the argument in a simple form, as it were, deleting subject matter.

If xxx, then yyy
It is not the case that xxx.
Hence, it is not the case that yyy.

Next, we can choose classes to use: {Abraham Lincoln}, {Libertarians}, {People who value freedom}. We create a false conclusion and the result is the following counterexample:

If Lincoln was a libertarian, then he valued freedom.	True
Lincoln was not a libertarian.	True
Hence, Lincoln didn't value freedom.	False

It will be noticed that the counterexample method is not a purely mechanical method for proving the invalidity of arguments. One has to be creative, to pick an appropriate subject matter for showing true premises and false conclusion. Take the "Freud" example above; the following classes would not have worked in a counterexample to that argument: {triangles}, {cubes}, {three-sided figures}, because the attempted counterexample argument would have been,

No three-sided figures are cubes.	True
All cubes are triangles.	False
Hence, no three-sided figures are triangles.	True

This argument does not have all true premises and a false conclusion, which is what one is attempting to derive with the counterexample method. This leads to the important point that just because one is, at the moment, unable to come up with a counterexample for some argument that one suspects to be invalid, that inability does not show that it is impossible to come up with such an argument. It may just be a matter of using a different subject.

To create premises that are clearly true, and a conclusion that is clearly false, it is best to choose one's subject matter carefully. For example, many people who would be interested in a counterexample to some argument would know that all dogs are mammals, that all brothers are siblings, that no cubes are triangles, that libertarians value freedom, and so on. Probably fewer people know that the seat of origin for the emotions resides in a part of the brain called the amygdala, or that Phil Edwards was the first person to surf a place called Pipeline, or that Michigan State University was founded in 1855. Hence, these facts are not very good candidates for inclusion in counterexamples, albeit, strictly speaking, they *could* be used as premises in a counterexample because they are indeed true. It might be guessed that the nature of one's audience can be of importance here, for a biologist is more likely to know about the amygdala than, say, a bass player for a punk band (though one might be surprised about this), and a person interested in water sports is more likely to know about surf spots than a person who is not interested in water sports. Notwithstanding all of the above, it is just plain easier to create counterexamples when one chooses very common objects of reference.

Exercise: Ch. 1.

Notes: 1. Solutions to starred exercises are to be found in the back of the book. 2. The words "sentence," "statement," "assertion," and "proposition" will be used interchangeably throughout the exercises.

A. Which of the following sentences are true and which are false?

1. No valid argument is an unacceptable argument.
2. "Aristotle was a philosopher" is a valid statement.
3. No argument with a true conclusion is invalid.
4. No valid argument can have one or more false premises.
5.* All sound arguments are true arguments.
6. No argument with a true conclusion is unsound.
7. All arguments with true premises are acceptable.
8. 'Since' and 'hence' are both conclusion indicators.
9. All arguments with false premises are invalid.
10.* No valid argument can have any false premises.
11. The conclusion of one argument may appear as a premise in another.
12. All arguments have either premise or conclusion indicators.
13. Validity has to do with form, not content.
14. Soundness has to do with form, not content.
15.* Acceptability has to do with content, not form.
16. The counterexample method is used to prove validity.
17. Inductive arguments that present a great deal of evidence for their conclusions are invalid but acceptable.
18. One can show a strong inductive argument to be strong on the basis of form alone.
19. The following argument is valid.
     Pat, a logician, says all valid arguments are deductive.
     So, all valid arguments are deductive.
20.* The word "so" is always used as a conclusion indicator.

B. Which of the following contain arguments and which do not? Specify the premise(s) and the conclusion of each argument.

1. I think it may be laid down quite generally that *in so far* as physics or common sense is verifiable, it must be capable of interpretation in terms of actual sense-data alone. The reason for this is simple. Verification consists always in the occurrence of an expected sense-datum . . . . [B. Russell, *Our Knowledge of the External World*]
2. The more different manifestations you observe of one phenomenon, the more deeply you understand the phenomenon, and therefore the more clearly you can see the vein of sameness running through all those different things. [Douglas Hofstadter, *Metamagical Themas*]

3.   Philosophers push or iterate a question, usually about justification, so far that they cannot find any acceptable deeper answer. [Robert Nozick, *Philosophical Explanations*]

4.   Fresnel's view of the dependency involved here (the intensity is dependent on the propagations along all possible paths of the wavefront) is endorsed in contemporary physics, his mathematics for articulating the dependency is enshrined in elementary texts and is embedded in a richer mathematical framework in advanced discussions. So, by contemporary lights, it is hardly surprising that his discussions of interference and diffraction were so strikingly successful. [Philip Kitcher, *The Advancement of Science*]

5.* A complementary objection would be that I have exaggerated the degree to which a fine-grained naturalistic view can accommodate traditional ideas about the authority of morality. It might be said, in this spirit, that I have not given any reason to think that the considerations that are authoritative for an individual will always be moral considerations, in any plausible sense of that term. For I have not said anything that would rule out the possibility of someone's treating considerations as authoritative that would ordinarily be regarded as amoral, or morally eccentric, or even immoral. [Samuel Scheffler, *Human Morality*]

6.   There is a long philosophical tradition of distinguishing between *necessary* and *contingent* truths. The distinction is often explained along the following lines: a necessary truth is one which could not be otherwise, a contingent truth one which could; or, the negation of a necessary truth is impossible or contradictory, the negation of a contingent truth possible or consistent; or, a necessary truth is true in all possible worlds, a contingent truth is true in the actual but not in all possible worlds. Evidently, such accounts aren't fully explanatory, in view of their 'could (not) be otherwise,' '(im)possible,' 'possible world.' So the distinction is some-times introduced, rather, by means of examples: in a recent book '7 + 5 = 12,' 'If all men are mortal and Socrates is a man, then Socrates is mortal' and 'If a thing is red, it is coloured' are offered as examples of necessary truths, and 'The average rainfall in Los Angeles is about 12 inches' as an example of a contingent truth. [Susan Haack, *Philosophy of Logics*]

7.   If I am asked, 'What is good?' my answer is that good is good, and that is the end of the matter. Or if I am asked 'How is good to be defined' my answer is that it cannot be defined, and that is all I have to say about it. [G.E. Moore, *Principia Ethica*]

8.   There is no hope whatever that man's biological nature can be changed enough to enable him to survive without the earth's atmosphere; in fact, the very statement of this possibility is meaningless. *Homo sapiens* achieved his characteristics as a biological species more than 100,000 years ago, and his fundamental biological characteristics could not be drastically altered without destroying his very being. He developed his human attributes in the very act of responding to the environment in which he evolved. The earth has been his cradle and will remain his home. [Rene Dubois, *So Human An Animal*]

9.   Not for a single instant can I believe that David's schoolfellows did not recognize his superior mentality and, to some degree, acknowledge it. Who does

not recall that the big and awkward Samuel Johnson, who also was to remain ungainly all his life, was occasionally carried to school on the shoulders of the pupils in honourable tribute to his intellectual attainments? [E.C. Mossner, *The Life of David Hume*]

10.* When we compare the individuals of the same variety or sub-variety of our older cultivated plants and animals, one of the first points which strikes us is, that they generally differ more from each other than do the individuals of any species or variety in a state of nature. And if we reflect on the vast diversity of the plants and animals which have been cultivated, and which have varied during all ages under the most different climates and treatment, we are driven to conclude that this great variability is due to our domestic productions having been raised under conditions of life not so uniform as, and somewhat different from, those which the parent species had been exposed under nature. [Charles Darwin, *The Origin of Species*]

11. We have not seized any foreign land: what we took is not the property of others, but our ancestral heritage which for a time had been unjustly held by our enemies. Now that we have the opportunity, we are holding on to the heritage of our ancestors. [Maccabees: 1,15,33]

12. Of every malice that gains hatred in Heaven the end is injustice; and every such end, either by force or by fraud, afflicts another. But because fraud is an evil peculiar to man, it more displeases God, and therefore the fraudulent are the lower [in the circles of hell], and more pain assails them. [Dante, *The Inferno*]

13. Sometimes I feel like I will *never* stop
Just go on forever
Till one fine mornin'
I'm gonna reach up and grab me a handfulla stars
Throw out my long lean leg
And whip three hot strikes burnin' down the heavens
And look over at God and say
How about that!   [Samuel Allen, "To Satch"]

14. The primary defect of utilitarianism is that it ignores the rights of individuals and always creates a minority group whose needs and desires go unfulfilled. I say this because the utilitarian believes it is the majority of the people who should receive the happiness attending any action by a moral agent.

15.* Since heat is a secondary quality, unlike, say, solidity, and since secondary qualities are not in the objects themselves, we can say without much doubt that fire is not hot.

C.   State the premises and the conclusions in the arguments in the passages below. Some passages contain more than one argument. Some passages may not contain any argument at all.

1.   We know that there is a level of naive, commonsense, grandmother psychology and also a level of neurophysiology—the level of neurons and neuron modules and synapses and neuro-transmitters and boutons and all the rest of it.

So, why would anyone suppose that between these two levels there is also a level of mental processes which are computational processes? And indeed why would anyone suppose that it's at that level that the brain performs those functions that we regard as essential to the survival of the organism—namely the functions of information processing? [John Searle, *Minds, Brains and Science*]

2.   Men are disturbed not by things, but by the views which they take of things. Thus death is nothing terrible, else it would have appeared so to Socrates. But the terror consists in our notion of death, that it is terrible. When, therefore, we are hindered or disturbed, or grieved, let us never impute it to others, but to ourselves–that is, to our own views. [Epictetus, *The Enchiridion*]

3.   When in broad daylight I open my eyes, it is not in my power to choose whether I shall see or not, or to determine what particular objects shall present themselves to my view; and so likewise as to the hearing and other senses, the ideas imprinted on them are not creatures of my will. There is therefore some other will or spirit that produces them. [George Berkeley, *Principles of Human Knowledge*]

4.   He spoke, and many were willing to go with Diomedes.
The two Aiantes were willing, henchman of Ares, and
likewise Meriones, and Nestor's son altogether willing,
and Atreus' son was willing, Menelaos the spear-famed,
and patient Odysseus to was willing to enter the multitude
of Trojans, since forever the heart in his breast was daring.
                    [*The Iliad of Homer*]

5.*   Alice was beginning to get very tired of sitting by her sister on the bank, and of having nothing to do; once or twice she had peeped into the book her sister was reading, but it had no pictures or conversations in it, "and what is the use of a book," thought Alice, "without pictures or conversations?"

So she was considering in her own mind (as well as she could, for the hot day made her feel sleepy and stupid), whether the pleasure of making a daisy-chain would be worth the trouble of getting up and picking the daisies, when suddenly a white rabbit with pink eyes ran close by her. [Lewis Carroll, *Alice's Adventures in Wonderland*]

6.   Ever since philosophy began among the ancient Greeks, mathematics has been one of the great sources of philosophical problems. For the Greeks, mathematics was pre-eminently geometry; and if one studies geometry in the traditional manner, a host of philosophical questions comes flooding in right from the very beginning. [S.F. Barker, *Philosophy of Mathematics*]

7.   Fires were burning in the town, tall, fierce flames leaping high into the air. It was pointless to order the troops to put them out. Here and there, smoke was rising from the fires which they had lit in ovens and out of doors. Having collected their loot, soldiers were sprawled around their camp-fires like gypsies. How the Narva regiment had changed in two hours. [A. Solzhenitsyn, *August 1914*]

8.   The regulation of aggregate demand, it will be evident, is an organic requirement of the industrial system. In its absence there would be unpredictable

and almost certainly large fluctuations in demand and therewith in sales and production. Planning would be gravely impaired; capital and technology would have to be used much more cautiously and far less effectively than now. And the position of the technostructure, since it is endangered by the failure of earnings, would be far less secure. The need for regulation of aggregate demand is now fully accepted. [John Kenneth Galbraith, *The New Industrial State*]

9.   It is traditional to think of the difference between an analog and a digital encoding of information as the difference between a continuous and a discrete representation of some variable property at the source. So, for example, the speedometer on an automobile constitutes an analog encoding of information about the vehicle's speed because different speeds are represented by different positions of the pointer. [F. Dretske, "Sensation and Perception"]

10.* The self presents itself, then, as an organized whole, an integrated structure, and experiences are related to one another not through but within the whole. For that reason, when the structure is modified the nature of the experiences and relationships between them are also modified. The interdependence of different experiential groups shows that the self is a structure which is organized and "makes sense" and that each member occupies its proper place within the structure. [Risieri Frondizi, *Nature of Self*]

11. Since 'conscious that' is at least unusual if not outright one of those things we 'do not say,' and since 'conscious of' and 'aware of' are as close to being synonymous—to my ear—as any terms we are apt to find in ordinary language, a step in the direction of clarity and order can be taken by abandoning 'conscious that' and rendering 'conscious of' always as 'aware of,' thus forming all the Intentional idioms with 'aware.' [D.C. Dennett, *Content and Consciousness*]

12. When we run over libraries, persuaded of these principles, what havoc must we make? If we take in our hand any volume; of divinity or school metaphysics, for instance; let us ask, Does it contain any abstract reasoning concerning quantity or number? No. Does it contain any experi-mental reasoning concerning matter of fact and existence? No. Commit it then to the flames: for it can contain nothing but sophistry and illusion. [David Hume, *Enquiry Concerning Human Understanding*]

13. There is no doubt that the formalism of theories *can* be interpreted in terms of iconic models and that doing so is heuristically fruitful in suggesting hypotheses, developing theories, and so on. Nagel's and Hesse's position, however, is not merely that such models *can* be given and are useful in such a way, but that they are *essential* and *integral* components of theories. [Frederick Suppe, *The Structure of Scientific Theories*]

14. Whatever features an individual male person has which tend to his social and economic disadvantage (his age, class, height, etc.), one feature which never tends to his disadvantage in the society at large is his maleness. The case for females is the mirror image of this. Whatever features an individual female person has which tend to her social and economic advantage (her age, race, etc.), one feature which always tends to her disadvantage is her femaleness. Therefore, when a male's sex-category is the thing about him that gets first and most

repeated notice, the thing about him that is being framed and emphasized and given primacy is a feature which in general is an asset to him. When a female's sex-category is the thing about her that gets first and most repeated notice, the thing about her that is being framed and emphasized and given primacy is a feature which in general is a liability to her. [Marilyn Frye, "Sexism"]

15. There are seven windows given to animals in the domicile of the head, through which the air is admitted to the tabernacle of the body, . . . two nostrils, two eyes, two ears, and a mouth. So in the heavens, as in a macrocosmus, there are two favorable stars, two unpropitious, two luminaries, and Mercury undecided and indifferent. From this and many other similarities in nature, such as the seven metals, etc,. we gether that the number of planets is necessarily seven. [J.J. Fahie, *Galileo*]

16. At that time, which we call the big bang, the density of the universe and the curvature of space-time would have been infinite. Because mathematics cannot really handle infinite numbers, this means that the general theory of relativity (on which Friedmann's solutions are based) predicts that there is a point in the universe where the theory itself breaks down. Such a point is an example of what mathematicians call a singularity. In fact, all our theories of science are formulated on the assumption that space-time is smooth and nearly flat, so they break down at the big bang singularity, where the curvature of space-time is infinite. This means that even if there were events before the big bang, one could not use them to determine what would happen afterward, because predict-ability would break down at the big bang. Correspondingly, if, as is the case, we know only what has happened since the big bang, we could not determine what happened beforehand. As far as we are concerned, events before the big bang can have no consequences, so they should not even form part of a scientific model of the universe. We should therefore cut them out of the model and say that time had a beginning at the big bang. [Stephen W. Hawking, *A Brief History of Time*]

17. At the present time, the philosophical world is curiously divided. If positivism be taken in its widest sense, the sense in which it embraces all shades of analytical, linguistic, or radically empirical philosophy, it is dominant in England and in Scandinavia, and commands considerable allegiance in Holland and Belgium, in Australia and the United States. Elsewhere, it makes hardly any showing at all. [A.J. Ayer, *Logical Positivism*]

18. The word "snob" has had many meanings since it surfaced in the late Middle Ages, none of them good. It began as an all-purpose insult, used to express contempt. By now it has certainly earned its evil reputation. For us snobbery means the habit of making inequality hurt. The snob fawns on his superiors and rejects his inferiors. And while he annoys and insults those who have to live with him, he injures himself as well, because he has lost the very possibility of self-respect. To be afraid of the taint of associations from below is to court ignorance of the world. And to yearn for those above one is to be always ashamed not only of one's actual situation, but of one's family, one's available friends, and oneself. Snobbery is simply a very destructive vice. [Judith Shklar, *Ordinary Vices*]

19. Relations of power are not in a position of exteriority with respect to other types of relationships (economic processes, knowledge relationships, sexual relations), but are immanent in the latter; they are the immediate effects of the divisions, inequalities, and disequilibriums which occur in the latter, and conversely they are the internal conditions of these differentiations; relations of power are not in superstructural positions, with merely a role of prohibition or accompaniment; they have a directly productive role, wherever they come into play. [Michel Foucault, *The History of Sexuality*]

20. Why cannot something be (seen as) red and green all over at the same time? Suppose that color is surface spectral reflectance (along with other objective wavelength phenomena), and that these physical properties have certain additional characteristics only in relation to human perceptual apparatuses. That is what an adequate reduction of the notion of color would hold. The color at a point (or small area) is the proportion of incident energy of each wavelength that is reflected at that point (or in that small area). No point (or small area) can have two different colors simultaneously because no point can simultaneously reflect different proportions of incident energy of a given wavelength. [Robert Nozick, *Invariances*]

21. Many scholars are attracted to . . . constructivist conceptions of truth and rationality independently of any overt concern with the doctrine of equal validity—the view . . . that there are many radically different "equally valid" ways of knowing the world, with science being just one of them. But whatever the source of their appeal, we are not in a position to lay out clearly why equal validity will seem plausible to anyone who finds even one of these constructivist theses true. Thus, if fact-constructivism were true, we couldn't just say that there is some fact of the matter out there about where the first Americans originated. [Paul Boghossian, *Fear of Knowledge*]

22. No individual is ever perfectly adapted, as was stressed early on by Darwin. The main reason for this is perhaps that every genotype represents a compromise of genetic variability and stability. [Ernst Mayr, *What Evolution Is*]

23. The network of internal principles and bridge principles is supposed to secure the deductive character of scientific explanation. To explain why lasers amplify light signals, one starts with a description in the antecedent vocabulary of how a laser is constructed. A bridge principle matches this with a description couched in the language of the quantum theory. The internal principles of quantum mechanics predict what should happen in situations meeting this theoretical description, and a second bridge principle carries the results back into the proposition describing the observed amplification. The explanation is deductive because each of the steps is justified by a principle deemed necessary by the theory, either a bridge principle of an internal principle. [Nancy Cartwright, *How The Laws of Physics Lie*]

24. In short, since he who merely believes in the word of God knows more than the greatest philosophers have ever known concerning the only matters of vital importance, we should feel justified in saying that the simplest among Christians

has a philosophy of his own, which is the only true philosophy, and whose name is: Revelation. [Etienne Gilson, *Reason and Revelation in the Middle Ages*]
25. The origin of the anthropologist is a mystery hidden in the historical mists. Indians are certain that all societies of the Near East had anthropologists at one time because all those societies are now defunct. [Vine Deloria, Jr., *Custer Died For Your Sins*]

D.   Refute the following arguments via the counterexample method.

1.   Some puzzles have solutions and some puzzles do not have solutions. So, some things with solutions are not puzzles.
2.   Franklin Delano Roosevelt was either a democrat or a New Englander. He was certainly a democrat, from which it follows that he was not a New Englander.
3.   All writers are literate and all poets are writers. We may conclude that some poets are literate.
4.   The last seven times Gary has added STP to his fuel supply, the pinging noise in his engine has disappeared. Since he just added another quart of STP, when he starts the car, the pinging noise will be gone.
5.* Oliver North either lied to Congress or had been brain-washed by some sinister Marxist group planning a takeover of the United States. North *did* lie to Congress. Hence, he wasn't brainwashed by the Marxist group.
6.   If Robert E. Lee had been born in Baton Rouge, then he would have fought for the South. But he did fight for the South. Hence, Lee was born in Baton Rouge.
7.   Buckingham Palace is not the most regal mansion in all England; but if it was the most regal mansion, every British girl would want to go to a slumber party there. It follows that it is false that every British girl wants to go to a slumber party at Buckingham Palace.
8.   If Darwin's Theory of Evolution is correct, then both the snake and the rabbit are descendants of a single-celled organism. Hence, the snake is a descendent of a single-celled organism.
9.   Some soldiers are pacifists. So, some soldiers are not pacifists.
10.* No tigers are cuddly. No skunks are cuddly. Thus, no tigers are skunks.

2. Informal Fallacies

2.1 Preliminaries

There are two kinds of fallacies of reasoning. Both kinds have to do with arguments. One kind has to do with the form an argument takes (called a *formal fallacy*). The other has to do with the content of the argument (called an *informal fallacy*). An example of a formal fallacy is one called *Affirming the Consequent*. It takes the following form:

Premise 1:   If A is true, then B is true.
Premise 2:   B is true.
Conclusion: A is true.

The first premise is in the form of a *conditional sentence* and the second part (that is, "B is true") is called the *consequent*. The first part of this premise ("A is true") is called the *antecedent*. The second premise is said to be an affirmation of the consequent, since the second premise is simply restating the consequent of the first premise. The conclusion drawn is simply the antecedent.

The argument given above is invalid. Here is a counterexample showing that it is possible for the premises to be true and the conclusion false with this argument form.

Premise 1: If the moon were a planet, it would be spherical.
Premise 2: The moon is spherical.
Conclusion: The moon is a planet.

The moon is a satellite of a planet but it is not itself a planet. Hence, we know the conclusion is false. We know that premise #1 is true because all planets are spherical (at least in our solar system). We know that premise #2 is true because of the findings of the world community of astronomers.

Notice how the first argument given above has no content. The letters "A" and "B" don't refer to anything at all in that argument, which shows that the fallacy *Affirming the Consequent* relies on the *form* of the argument, not the content. The counterexample does rely on content, of course, because that is one good way to show how premises can be true and the conclusion false.

Another very common formal fallacy is one called Denying the Antecedent. Its form is as follows:

Premise 1: If A is true, then B is true.
Premise 2: A is false.
Conclusion: B is false.

Here is a counterexample showing that it is possible for an argument of this form to have all true premises and a false conclusion, which then proves it to be invalid.

Premise 1: If Thomas Kuhn coined the phrase "paradigm shift," then studies in the history of science have shown that a paradigm shift took place late in the 18th Century with the work of the great chemist Lavoisier.
Premise 2: Kuhn did not coin the phrase "paradigm shift."
Conclusion: Studies in the history of science have not shown that Lavoisier's work in chemistry inaugurated a paradigm shift in chemistry.

Lavoisier, sometime around 1777, began to put forth the "oxygen theory of combustion." In time, this theory replaced the then current theory of combustion, in which it was alleged that phlogiston was the substance responsible for combustion. A new way of looking at a specific part of the chemical world was inaugurated. So, the consequent of the condition of premise 1 is true, thus making that premise itself true. Further, premise 2 is true because Kuhn coined the term "paradigm" but not the term "paradigm shift." The conclusion is, of course, false. We can see that because it denies what the consequent in the first premise affirms.

Informal fallacies, on which we will focus in this chapter, rely on content and not on form. The goal of the present chapter is to get us well acquainted with some common informal fallacies so that we will be able to analyze an argument in terms of 1) whether or not it commits one or more informal fallacy, 2) which fallacy or fallacies it commits, if it commits any, and 3) why it commits the fallacy or fallacies it does commit. We will study sixteen of the most common fallacies (over two hundred have been named).

A *fallacious argument* is a defective argument and a *fallacy* is the defect in the argument itself. The formal fallacy *Affirming the Consequent* just discussed is defective in that to affirm the consequent of a conditional and then draw the antecedent as a conclusion yields an invalid argument. As with the formal fallacies, an argument committing one of the informal fallacies is an argument in which the conclusion does not, in most cases, follow conclusively from the premise(s). The presence of a formal fallacy in an argument precludes the premises leading to the conclusion in a decisive way. We call such arguments invalid, though that term is misleading at times. There are two instances of informal fallacies where the argument itself may be valid in the formal sense of that term, but the arguments are unacceptable because of the presence of the fallacy. These will be discussed in due course.

Informal fallacies differ from *formal* fallacies primarily in that the former do not, whereas the latter do, arise from the specific forms of arguments. To detect an informal fallacy, one needs to have a subject matter with which to deal. This is to say, again, that the argument must have content, unlike the examples of Affirming the Consequent Denying the Antecedent above, each of which commits a fallacy regardless of the actual subject matter of the argument.

Another difference between formal and informal fallacies has to do with the psychological effect an argument committing an informal fallacy may have on the hearer of the argument. Many fallacious arguments can be quite persuasive because of the way they are presented. As with all natural languages, English is very rich, and many people have such a command of the language that they can "make the worse argument seem the better." Whenever the worse argument does seem the better, a fallacy is being committed, because the worse can only seem the better if there is some sort of defect in our thinking about, or recognition of, which argument *is* better. This defect in thinking about the arguments is due to our having missed the defect in the worse argument. For example, imagine for a moment that Dustin Hoffman is your favorite actor. Imagine Hoffman in a television commercial for, say, Bayer Aspirin. If the commercial is done with taste, which you probably will think it is, given that Hoffman is in it, you might think, "Well, if Bayer is good enough for Hoffman, it's good enough for me." Or, you might think, "If Hoffman takes Bayer, and says it's a good pain reliever, it must be all right, since he wouldn't say it if it wasn't true." In a case such as this, you would have missed something crucial in the argument being presented. First, you would be thinking exactly what the Bayer company probably wanted you to think when the commercial was conceived. (That in itself is not a sufficient reason for rejecting the argument, however, for many times an arguer will present an argument and will want another person to come to believe something through the argument and the argument will be a good one.)

Second (and this is the important part), you would have missed the point of asking whether Dustin Hoffman is an expert in pharmacology. That is, is Hoffman an authority in the properties of the various chemicals used in Bayer and other types of pain relievers? What you need is detailed information (that a layperson can understand) about the pain relieving qualities of Bayer. Although you admire Dustin Hoffman very much as an actor, you may not be convinced of his prowess in the chemistry lab. (This, of course, is not to say that you are right about Hoffman. Perhaps you are ignorant of the fact that he is a highly respected person in the field of pharmaceuticals. If you have jumped to an incorrect conclusion about Hoffman, then it must be admitted that you should take the commercial more seriously.)

The point is that we should look closely at what the argument is, as well as at the motive and expertise of the arguer. But when you see Dustin Hoffman on the TV, you are probably already interested in what he's going to say because of your respect for him as an actor. If we don't use our knowledge that acting skills have very little to do with skills in chemistry, then we could be led to believe that Bayer Aspirin is the best pain reliever *just because* Dustin Hoffman says it is. And this is a fallacious argument.

There are a number of different categories of informal fallacies. There are fallacies of inconsistency, fallacies of grammar, fallacies of relevance, analogical fallacies, and so on. We are not so much interested in the various classes of fallacies as we are with the fallacies themselves. However, since understanding the nature of a fallacy is helpful for understanding each particular instance of fallacious reasoning, the fallacies will be grouped in terms of the classes of fallacy.

2.2. Fallacies of Relevance

All fallacies of relevance have at least one thing in common, to wit, the premises in the arguments that commit one of these fallacies are logically irrelevant to the conclusions they are intended to support. However, though these arguments are logically fallacious, they sometimes have great psychological appeal to the listener. The earlier example of Dustin Hoffman is applicable here. Even though the conclusion may seem to follow from the premises, closer attention will show that it in fact does not follow at all. In attempting to detect fallacies of relevance, it is helpful to pay attention to "why" one thinks some argument is a good one. Ask, "Is the arguer appealing to my emotions or to my sense of logic?" If the former, then it is likely that a fallacy of relevance is being committed.

A. Argumentum ad Vericundiam

This fallacy is commonly known as the Argument from Authority. There are three sorts of *ad Vericundiam* fallacies. The first is the most typical and involves an arguer who cites someone as an authority on some topic who is not an authority on the topic at all. We call this type of *ad Vericundiam False Authority*. The Dustin Hoffman example, discussed above, is of this kind. Consider the following argument.

> Since Albert Einstein was a thoroughgoing advocate of a Zionist state, and since Professor Einstein's reputation for being an intelligent man is beyond reproach, we can only conclude that a Zionist state is something to be advocated.

There is no doubt that Einstein was a remarkable man. One needs only to read his biography to see this. But Einstein is famous for his work in physics, mathematics, and related fields. He is not known for his political or religious polemics. Einstein is considered an authority in science, not an authority in religion and/or politics, and when one uses Einstein's esteemed name to get someone to accept an argument having to do with religion and/or politics, then the arguer has committed the argument from false authority.

The second kind of fallacy of authority is related to the first, but is different in that the arguer refers to a person who *is* an authority and says that just because this person said X, X must be true. This sort of *ad Vericundiam* is called *Absolute Authority*. An example:

> John Stuart Mill believed that pleasure is the highest good, and built much of his ethical theory around this idea. Mill was considered a genius by many of his peers. Hence, since he believed it, pleasure must be the highest good.

In his *Utilitarianism*, Mill writes, ". . . pleasure and freedom from pain are the only things desirable as ends; and . . . all desirable things (which are as numerous in the utilitarian as in any other scheme) are desirable either for pleasure inherent in themselves or as a means to the promotion of pleasure and the prevention of pain." We see, then, that the first premise of the argument is correct, i.e., that Mill did in fact think that pleasure is the highest good. We also know that Mill was, and is, considered an authority in ethics. However, being an authority in some field does not mean that one knows everything there is to know about that field, nor does it mean that one cannot be wrong. There is a great difference between being an authority and being a complete or absolute authority. There is simply no such thing as a complete authority in the sense in which it is being used in the above argument, i.e., in the sense of someone knowing everything there is to know about any given topic and being infallible about it. (I leave it to the reader to contemplate what has just been said in light of the widespread belief in the authority of some religious figures and books.)

One of the best examples of the use of the fallacy of Absolute Authority comes from the veneration many medieval scholars had for the ancient Greek philosopher Aristotle. St. Thomas Aquinas cites Aristotle's *Physics* without argument when he writes,

> And if it be said that the statue in question is endowed with some vital principle by the power of the heavenly bodies, this is impossible. For the principle of life in all living things is the substantial form, because, as the Philosopher says, *in living things to be is to live*. Now it is impossible for anything to receive anew a substantial form, unless it lose the form which it had previously, since *the generation of one thing is the corruption of another*. (Aquinas' italics of Aristotle's text)

Note here that in this one paragraph Aquinas refers to Aristotle, not as Aristotle, but simply as "the Philosopher." Also note that Aquinas does not back up his double use of Aristotle's words with any argument at all. It's as though "just because Aristotle said it, it must be true."

The third type of *ad Vericundiam* fallacy has to do with an arguer appealing to custom or tradition as authoritative. A good example of this occurs sometimes when one takes a new job and tries to change the way things are done only to hear, "we've always done it the other way, so let's stick with that."

Few would deny the importance of custom and tradition in shaping our attitudes, practices, life styles and cultures. And many of us see the importance, the virtue, of retaining cultural traditions. However, even with that said, it does not logically follow that custom and tradition are in themselves reason enough for continuing a practice. When someone does appeal to custom or tradition in this way, we call it *Authority of Custom* (or Tradition). Consider the following argument.

> Segregation has been the way of the Southern states for generations.
> Hence, this practice must continue, in such forms as "white only"
> drinking fountains, for example, and "colored only" restaurants.

Many people are simply dumbfounded by such arguments. It is hard to believe that such reasoning could be taken seriously. Of course, what is missing from the above argument are the "real" reasons people have advocated segregation. When those reasons are brought in, the argument changes and it will no longer commit Authority of Custom. To see what fallacy or fallacies the altered argument would commit, we would need to see, and assess, the set of premises offered in support of the conclusion.

Consider the following argument, similar to those given by some members of Major League Baseball when the American League was considering adopting what is known as the "designated hitter" rule (which specifies that the team may designate some player, not playing a position in the field, to bat in place of the pitcher each time the pitcher's turn to bat comes around):

> Baseball, as conceived by Alexander Cartwright in 1825, required all players holding positions on the field, to take a turn at bat. This includes the pitcher. That has always been the way of baseball and to change it now would be as wrong as filling in the Grand Canyon. Change baseball and it's no longer baseball. It's the way it's always been and it's the way it must continue to be.

There seem to be a number of arguments here, all of which point to some kind of reverence for tradition. Hence, it commits *ad Vericundian.*

Even if the argument above is a bad argument, one might consider other reasons for holding the position that the designated hitter rule not be allowed. For example, some have argued that teams with the most money can hire the best hitters, thereby making the teams more uneven in terms of their offensive strengths. Or, one can argue that baseball has become too specialized and that the designated hitter rule allows further specialization, with the designated hitter only hitting and never playing the field and the pitcher only pitching and never hitting. Both of these arguments are interesting and deserve analysis, but neither commits *ad Vericundiam.*

Another name for *ad Vericundiam* arguments is the general phrase "appeal to authority." It is true that we do appeal to authorities in our daily lives. People we recognize as either having an advanced degree in some field, or considerable practical experience, or both, are usually deemed by us to be authorities. If you want to know something about political liberalism, perhaps a good person to see would be a political scientist; if one has questions about subjunctive conditionals, see a linguist; if one has a pulled muscle, seeing a physician would seem to be a reasonable choice; and so on. We do, however, have the practice of getting a "second opinion" on matters, whether they be in medicine, history, art criticism, chemistry, or whatever. We take these authorities to be "the people most likely to know," but not as "infallible sources of information." To treat anyone (or custom) as an incontestable authority, or to cite someone as an authority who isn't one, is to commit the fallacy of authority.

B. Argumentum ad Populum

This fallacy is commonly known as the "appeal to the people," or "argument from the populace," and is committed when an arguer appeals to the listener's need or desire to be "one of the group" to get the listener to accept an argument. There are certain reasons people need or want to be part of a group, most of which involve the values we possess. However, appealing to those values does not establish an argument as reasonable or acceptable. It is only when the premises lead to the conclusion that an argument is reasonable or acceptable.

There are two sorts of appeal to the people. One occurs when a speaker is trying to evoke the emotions of a crowd of people, as, say, when a politician uses such phrases as "the threat of terrorism," or "the American way" in an attempt to get the audience heated up. When banners are flying and everyone is listening to a speech on the "evils of socialism," it is then that one needs to be on guard for an argument appealing to our emotions rather than our reasoning faculty.

Can we take another four years of a government bent on destroying the American Dream? Will we allow the further destruction of our children's future by continued no-growth in social reform? Will we stand for higher taxes and higher budget deficit? The answer to these questions is a resounding *NO!* We can be *true patriots* and take back the freedom we had when this great nation offered our children the hope of a future ripe with happiness and success. We can do it and do it together – as a people, as a community. How? There is only one way: We can vote for Rose Johnson!!

This argument is like many we have heard in the past. It may be that Johnson is the best candidate. The point is that the argument itself does not present us with the facts we need to judge. This argument appeals to our patriotic and parental emotions, not to logic and not to evidence, which is what is needed for acceptable argumentation.

In the above sort of situation, the members of the audience may be caught up in the words, music, and actions of the present situation. They may be carried away by the scene, being led to accepting conclusions on the basis of the rise of emotion, the sense of purpose, and the fervent shouting and emotion being displayed by the other people in the audience. The speaker's words are intended to heighten these emotions, not to present a cool, calm, and rational account of why Johnson should get the vote. Some of the things we would want to know, if we were to vote for Johnson, would be what her qualifications are, her voting record, where she stands on issues important to us, her economic policy, her foreign policy perhaps, and so on. The argument above provides none of this information.

The other type of appeal to the people commonly has as its audience one person. This fallacy has the same purpose behind it as the one above, except that it is not intended to stir our emotions to frenzy, but rather is supposed to work in a more subtle way. Many advertisements commit this fallacy and, though sometimes in an indirect way, they are all designed to appeal to various emotions we have about belonging to a group. For example,

> Everyone here at the Institute is reading the works of Maya Angelou right now. You certainly don't want to be out of it, so you need to do some reading of Angelou's work.

The phrase "out of it" says a lot. No one wants to be out of it, and if being out of it means one is not reading or has not read Angelou, then perhaps we should all get a copy of one of her books. There is a certain legitimate appeal here, it would seem. If one is to be able to converse with the members of one's community, from necessity, then perhaps one ought to get acquainted with Angelou's work. However, this is far from the sense of avoiding being out of it as displayed in the above passage. The argument is appealing to our *sense* of being out of it; it neither appeals to our wanting to read Angelou because there is value in her work, nor to any supposed value the works of Angelou may possess. The appeal here is to our sense of wanting to be part of the group.

The number of examples of arguments committing *ad Populum* is vast. They range from a parent trying to persuade a child to eat liver and peas so the child can grow up to be like Wonderwoman or Spiderman to a computer salesperson trying to sell a customer a "state of the art" machine because that's what "computer people" use. Some of the arguments are quite direct and open, some are subtle and seductive. But the one thread running through each argument, overt or covert, is that appeal to our sense of wanting to be a member of "the" group, the "in-crowd," the "people in the know," the "gang."

Take another example, somewhat more indirect but, by this time, not fooling many. I'm watching TV and an ad comes on with this young, attractive man driving a shiny, new sports car. (The background music is soft jazz, kind of hip.)

He pulls up to a stop light. Another car pulls up next to him in which there is a very attractive young woman who notices, first, the car he's driving, and then him. She gives him a sexy smile, we hear the revving of engines, the screen fades to black and the caption reads,
NOW WHAT WOULD YOU DO?
Well, the first thing I'd do is smile back. That is, *if* I had one of those sports cars. But since I don't have one, I'd better get hopping and buy one. I'd better get myself into the group of guys (young and attractive or not) who own one of those sports cars. Then I'll get the girl, right? Well, I might get the girl, if she doesn't suspect the fact that I accepted a fallacious argument. The point is that the ad is not appealing to the quality of the car (which is what is being advertised), but rather to my desire to be accepted as a member of a class of people. Hence, *ad Populum*.

C. Argumentum ad Misericordiam

This fallacy, commonly known as the "appeal to pity," relies on evoking pity in the listener. The listener is then asked to accept some conclusion on the basis of this emotion. For example,

> *Tom:* My friend Tony was abandoned by his real parents and sent to an orphanage when he was three.
> *Rob:* I'm sorry to hear that.
> *Tom:* He never had the money to go to college and had learned none of the ordinary skills at the orphanage because the people there didn't care about anything but themselves. He was neglected and had to fend for himself, picking up odd jobs where he could get them. He injured his hand and foot in a railroad accident and spent two years in hospital.
> *Rob:* He's sure had a rough time of it.
> *Tom:* So, won't you give him a job on your fishing boat?

The conclusion here comes in the form of a question: Won't you hire Tony to crew your fishing boat? Stated in non-question form, the conclusion would be something such as: You should hire Tony to crew your fishing boat. It is obvious that Tom's story has caused Rob to feel sorry for Tony. But the relevant question is: Is that good reason, by itself, to hire Tony? Probably not, for the crew of a fishing boat is a highly skilled team of individuals. Tony, who has none of the skills required, could not do the job, no matter how much pity one feels for him.

Notice, as in *ad Populum* and *ad Vericundiam*, that the premises are really irrelevant to the conclusion; they don't have anything to do with one another. From this perspective, one can accept the premises and reject the conclusion. Or, it is possible that the premises are true and the conclusion false.

Another example of *ad Vericundiam* comes sometimes with the appeal for money to assist with famine relief, or help the plight of the homeless; generally, the needy. A television or film personality is seen crying about the deplorable circumstances of people who don't have nutritionally adequate and/or enough food to eat. Film is shown testifying to this. Is the intention to evoke pity from the viewer so he/she will send money? If so, the argument behind this commits the fallacy. However, one might detect a "moral" argument here as well. If one's moral code includes the principle that one should help other people if one can, and if that is the principle upon which the appeal is made, then *ad Vericundiam* is not committed here.

D. Argumentum ad Baculum

An "appeal to force" occurs when someone threatens another in order to get a conclusion accepted. As examples,

> People who don't vote for Wayne Winger for "Associated Student President" will find certain doors closed to them in Spring semester. Unless you believe that the Ford Cobra is the fastest car on the road, we'll have your gas tank filled with sand.

> If you don't do your homework, you'll not go to the game.

In the first case, the consequences referred to are rather vague. We ask, What doors? Nonetheless, the threat is evident here and constitutes a clear *ad Baculum*. In the second case above, it seems absurd to try to *make* someone believe something on the basis of a threat. Beliefs are usually arrived at on evidence in favor of that which is to be believed. It may be the case that a person will "say" that the Ford Cobra is the fastest car, but that does not mean the person "believes" it. The third case is different, however. We have all done things to avoid something happening that we consider bad. This does not, in itself, make the threat a *logically* good reason for doing, or not doing, the thing in question.

> This gun just might go off unless you tell me where the money is. It's got a hair-trigger, and I'm the nervous type.

Prudent advice would probably be to tell the threatener where the money is located. But this doesn't mean we take the argument to be valid, or even as acceptable (this deserves discussion, of course), the point here being that if we feel forced to give in and tell where the money is, that is tantamount to feeling forced to "act as if" we accept the argument. The argument above, spelled out, is:

> Tell me where the money is or I'll shoot you.
> You don't want to be shot.
> Therefore, you want to, and will, tell me where the money is.

This is simply an invalid argument. If we accept it, it is because we are forced to, but not because it is acceptable "as an argument."

Argumentum ad Baculum is committed anytime a person threatens to harm another person (physically or psychologically) in order to get the other person to accept a conclusion (which may or may not lead to action on the part of the listener). It is important to note that the premises to any argument committing *ad Baculum* are *logically* irrelevant to the conclusion. This is not to say they are *practically* irrelevant, however. This should be obvious from the fact that we do sometimes feel forced to accept, and act on, an argument committing this fallacy.

E. Argumentum ad Hominem

Sometimes called "argument to the person" or "personal attack," there are three distinct versions of the *ad Hominem* fallacy: *Abusive, Circumstantial*, and *Tu quoque*. The situation in which a person commits this fallacy always involves at least two arguers. Typically, it goes like this: One person presents an argument. The second person then presents what is to be taken as a refutation of the first argument. However, the second arguer does not attack the first arguer's argument, but rather attacks the arguer her/himself. The crucial background point here is that an arguer and an arguer's argument are separate entities. A very nice person can present the most invalid of arguments, just as the meanest of villains can present a sound argument. *An argument must be judged on its own merits, quite apart from merits or demerits of the person who puts it forth.*

Ad Hominem Abusive is committed when the second arguer makes abusive statements about the first arguer. For example,

> The Senator has made the absurd argument that we need to rewrite the legislation on campaign contributions because there are loopholes allowing tax write-offs on undisclosed amounts. It is beyond me how you could seriously consider the reasoning of a man who cannot even balance his own checkbook, who has been seen sneaking around Second Street late at night talking to known dope addicts, and who is simply the laugh of the town.

So the Senator has trouble with mathematics, and talks to drug addicts. Does that mean that the legislation shouldn't be rewritten? Clearly, no. What needs to be done here is to investigate the plausibility and ramifications of a rewriting the legislation. The Senator and the Senator's argument are different things; they are not, and are not to be, judged by the same criteria. The following example is much the same,

> Jack Kerouac was a marijuana smoking, beatnik bum who advocated a life of the homeless, vagabond rogue, searching for experiences having nothing to do with growth and learning. His book *On The Road*, there-

fore, cannot be taken as serious literature and should not be read by serious students.

What has been said about the separation of the argument from the arguer holds good here. However, there are a number of points to consider. First, we must question the nature of "abuse" in any supposed *ad Hominem*. Calling Kerouac a marijuana smoking beatnik, for example, just may not be considered abusive by everyone. The important thing here is that the one committing the fallacy "intends" to abuse. If intent cannot be known, or proven, in any given situation, then one cannot be sure the fallacy is being committed.

Second, one has to wonder whether the things said about the person are in fact true. But, true or false, the things said are said about the person, not about the person's argument. And this means that the argument itself has not been refuted. Many times criminal attorneys are portrayed as people who will try to discredit a witness' testimony by calling into the question the character of the witness her/himself. This kind of ploy, whether the witness is shown to have unappealing qualities or not, is a perfect example of *ad Hominem* Abusive Attention is diverted away from the witness' testimony toward the witness proper. The idea behind such tactics is that if the attorney can show the witness in a bad light, perhaps the jury or judge will discount what the witness has said in the testimony. The fact that the witness may not be a model citizen has little to do with the truth or falsehood of the testimony of the witness. Even though we will question the truth or falsehood of the testimony of a witness who is shown to be, say, a persistent liar, that in itself is not a good reason for discounting altogether the testimony. The witness may, this time, be telling the truth.

The second variant of the *ad Hominem*, the Circumstantial, is the same as the Abusive except the first arguer is not abused, but rather it is pointed out that the first arguer's argument ought not be accepted because the first arguer stands to gain something if it *is* accepted. This is to say that the second arguer appeals to the first arguer's special circumstances to show that the first arguer's argument is to be rejected. For example,

> I know your advisor, Professor Slagel, said that you should take English 415. I also know why; because Professor Slagel is an English teacher and he will get in good with the Dean if more students take the course.

If you think about it, sometimes that is exactly how it works: the Dean will usually be happy when the enrollment increases in departments. And if the Dean is happy with a department, it can benefit that department. The faculty, students and staff in the department, then, will in turn benefit as well. Your physician recommends surgery; your mechanic advises a tune-up on your car; your stock broker recommends buying Intel stock; your butcher recommends T-bone . . . . All these people make money from their services, but that does not mean that you should not invest in Intel, have surgery, a tune-up, or T-bone.

The focus in the passage above directs attention away from the idea of taking a certain course toward the advisor, who is the first arguer. No mention is made about the prudence of taking English 415. Even though the special circumstances of the advisor entitle her/him to benefit if you do take the course, it just may be a good idea to take the course anyway, given that you want to benefit from your advisor's advice.

The third version of *ad Hominem*, the *Tu quoque*, is what I call the "children's fallacy." It consists in one arguer charging someone with having said or done a certain thing, and the second arguer charging the first arguer with having said or done something similar. A typical example:

Caleb: You wrecked my fort.
Faith: Well, you wrote all over my homework.

So Caleb wrote all over Faith's homework and Faith wrecked Caleb's fort. Faith is presenting a *Tu quoque* here, in that she is not responding to Caleb's charge that he ruined the homework. Faith is coming back with a charge of her own. Caleb accuses Faith of being guilty of something, and instead of defending herself against that accusation, Faith diverts attention away from herself and her alleged/supposed guilt, toward Caleb and Caleb's alleged/supposed guilt.

This fallacy is also known as the "you, too" fallacy because the one who commits it is responding to someone's charge of guilt by saying, essentially, "you are guilty too," i.e., not denying guilt but trying to show that someone else is also guilty. No one is fooled here. Even if Caleb is guilty, that does not mean that Faith is innocent. The point is that Faith tries to get the focus of attention away from herself, by arguing against the person of Caleb, and that is how she commits *ad Hominem, Tu quoque*.

F. Argumentum ad Ignorantiam

The "appeal to ignorance" fallacy is committed when someone argues that nothing is known, or can be known, about X and then goes on to make a positive statement about X. This commonly involves a denial of evidence about, or proof of, X. For example,

Some of the greatest thinkers of our time have worked long and hard trying to find a solution to Russell's Paradox. No one has come up with a solution acceptable to everyone in the academic community. We can conclude that there is no solution.

It is clear that the conclusion of this argument does not follow from the premises. Many of the best minds had, for centuries, wrestled with Zeno's puzzles about motion, and it was only in the 20th century that they were finally put to rest. It would have been false in, say, the 17th century for someone to say that since no one had solved Zeno's Arrow Puzzle, no one ever would.

The premises in the above argument are true. But if/when someone does come up with an acceptable solution to Russell's Paradox, the conclusion will then be known to be false and the argument will be shown to have true premises and a false conclusion, which violates our definition of a valid argument.

There are many instances of this fallacy being committed. Some of the topics have been: ghosts, the soul, the claims of astrology, parapsychology, a Northern route to the Indias, extra-galactic visitors in ancient times, and so on. Some of these topics are still under close scrutiny by interested individuals, with books and articles appearing every year claiming "new and conclusive evidence." The crucial question is, What is the evidence and how was it discovered?

This question leads to a situation many believe to be a legitimate exception to the fallacy. When a group of people (or a person) is engaged in the pursuit of knowledge regarding the existence of a certain thing, and when these people are considered experts in the field in which they are studying, then if this group makes some claim to the effect that there is no evidence to show that X exists, this claim is thought to be acceptable. For example,

> Scientists for many years worked under the theory that phlogiston, a chemical thought to be released during combustion, existed. After much research, this phantom "stuff" has never been found. Therefore, phlogiston does not exist.

The conclusion here is taken to be true within the community of scientists. But it is not the case that this is proven by the fact that many scientists were unable to discover it. Rather, it is proven by further research into combustion itself, and determining exactly in what this process consists. We have a tendency to believe what those who are supposed to know, i.e. the experts, say. It seems we commit two fallacies at once here, to wit, *ad Vericundiam* and *ad Ignorantiam*. Just because they haven't found X does not lead to the conclusion that X isn't there to be found. It seems most likely to us, when a group of trained people are working on such a project, that if they fail to locate X, then *probably* X doesn't exist. This seems an acceptable argument, when the 'probably' is inserted. Presumably these people know pretty much where and how to look for X. This is so if they are correct about the properties X is supposed to possess. However, we must admit that it is always possible for a group of people to overlook crucial facts in any research project.

Another accepted exception to the *ad Ignorantiam* fallacy has to do with the United States justice system, where, *in the eyes of the law*, an individual is innocent until proven guilty.

> Lawyer to jury: As you have seen, ladies and gentlemen, the prosecutor has failed to establish, beyond any reasonable doubt, that the defendant had any connection, public or private, with the deceased. Not one bit of evidence places my client at the scene of the crime, nor has anything

pointed to a possible motive on her part. Therefore, in accord with the law of the United States, Rita Paar is innocent of the murder of John Hirsch.

In the most strict usage of *ad Ignorantiam*, this is not an exception, since if someone is guilty of a crime, whether proven so beyond a reasonable doubt or not, still the person is guilty. However, as the presumption of innocence is taken to be a basic and indispensable element in legal proceedings in the United States, we admit to the good sense of the presumption, and hence, we tacitly agree to overlook the fallacy for practical purposes. The best reason I've heard for this agreement is that the consequences of the opposite presumption would be completely disastrous for truly innocent people.

G. Accident

When a general rule is applied incorrectly to a specific instance, the fallacy of accident has been committed. The general rule referred to here is usually one thought to be a good rule, i.e., one that is worth adhering to. For example,

Since you promised not to disclose the nature of this case, it does not matter whether someone's life depends on the knowledge only you possess. You cannot talk about it because everyone knows that breaking a promise is wrong.

This is one of those "hard cases" we all know about. It is true that we go by the rule that one should not break promises. It could be argued, and has been, that the reason we call the rule against breaking promises a "general" rule is that it holds in many, or most, cases, but not in all cases. Consider this situation carefully, however. There seems to be two alternatives: first, keep the promise and someone dies; second, break the promise and a life is saved. It would seem that saving a life trumps keeping a promise. If that is true, then the rule that says we should keep our promises is shown to be truly a general rule, one that may be overridden under certain circumstances. Here is another case, one that involves the general rule that we should not tell lies.

Senator Smith was urged by Congress to divulge the information she had about the internet scam. In the subsequent days, Smith lied to Congress in order to secure the freedom of seven young people who had been kidnapped by a well-known cult in Missouri. Senator Jones is now bringing Smith before the House Ethics Committee for her lies. Jones' argument is that since Smith lied to Congress, and since lying is always wrong, no matter whether it has beneficial consequences to both life and country, Smith ought to be recalled from the Senate.

Lying to Congress is something one would presumably do only under the most dire of situations. It would appear that Smith thought lying to Congress was a better thing to do (Smith never said it was right) than allowing a Missouri cult to dictate the fate of seven people. If the prohibition on lying were thought to be an absolute rule, then Jones' argument would carry much more weight than it does when one views "lying is wrong" as general rule. Taken as a general rule, Jones' argument commits Accident.

One might suspect that those typically called "white lies" are specifically designed to override any ruling that lying is always wrong. Take another example:

> The rule of freedom of religion and worship are absolutes in this country. Hence, there is really nothing we can do about the religion that advocates sacrificing two human teenagers per year to their god.

Freedom of religion seems to be a reasonable general rule. However, when values conflict, as here and in the case above, one usually points to a hierarchy of values. If we take the value of human life to be greater than the value of freedom of religion, this argument commits Accident.

H. Hasty Generalization

The fallacy of Hasty Generalization is the opposite of Accident. That is, one commits Hasty Generalization when one reasons to a general rule from a limited number of specific instances. For example,

> Karen and Jan and Nancy each bought a 2003 Ford Mustang GT. The clutch cable kept snapping and the crankshaft ripped apart on Karen's Mustang; the fuel line repeatedly clogged up and the front axle cracked on Jan's Mustang; the carburetor valve got stuck, the gas tank leaked, and the headlights wouldn't work on Nancy's Mustang. We can therefore conclude that 2003 Ford Mustang GT's were ill-made vehicles.

Here the general rule is that 2003 Ford Mustang GT's were ill-made. This is supposed to follow from three examples of people who had trouble with theirs. The conclusion does not follow, since there is no vehicle on the road which is free from problems. It is to be suspected that everyone who bought an 2003 Ford Mustang GT had to have it worked on by a mechanic at some time or other, even if it was something as minor as replacing the shock absorbers. That Jan, Karen, and Nancy had so much trouble with their Mustangs does not indicate that *all* 2003 Ford Mustang GT's were faulty or ill-made. What it indicates is that *some* were faulty. The above argument is typical of Hasty Generalization, going from a limited number of instances to a general rule.

Another way of representing this fallacy is to say that when one picks out a number of atypical cases and then concludes with a general rule based on the cases, one generalizes hastily. The above argument picks out three Mustangs owned by three different people. Given that the Mustangs were each made at the same factory, along with hundreds of other Mustangs, the cases are *not* at all atypical. But, consider the following argument:

> José spoke up in the City Council meeting yesterday for the first time since he was elected over two months ago. His comments were neither relevant nor well-spoken and Kalin drew the conclusion that José is not a good public speaker.

This conclusion may be false. Add the following facts: 1. José was very nervous; 2. The topic of José's comments is very controversial and complex. In the first place, we might say that Kalin is guilty of Hasty Generalization by basing his argument on an unfair sample. In the second place, we can say that it is very unusual to find José speaking before that particular crowd and, therefore, the argument that Kalin is using commits Hasty Generalization based on an "atypical case." As with the cliché regarding summers and swallows, we might say here that one ill-presented set of comments does not a bad orator make. We can say, then, that Kalin's argument is guilty of Hasty Generalization both regarding the limited number of cases as well as picking out an atypical instance and generalizing from it.

I. False Cause

When someone reasons to a conclusion on the basis of there being some causal connection between premises and the conclusion, or between certain facts about the world, *when in fact the causal relationship does not hold*, one commits the fallacy of False Cause. If one suspects that some argument rests on a false cause, one should be able to pick out the incorrect causal relationship referred to in the argument. For example,

> For over a year now, Harper's television picture has been fuzzy and dark. At about the same time the television started to malfunction, Harper began a rigorous program of cataloging his considerable CD collection. Every day he works on the CD's and sits in a chair with his shoulders slumped forward. At the end of the day he has a great deal of back pain and uses a hot water bottle to give him comfort while he watches television. If he would just stop using that hot water bottle, Harper's television would work just fine.

So far as is presently known, there is no causal relationship between the use of hot water bottles and the operation of televisions. This should clue us in on the False Cause here.

The fallacy of False Cause can be quite persuasive at times, because we are sometimes ignorant of the exact causal relationship between events, i.e., whether two or more events are in some way causally related. For example, AIDS is linked with blood transfusions, unsafe or unprotected sex, and with the sharing of needles. It is not known conclusively, at present, whether these are the only methods of transmitting AIDS. HIV, the virus that causes AIDS, has been found in virtually every bodily fluid. Hence, arguments like the fictional example below may, without our knowing it, commit the fallacy of False Cause.

> Maria, a periodontist for many years, recently contracted AIDS. She recalls discovering, after one of her treatments of an HIV infected patient, that one of her plastic gloves had a tear in it. She also recalls that she had two small paper cuts on one of her cuticles. She is certain that some of the saliva from her patient made contact with her cuticle. We can conclude that Maria became HIV infected as a result of the contact between the saliva and the cuticle.

Now, if AIDS cannot be transmitted through contact with an infected person's saliva, then that cannot have been the cause of Maria's HIV and a different cause must be discovered. The point is that no one is *absolutely* sure at this point. This is much different in the case of hot water bottles and televisions. There is simply no evidence whatever to link these two things in terms of causality.

J. Straw Person

The Straw Person fallacy is committed when someone tries to refute an argument (or a position) that is attributed to a person when in fact the argument (or position) being attributed to the person is not the argument (or position) held by the person. What happens in a Straw Person fallacy is that the arguer tries to refute an argument not held by the specific person to whom it is attributed. For example, let's say that Loren holds the position that marijuana ought to be legalized for medical purposes. If Tim were to misrepresent Loren's position in such a way that Tim gives the impression that Loren holds that marijuana ought to be legalized generally, and then goes on to argue against *this* position, then Tim is guilty of committing the Straw Person fallacy. Here is an example. The arguer is Bausch.

> It is very difficult for me to fathom how Turnbull could argue that people ought to be allowed to come to class with hand guns and submachine guns. But that is just what his argument amounts to when he argues in favor of the right to bear arms. My conclusion is that we must reject Turnbull's position.

Assume here that Turnbull has argued in favor of the right to bear arms. Further assume that Turnbull's argument took into account such things as not allowing firearms to be brought into situations where there is typically little threat of the need to defend oneself; for example, Turnbull never mentioned schools directly, or grocery stores, or basketball games, or places and situations of that nature. For Bausch to argue that Turnbull's position amounts to allowing guns in the classroom is to change Turnbull's position. That means that Bausch is *not* arguing against Turnbull's position but is arguing rather against another position, perhaps similiar to Turnbull's, but definitely not Turnbull's.

In another example, we have a centuries old argument from René Descartes, the great French philosopher. Descartes argued that it is possible to doubt our senses because we have been deceived by them before and can't be sure that we are not being deceived now. Descartes was arguing that the senses do not give us absolute certainty about things; so, for example, if I see someone across the street that looks very much like my brother John, Descartes would say something such as "you would do well to take a closer look, to be as sure as can be." Imagine Janet making the following argument, trying to refute Descartes' argument:

> The argument which Descartes puts forth for being able to doubt our senses is pure nonsense. It leads to absurd consequences, such as my not being able to be sure that I am looking at my own hands when I am looking at hands that are attached to my own arms. I know that I can doubt my senses, but *this* would be ridiculous.

Descartes' argument is not designed to get us to doubt our normal, everyday sense perceptions, those many perceptions that take place in good light and at a distance that would cause us to be pretty sure of what we are seeing (such as in a grocery store, reading the label on a quart of milk and seeing that the label says the milk is homogenized and pasteurized). Descartes was engaging in a process by which he tried to see whether there was something that was impossible for him to doubt, so that, if there was, then he would know that thing (that which is impossible to doubt) with absolute certainty. Janet is not being true to Descartes' original argument and position because we are rarely, if ever, called upon to have absolute certainty. Rather, it is usually the case that strong and justified belief, based on good evidence, is what stands in good stead of knowledge, or, for many people, simply *is* knowledge.

To detect the Straw Person fallacy, one needs to know what the original argument or position is that is being misrepresented. Without that, it is quite impossible to know that the argument (the one Janet gave, for instance) is not being fair to the other, original argument.

2.3. Fallacies of Ambiguity

Natural languages are, of course, very rich in meaning and nuance. Many words and phrases can be used in a number of different senses, and when used in such a way as to admit of various ways of understanding what is being said, we call that being ambiguous, or, not saying explicitly what you mean. The following fallacies each involve some ambiguity of terms and/or phrases. The problem with arguments with ambiguous components is that different conclusions can be drawn depending on the meaning of the ambiguous terms.

K. Equivocation

When an argument is presented in such a way that one of its terms or phrases is actually used in two, or more, different senses, the fallacy of equivocation is committed. For example,

> All rabbits have tails.
> Edgar played a rabbit in the school play.
> It follows that Edgar has a tail.

Obviously the term "rabbit" is being used here in two different senses. One sense is that of the lagomorph mammal. The other sense is that of a person who acts in creative works called plays. This is not a valid argument, even if its *form* might suggest that it is. That is, because of the equivocation on the word "rabbit" the argument would be invalid and unacceptable. It must be noted that each premise could be true, given the different senses of 'rabbit' in each premise. This is to say that it is true that all rabbits, the mammals, have tails, and it is true that there is a human person named Edgar played the part of a rabbit in a play. True premises, however, while necessary for an acceptable argument, are not sufficient

It is curious to note that a great number of jokes turn on equivocation. We have a tendency to groan when the joke is very silly, for example, Q: Why did the chicken cross the road once but not twice? A: Because it didn't want to be a double-crosser. Equivocation in jokes are fun; in arguments, not.

The next example is kind of tricky.

> Though I have only been here one term, I can say with some assurance that the university must be haunted. The reason I believe this is because people here, some of the students, some of the faculty and the staff and even some of the administrators continually talk about how we need to get involved with activities, such as student government, sports, clubs, and such like, and we need to let the spirit move us.

Now, the conclusion is the second part of the first sentence. It refers to the university as being haunted. Presumably, the haunting is done by ghosts or spirits. But the premise is referring to a spirit of a different sort, namely, a frame of mind in which we act with some excitement or seriousness about the activities in which we are engaged. Clearly, this is an equivocation on 'spirit.'

L. Composition

The Fallacy of Composition is committed when an argument is presented which proceeds from the attributes of the parts of something, as premise(s), to the attributes of the whole of something, as conclusion. We can call this the "part-to-whole-fallacy." For example,

Monica's library contains only books that are well-known.
We conclude that Monica's library is well-known.

Let's say that Monica owns only books that were written by famous authors, for example, books by Virginia Woolf, Thomas Pynchon, John Stuart Mill, W.E.B. Du Bois, Stephen King, William Shakespeare, Vine Deloria, and so on. That each book in Monica's library is well-known refers to an attribute of the books themselves. Many other people, however, own just those sorts of books. It does not follow that Monica's library is special and hence well-known itself. We have gone from an attribute of each of the parts of Monica's library to an attribute of the library itself. The premise may be true, but the conclusion false. This is an invalid argument; it commits the fallacy of Composition. Another example is:

Each player on the Oakland Raiders football team is an outstanding player.
Hence, the Oakland Raiders is an outstanding team.

Here, of course, it would be pointed out that even if each player is outstanding, unless the players play/work "as a team," then the Raiders won't be outstanding.

The next example is one which does not commit Composition but which has the same form as the above arguments.

Each brick in the brick wall is made of mud and straw.
So, the wall is made of mud and straw.

Note here that the author of this argument intends us to understand that each brick in the wall is made only of mud and straw and that the wall is itself is made up entirely and only of the bricks. The attributes here are "being made of mud and straw." The argument proceeds from the parts (the bricks) to the whole (the wall). This is an excellent example to show that informal fallacies of reasoning rely on *content* rather than *form*.

One must take care not to confuse Composition with Hasty Generalization, for though the latter may seem to go from parts to whole, two factors distinguish these fallacies: 1) Composition refers to the *attributes* of the parts and the whole, not generalizing, and 2) Hasty Generalization relies on premises that are either atypical or of a limited scope, with a conclusion that is a generalization.

M. Division

The Fallacy of Division proceeds in the opposite direction as that of Composition. We might call it the "whole-to-part-fallacy," because when someone presents an argument wherein the premises refer to the attributes of a whole leading to a conclusion referring to the attributes of the parts, Division is committed. For example,

> Oxford University's Bodleian Library is well-known.
> Hence, every book in the Bodleian Library is well-known.

The Bodleian Library contains some rather obscure books, books of which many of the most well-read of scholars are unaware. There are books and manuscripts in the Bodleian known perhaps to only one or two people. Of course, the locution "well-known" is relative, but generally speaking, we might say that within a certain very large circle, the Bodleian Library is well-known and attracts many more visitors than, say, a local town library. Another example is:

> The Toledo Mudhens is an outstanding team.
> Hence, every player on the Mudhens is an outstanding player.

It is not always true that outstanding teams have only outstanding players. Sometimes the high level of ability of some of the players will make up for the inadequacy of other players. It must also be said that there are outstanding teams and then there are *outstanding teams*, 'outstanding' being another somewhat relative term.

As the fallacy of Composition must not be confused with Hasty Generalization, so the fallacy of Division must not be confused with Accident. The reasons are parallel. While Accident runs from a general rule to specific instances wherein the rule is incorrectly applied, Division makes no mention of a general rule, but refers rather to attributes of some whole to draw a conclusion about the attributes of the parts of this whole.

N. Petitio Principii (Begging the Question)

Essentially, there are three ways to "beg the question." One way is to more or less assume as true the very conclusion for which one is arguing. Strictly speaking, all these sorts of "petitio" arguments are valid in the sense that if at least one of the premises is true, i.e., the question-begging one, then the conclusion is also true, or, since one of the premises says the same thing as the conclusion, it is impossible for the premises to all be true and the conclusion false. For example,

> It is morally permissible for a psychiatrist to betray the confidential relationship between client and physician when the psychiatrist has in-

formation about the intentions of the client that, unless disclosed, would result in harm to a third person. This is so because a psychiatrist, even though bound by the confidentiality of the client/physician relationship, cannot be held ethically responsible for violating a trust when not doing so would cause another person to be harmed.

The first sentence is the conclusion and the second sentence the premise in the above argument. Notice that 'morally permissible' and 'cannot be held ethically responsible for' have the same connotation. These two sentences "say" essentially the same thing. Hence, the argument begs the question. Consider the following:

Ektelon racquetball racquets are the best racquets made. We can see that this is so because Ektelon racquets are made with only the finest materials. They are made with only the finest materials because professional racquetball players demand high performance and endurance in their racquets. These players can be sure that Ektelon racquets perform well and last long because Ektelon racquets are the best racquets made.

This is an example of an argument based on "circular reasoning," beginning and ending with the same sentence. Since *one* of the premises is precisely the same as the conclusion, this argument begs the question.

The second way an argument can beg the question is by failing to state all of the premises explicitly. That is, some arguments have "hidden" or "suppressed" premises. These premises are hidden because they are false, or, at least, questionable or debatable. For example,

The elephant is a protected species and whoever kills one is guilty of poaching. Carleton, who works for the Gobi Wildlife Service Program, killed an elephant. Hence, Carleton is definitely guilty of poaching.

In this case, one hidden premise is that the elephant killed by Carleton was a rogue and had destroyed much property and killed many people. The second hidden premise is that the Wildlife Service has a policy which permits destroying rogue elephants. We can see that if these two premises were to have been included in the original argument, then no fallacy would have been committed. Another example of "hidden premise *petitio*" is below.

Advocating the violent overthrow of the government is a crime of treason, punishable by exile or death. It follows that Bernard may be banished or executed for his riot-causing speeches about impeaching the president.

The hidden premise here is that Bernard's speeches, which cause riots, can be construed as advocating the violent overthrow of the government. This is not explicitly stated in the argument, but is obviously being used in reasoning to the conclusion. The problem is that the sort of behavior Bernard is engaging in is arguably *not* promoting the violent overthrow of the government, but is rather designed to get people angry enough to demonstrate a certain dissatisfaction with the President or Congress or what have you. The fact that the speeches cause riots may be reason enough to arrest Bernard. But the question of whether his acts are treasonous is open to interpretation. This argument begs the question in that it fails to point out the crucial premise upon which the argument relies.

The third way an arguer can beg the question is to state a controversial premise as though it is not controversial. As examples, consider the two following arguments.

Infants born with birth defects are of little value to the society. They require a great deal of the scarce resources and therefore should be terminated and not treated.

Research by a professor at a university specializing in teaching should always be directed toward improving her/his teaching. Ivan, who works at an institution whose primary mission *is* teaching, has an outstanding teaching record but insists on doing research in areas outside his teaching areas. Hence, Ivan will never be awarded tenure.

The first premise in each of the arguments above is controversial. To establish them as true would presumably require much argumentation. Both premises are stated in a more or less dogmatic way, thus, closing the door on dispute. If any listener detects this, the argument could legitimately be rejected on that basis alone.

O. Limited Alternative

The fallacy of Limited Alternative is committed when one is given a choice between two (or more) options when there are clearly more options than are presented. For example,

If you study Philosophy in graduate school, you can specialize either in epistemology, metaphysics, or ethics. If you concentrate on epistemology, you are in danger of losing sight of many of the most important issues facing the world today. If you concentrate on ethics, you will be unable to sustain the epistemic arguments for your positions. Hence, that it would be better for you to specialize in metaphysics.

Like any major discipline at a university, Philosophy offers a wide range of possibilities with regard to specialization. The following are some examples: ancient Greek philosophy, philosophy of language, philosophy of science, logic, modern philosophy, 20th century philosophy, medieval philosophy, the empiricists. Clearly, then, the first premise in the argument above gives limited alternatives. Hence, the fallacy of Limited Alternative is committed here. Another example of this fallacy is:

> Either you vote for a Democrat or you vote for a Republican in the presidential election. Since all the Republican candidates are equally unappealing, you can't vote for any of *them*. We can conclude that you will vote for a Democrat.

There is one thing we can pretty much predict in an election year, and that is that there will be many more sorts of candidates for office than just Democrats and Republicans. There will be Peace and Freedom, Libertarian, Green Party and Independent Party candidates, just to name a few. Hence, in the above argument, one is given a limited number of alternatives, i.e., one might not vote for a Democrat *or* a Republican, but rather one of the others. Or, one might not vote at all – another alternative.

Note, however, that the above argument is valid. This is to say that *if* there were only Democrats and Republicans to choose from in the election, and *if* one found each of the Republicans to be so unappealing as to be unable to vote for any, and *if* one were definitely going to vote, then it would follow that one would vote for a Democrat. Recall one of the ways mentioned in Chapter 1 that an argument could be unacceptable was if one or more of the premises were unacceptable. This is precisely the case in the above argument. The first premise is unacceptable *because* it presents a limited alternative.

P. Deontic Fallacy

The Deontic fallacy is otherwise known as the "normative" or "moral" or "Naturalistic" or the "is/ought" fallacy, and is committed when one presents an argument in which the premises are *descriptive statements* (asserting that something *is* the case) but where the conclusion is a *prescriptive statement* (asserting that something *ought to be* the case). There is sometimes a hidden premise in an argument that commits the Deontic fallacy, and this hidden premise is sometimes a *value statement* (asserting a value one holds). For example,

> Black South Africans have been seen by White Afrikaners as second-class citizens and nonpersons for hundreds of years. This is an outgrowth of the way South Africa grew, historically, as a nation. Therefore, this is the way it should be.

A possible hidden premise here is that history always works out for the best, an assertion of value. The truth of this hidden premise is, of course, debatable, as are many (if not all) value judgments we encounter. One can attack this argument from at least two sides: 1) by attempting to show that the hidden premise is false (if there indeed *is* a hidden premise), and/or 2) by attempting to show that the conclusion itself is false. Another way of showing its unacceptability is to present a counterexample, such as,

> Jews have been considered by many to be second-class citizens and nonpersons for hundreds of years. The Third Reich's treatment of Jews was an historical outgrowth of this attitude toward the Jews. We conclude that this treatment was the way it ought to have been.

One of the distinct problems with this argument as a counterexample to the argument above is that it also relies on a value judgment, one perhaps not shared by all readers of this text. I take the position that the conclusion is false and that the premises are true; otherwise, I would not have selected this argument as a counterexample. Perhaps the most that can be said here is that the argument itself is simply formally invalid, which means that the conclusion does not follow from the premises.

A word about hidden premises relative to the Deontic Fallacy is in order. Any argument that contains a hidden premise that is controversial begs the question. Hence, some arguments that commit the Deontic Fallacy also commit *Petitio Principii*. But, if any argument commits the Deontic Fallacy but does not contain a hidden premise, or if it contains a hidden premise but the premise is not controversial, then that argument does not also commit *Petitio Principii*.

The Deontic fallacy, being one of the most common of all fallacies, is many times persuasive. The primary reason for this is that the hidden premise is many times one we would presumably accept. Consider:

> Smoking cigarettes causes shortness of breath, diminishment of circulation, heart disease, bronchial infections, and lung cancer. Hence, one ought not smoke.

The hidden premise here is that one ought to avoid all of the stated effects of cigarette smoking. This is a case in which, if the hidden premise is added to the argument, the argument becomes more or less acceptable. However, it is possible that the hidden premise might be rejected by a person who could present an acceptable argument for doing so, say, in a situation where a number of people had agreed (having been informed of the possible consequences) to smoke cigarettes for a research project studying the effects of cigarette smoking on distance runners. The point is, again, that value judgments are open to question as to their truth. They are not simply statements of objective fact (whatever that is). That is, a value statement, such as, "New York is as beautiful as New Orleans," is not in the same category with such sentences as, "Chicago is further from San Diego than Detroit is from Toronto," in terms of discovering their truth.

When there is differing opinion about the truth value of a sentence in an argument, the acceptability of the argument is also in question. To understand the disagreement usually requires getting clear on what values are being pulled in to the arena of judgment about the argument. When the values themselves are made explicit, further new arguments will result, having to do with the acceptability or unacceptability of these values, and so on. It is only when agreement is reached on these values that the original argument itself can be agreed upon as acceptable or the reverse.

One of our jobs here is to try to discover when an argument is valid and when not. The fact that one cannot validly go from a fact to a value indicates that any argument containing only *factual* statements in the premises and a *value* statement in the conclusion is not valid, no matter whether one thinks it acceptable or not. Thus, for example, many people have argued that,

> Lying, in any form, creates distrust. Literally no one wants to be distrusted. Therefore, one ought never lie.

I think it cannot be denied that anyone caught in a lie is usually thereafter, to some extent, distrusted. And it is probably true that the vast majority of people would prefer to be trusted rather than distrusted. Does it logically follow that one ought never lie? It does not, since perhaps there are cases in which one might attempt to show that it is *better* (a value term) to lie, be found out, and be distrusted than tell the truth and avoid the risk of being distrusted. Just from the practical point of view, it seems the above argument cannot be defended against all situations. But, further, those who heartily agree with the idea that one cannot derive an 'ought' from an 'is' ask, What could it be in the premises that might possibly lead anyone to think the conclusion follows? So smoking *is* bad for one's health. Does it *logically* follow that one ought to stop smoking? So polluting the environment will kill seventy-five percent of the wildlife. Does it *logically* follow that we ought not pollute? The strictly logical answer to these questions is "no." So that black widow spider is crawling up the nape of your neck. Does it logically follow that you should try to remove it? No! But, behind all these "oughts" are values which influence our accepting the inferences we do accept. From the point of view of logic alone, the arguments are not valid, but from the view of one who holds the various values indicated, there is no hesitation to accept the argument. The moral here is that one must take care to make one's values explicit, so there is no confusion about the "hidden" values present in any argument that might be charged with committing the Deontic fallacy.

4.4. Avoiding Fallacies

The best way to avoid committing a fallacy, which is also the best way of avoiding falling prey to someone else committing a fallacy, is simply what your mother used to say to you every time you left the house: *"Be Careful!"* One must attempt to understand precisely what is being said in an argument, whether the conclusion actually does follow from the premises, whether there are one or more hidden (suppressed/unspoken) premises, whether the arguer is appealing to one or more of our emotions, and whether there is either ambiguity or irrelevance in the relation between the premises and the conclusion. Consider, for example, the following argument:

> If I run day-care from 8am to 4pm, with 10 children, then my own family will suffer from my not being able to spend much time with them alone. If I run day-care from 9am to 2pm, with 10 children, then I will have much more time to spend alone with my family. If I run from 9am to 2pm, I will be making less money than if I run from 8am to 4pm, money that is sorely needed by the family. Either way, the family will suffer, because if I don't spend time with my own children, they will not receive the care and attention they want and deserve, and if I don't make enough money, we will not be able to make our house payment and could lose it. For the next two years at least, the money is more important than spending time alone with my family. Hence, I'll run day-care from 8am to 4pm.

Valid or invalid? Acceptable or unacceptable? You might have guessed that the last premise is the most important here. It states a value judgment, and one perhaps not everyone would share. The argument will be unacceptable for anyone who denies the last premise. For another person, however, it may be unacceptable because perhaps there is a third alternative, say, running day-care from 9am to 2pm with 12 children, yielding shorter hours but more paying customers, as it were. In terms of strict validity, however, discounting all other factors, if the premises are true, then the conclusion will also be true.

To avoid fallacies, we need first of all to be aware of them. We need to be able to call on our knowledge of the fallacies when attempting to analyze an argument, to have the fallacies in mind. But just knowing the fallacies does not always get the job done. Sometimes arguments are presented in such a way as to hinder exact analysis, usually because there is ambiguity in what is being said, or because of the lack of articulation of the arguer. This can happen especially where someone is trying to slip in a value judgment unnoticed. It is very difficult to state a value judgment which would be unquestioned by a great majority of people. The fact that there is a value judgment in an argument does not automatically make it invalid or unacceptable. Consider the following:

> If "open marriage" is psychologically healthier for a couple than "closed marriage," then adultery, consented to by each partner, is not morally wrong. But that is absurd. Adultery, in all of its many forms, is always morally wrong. Therefore, open marriage is not psychologically healthier than closed marriage.

This is a valid argument. That is, there is no possibility here that if the premises are true the conclusion is false. This is not to say that the premises *are* true in fact, but rather that *if* they are, then the conclusion is also. So, here is a valid argument with the second premise, i.e., adultery is always morally wrong, that is a value judgment. If one is unhappy with the argument, there a number of ways to analyze it. One might go through each of the informal fallacies to check whether one or more has been committed. In this case, however, I think none has been. One might ask, Is the implication of the first premise a good one? That is, does open marriage being psychologically more healthy than closed marriage *entail* that adultery is not morally wrong? One could challenge the first premise on this score. One might also challenge the truth of the second premise. It is one thing to say that *if* the premises are true, then the conclusion is also true. It is quite another to establish the premises as true. Showing, then, that the entailment of the first premise fails to hold would be tantamount to showing the argument to be unacceptable. Showing the second premise to be false would have the same result. Hence, even when one does succeed in avoiding each of the fallacies, and even when one is able to show the argument to be valid, these things in themselves do not insure that the argument is acceptable.

Any argument that commits a fallacy is suspect. Even though some arguments that commit fallacies may be more or less acceptable to some people, that is not a good reason not to avoid fallacies. And to avoid them, listen and read carefully and for content. Know the fallacies and know what the arguer is attempting to say, whether you are analyzing an argument of your own or the argument of another person.

Exercise: Ch. 2.

A. Identify the fallacy or fallacies committed in the following passages/arguments. Some passages may not contain fallacies.

1. The dominant view of the universe among working physicists is that the universe is expanding. Since the Empire State Building, the Tower of London, and the Clock Tower at Humboldt State University are each part of the universe, it follows that these objects (and all others as well) are expanding.

2. The dominant view of the universe among working physicists is that the universe is expanding. With the recent budget cuts that have halted any new book acquisitions, it is clear that the Fallbrook County Library is *not* expanding. Hence, the physicists of today might want to rethink their theory.

3. "Subway! Where winners eat."

4. Crow #1 is black, crow #2 is black, crow #3 is black . . . crow #2735 is black. We conclude that all crows are black.

5.* I would recommend that you take care not to damage the reputation of our client with any of your comments in the newspaper column. Remember what happened to Adrian Lester after he wrote those lies about Kyle Anders. He got dumped in the river, wearing cement shoes.

6. Our water is polluted, our air is polluted, the wildlife in the forests and deserts are no longer safe from the consequences of our high-tech society, sea-life has become increasingly more difficult to stabilize, and our children can no longer roam the fields and hills by themselves. These things can be changed if we will only remember our roots and "get back to nature." Hence, we have a

moral duty to limit the use of automobiles, factories, and any other thing that destroys what is "natural."

7.   Avoid broccoli at all costs! My sister once ate three stalks of broccoli, got sick, and had to go to the hospital for an appendectomy.

8.   Plastic surgery costs are the highest in the medical profession, up to $6,000 for one-half hour of the staff's time. Hence, unless one has unlimited wealth and doesn't care how one spends it, it may be advisable to seek a second or even third opinion, and find out about prices, prior to hiring a plastic surgeon.

9.   Hegel thought he was God. Now, anyone who is such a deluded egotist cannot be taken seriously as a philosopher, and that person's writings are better left to rot on the moldy shelves in the back rooms of libraries.

10.   The United States Senate is a distinguished body of men and women. We can only conclude that every senator is a distinguished person or that senators have distinguished looking bodies.

11.* My Uncle Zeb just got back from a visit to Peking. He was telling me about the way the upper class Chinese women wear their hair these days. They first part it straight down the middle, front to back. They then comb the left side to the back, with a pink or gold colored ribbon tying it to the short hairs on the nape of the neck. They comb the right side to the front with a purple or blue ribbon tied in a bow and hanging just beside the eye. Hence, if you want to be considered *chic* in the Chinese style, you might try this hair style.

12.   "The origins of the anthropologist is a mystery hidden in the historical mists. Indians are certain that all societies of the Near East had anthropologists at one time because all those societies are now defunct." [Vine Deloria, Jr., *Custer Died for Your Sins*]

13.   If the industrial revolution is to be thought of as having significantly altered the lives of the common person, the entire population will have to be considered in their economic, cultural, and linguistic aspects.

14.   Lyndon Johnson was as powerful a president as this country has ever known. He was powerful because he had markers (IOU's) from just about every government official during the years 1959-1965. And the reason he had all these markers was because he was the most powerful president.

15.   Pierre Teilhard de Chardin, 1881-1955, is thought to have been part of the great "Piltdown Conspiracy" that occurred in the early part of the 20th Century. Letters from him to his parents and friends, as well as witnesses concerning dates, times and places of Teilhard's meetings with Charles Dawson, the originator of the hoax, point to many inconsistencies in the records. Not only that, but it appears that Teilhard attempted to cover up his own part in the hoax. At least two facts follow, to wit, 1) that Teilhard is considered part of the conspiracy, and 2) that the works of Teilhard hardly merit all the attention they have received since his death.

16.   ". . . To die, to sleep –
       To sleep, perchance to dream – ay, there's the rub,
       For in that sleep of death what dreams may come,
       When we have shuffled off this mortal coil . . . ." [Shakespeare, *Hamlet*]

17. One of the greatest sportscasters of our time, Vin Scully, made some comments about the possibility that the Persian Gulf shipping lanes are perhaps the most dangerous place to be right now. If I were you, I'd take my vacation on the other side of the world this year.

18.* It seems absolutely incredible that the people of California could believe in a man, and believe the things he says, who stands to gain so much my being elected governor.

19. Sociology 304, Biology 303, and Philosophy 306 each satisfy a General Education requirement at the University. It follows that if we teach those classes as essentially one class, then that one class would also satisfy the General Education requirement.

20. Since we cannot read other people's minds but can interpret their actions, and since all we need for an acceptable scientific theory is a plausible set of hypotheses, that is, ones that will yield good explanations and reliable predictions, we can see that behaviorism is an excellent theory. After all, though behaviorism can deny the existence of minds by just focusing on the actions of the person being studied, it has a tendency to make very reliable predictions of human action.

21. Each and every college in this university is headed by a person who has over fifteen years of experience in administration. Each and every person on the list has a reputation for excellence in her/his respective area of specialization. We may conclude that the university as a whole shares this reputation.

22. It is quite unreasonable to believe that peace and harmony can be the normal way of human life. Acts of violence have always been part of living. In addition, there is no one who has never committed an act of violence. Our society itself breeds violence in such popular sports as American football, boxing, wrestling, and even in some instances basketball and baseball.

23. We can choose either nuclear war or nuclear peace. If we opt for the former, billions of people will die the death of violence. If we opt for the latter, billions of people will die the death of fear, greed and starvation. In the end, then, there is no way to win.

24. There can be no doubt that each of the candidates is qualified for the job. But let me make a special plea for candidate #5. This person has just gone through a thoroughly destructive divorce, one of her children was hurt in a bus accident three weeks ago, her self-esteem is waning, and she learned yesterday that her property in Arizona has been seized by the government for payment of back taxes, the fault of her former husband.

25.* I have received notice that there has been a grievance filed against my colleague because she allegedly failed to turn in her grades on time. This is sheer harassment. I happen to know, and can prove with the documents in this folder, that the person who filed the grievance, on two occasions, destroyed student evaluations from his file which would have cast a disparaging light on his performance as a teacher.

26. The question is not whether Grape Nuts is right for you, the question is whether you are right for Grape Nuts.

27. Glenn really has no right to bring a law suit against Harry. Even though Harry secretly had Glenn's father's Will altered to give him (Harry) 60% of the company, one has to consider, Glenn and Harry have been friends since they were eight years old, and you know the old adage: Once true friends, forever true friends.

28. Every time Matt and I go to a professional baseball game, the team we want to win loses. For the sake of our favorite teams, we should stay away from the baseball park.

29. Every time Matt and I go to a professional baseball game, the team we want to win loses. We went to see the Giants and the Mets and the Giants lost. We went to see the Giants and the Cubs and the Cubs lost. We went to see the A's and the White Sox and the White Sox lost. Hence, our favorite teams lose all the time.

30.* If the goal of human sexuality is procreation, then all sexual acts which one participates in that could not lead to procreation are perversions of human sexuality.

31. The goal of human sexuality is pleasure.

32. Imelda promised to have the truck back here by Thursday. She therefore has an obligation to have it back by Thursday.

33. "There's something about an Aqua Velva man."

34. "We are here for the Peace Rally! What I don't understand is why we are going to listen to such a person as Conrad Welsh. He's known to be a pro-Contra radical, a Gay activist, a liar and a back-stabber. His bit about how we should spend three million dollars on media coverage for the fight in Latin America is just another one of his shady, self-serving, tricks. His family owns fourteen television stations in seven western states."

35.* The Holocaust took untold numbers of innocent lives. We have a moral duty to our children, and their children, that this devastation never happen again–and never be forgotten.

36. Consider the abolitionist (John) who has two choices: He can give up the runaway slave (William) to the authorities, thereby avoiding the risk of being caught and hanged himself, or he can lie to the authorities and save the life of the slave. He cannot give up the slave because he knows that the slave will be hanged himself. And he cannot lie because lying is wrong. No matter what he does, he does wrong. But wait! That last sentence is false. Whichever action he does is the right action, because when given a choice between two evils, when one chooses to act, the evil that one does turns out to be the thing one ought to do. And since no action that one *ought* to do is wrong, John will commit the right action by doing either one.

37. Very few people will take wise advice from an elder. But everyone will take money from an elder. We can conclude that money is more valuable than wisdom.

38. Nature is uniform. Hence, when it comes to events in the natural world (the seas, the atmosphere, the forest, etc.), the future will be like the past.

39. Pragmatism is most definitely the most distinctively American philosophical perspective there is. William James, C.I. Lewis, John Dewey, W.V. Quine,
Oliver Wendell Holmes and dozens of other justifiably famous Americans have
adopted it. Since these men embraced pragmatism, and since their considered
judgments are not to be discounted, we ourselves ought to study pragmatism in
depth and adopt it ourselves.

40.* Descartes argued that we cannot trust our senses. But that is utterly ridicu-
lous. We trust our senses every day and all day long. When you go to the store
and look for produce, what you do is thump the watermelon to see if it is ripe,
gently squeeze the avocado, smell the orange, and so on. You are using your
senses for all these things, for signs of freshness. When you have lost your keys,
what do you do? You "look" for them. You look on the tables, under the couch,
on the dresser; you put your hand under pillows and cushions, and so on. Can't
trust our senses – that's absurd.

3. Translations

3.1. Preliminaries

Beginning with the present chapter, our study will focus on what is commonly known as *sentential logic*. It is also known otherwise as *propositional, symbolic, or formal logic*. The main concern here is with sentences and arguments, which may be expressed in symbolic notation. Using the logical techniques of truth tables and truth trees, in Chapters 3 and 5 respectively, we will be able to determine the logical status of sentences. Also, we will be able to determine whether arguments are valid or invalid by using truth tables, truth trees, and, in Chapter 6, natural deduction.

The major difference between our subject matter in the present and later chapters and Chapters 1 and 2 has to do with the distinction between formal and informal logic. Whereas the first two chapters were concerned with definitions and the content of arguments (that is, what the arguments are actually about in terms of subject matter), in the following chapters our focus will be on the *forms* of sentences and arguments, where content takes a back seat (or no seat at all).

The name "sentential logic" derives from the fact that we must begin by studying sentences themselves. We will be naming, defining and classifying the sentences of symbolic logic. We will also be combining sentences to form arguments.

One guiding principle for this study is that *every sentence is either true or false; no sentence is neither true nor false; and no sentence is both true and false*. This principle is called *The Law of Excluded Middle*. The principle will be unproblematic if we adopt the definition of a "sentence" as an assertion made about the world (that is, what we mean by 'sentence' is "declarative sentence"). An example here is:

(1) John Kennedy was the U. S. President in 1961.

This is a sentence which states something about the world. In line with the Law of Excluded Middle, we see that it is either true or false that Kennedy was President in 1961; that it is false that Kennedy was neither the President nor not the President in 1961; and also false that Kennedy was and was not President in 1961.

Further along, we will be referring to the *truth value* of sentences. There are only two truth values: True and False. The truth value of (1) is true, since Kennedy was indeed President in 1961. It often happens, however, that a sentence changes truth value. If someone had said, in 1950, that Hawai'i is one of the

United States, for example, its truth value would have been false, for at that time Hawai'i was not a state. However, if someone should utter that sentence now, the truth value of that sentence would be true. Examples abound.

There *are* things that people utter that are neither true nor false, but we do not count these utterances as sentences in the sense in which that term is used here. For example, if you pass a friend on the street and say "Hi!," you have not uttered anything that is either true or false. Truth and falsehood do not apply to salutations and greetings. Nor do they apply to commands, as "Mow the lawn" and "Tie it down securely." Nor do they apply to questions, such as "Have you seen my keys?" and "Do you like to swim?" These utterances do not assert anything about the world directly and hence are not counted as either true or false.

To see the importance of the concept of truth value, and of knowing which sentences are and which are not true, recall our definition of validity. We say that an argument is valid if it is impossible for the premises to be true while the conclusion is false. Truth tables, to be encountered in Chapter 4, is a most conspicuous way to use truth values to determine which arguments are valid and which are not. We will also be able to determine, in many cases, that some given sentence is true, or false.

3.2. Truth Functional Connectives and Translations

To make the work of analyzing sentences and arguments less reliant upon the ambiguities of *natural language* (Arabic, Spanish, Yurok, Russian, English, Chinese, German, Greek, etc.), and to seize a bit of control over the size of the sentences and arguments to be analyzed, we use specially designated symbols to represent certain terms, phrases, and sentences. In essence we will be laying out the rules for what we will call an *artificial language*. For example, the sentence

(2) Rose is a teacher.

could be represented by the capital letter "R." Contrast (2) with

(3) Rose is a teacher and Ester is a student.

We can represent 'Ester is a student' with 'E' and derive the following partial symbolization for sentence (3):

(4) (R and E)

We call (2) a *simple sentence* because it expresses essentially one idea. We call (3) a *compound sentence* because it contains two simple sentences as components, namely, "Rose is a teacher" and "Ester is a student." Any sentence that contains two or more simple sentences as components is a compound sentence. The parentheses around (4) are to be understood as representing punctuation marks. They are also used as "groupers," as in (6) below:

(5) Samantha and Katie must both arrive late, or the party will be ruined.
(6) [(S and K) or R]

where 'S' stands for 'Samantha must arrive late,' 'K' for 'Katie must arrive late,' and 'R' for 'the party will be ruined.' Parentheses ('( )'), brackets ('[ ]'), and braces ('{ }') will also be used as punctuation and for grouping. It can be seen that the symbolizing of sentences greatly reduces the size of the sentence. This is a singular benefit when one is working with many sentences at once, as we will be doing further along. It will also help when the sentences we work with in natural language are large and complicated.

At this point, the notion of a *sentence connective* can be introduced. Connectives are symbols used in place of specific "logical" words and phrases found in natural language. There are five connectives. Consider the following sentences:

(7) Seven is less than ten and greater than five.
(8) Bruce got the sabbatical but turned it down.
(9) The road was flooded, yet passable.
(10) Baby seals are hunted; however, they should be protected.

Conjunctions

Each of the sentences (7)-(10) is called a *conjunction*. A conjunction is a compound sentence in which the word "and" (or some variant such as 'yet' or 'but') *connects* the simple sentences.

To symbolize the conjunction, we use the "dot," (•) which has the same shape as a period but appears in the middle of the line rather than at the bottom. The dot in the translated (symbolized) sentence is located between the **conjuncts** of the conjunction. The conjuncts in a conjunction are the simple sentences which are "conjoined." Thus, (7)-(10) are translated as follows:

(7a)   (T • F)   The conjuncts are "T" and "F"
(8a)   (S • T)   The conjuncts are "S" and "T"
(9a)   (F • P)   The conjuncts are "F" and "P"
(10a) (H • P)   The conjuncts are "H" and "P"

We may now introduce the notion of a *translation dictionary* to specify the exact designations of the component sentences found in the original sentences. Dictionaries are to be constructed on the following models for (7)-(10):

(7) Seven is less than ten and greater than five.
Dictionary: 'T' = 'seven is less than ten'
              'F' = 'seven is greater than five'
Translation: (T • F)

(8) Bruce got the sabbatical, but turned it down

Dictionary: 'S' = 'Bruce got the sabbatical'
'T' = 'Bruce turned the sabbatical down'
Translation: (S • T)

(9) The road was flooded, yet passable.
Dictionary: 'F' = 'the road was flooded'
'P' = 'the road was passable'
Translation: (F • P)

(10) Baby seals are hunted; however, they should be protected.
Dictionary: 'H' = 'baby seals are hunted'
'P' = 'baby seals should be protected'
Translation: (H • P)

In constructing a dictionary, the letter one chooses to represent each simple sentence is arbitrary. However, it is useful to pick some letter that can readily identify the sentence being represented. *The translation dictionary must contain only simple sentences, stated in the affirmative or positive. There must never occur any term in a translation dictionary which would be translated with one of the five truth functional symbols.* Hence, for example, the word "and" (used in its conjunctive sense) would never appear in a translation dictionary. More on this as we proceed.

Note how, in the above translations, the dot replaces the words "and," "but," "yet," and "however." Other *conjunctive words* are: "moreover," "also," "still," "nevertheless," and "although." These words are normally translated with the dot.

Not every occurrence of the word "and" can be straight forwardly translated with the dot, because some sentences containing 'and' are not straightforward conjunctions. For example,

(11) Oil and vinegar make a great tasting salad dressing.

This sentence is not an ordinary conjunction. This is where the dictionary comes to be very important. In (11), if our dictionary is 'O' = 'oil makes a great tasting salad dressing,' 'V' = 'vinegar makes a great tasting salad dressing,' we derive the following:

(11a) (O • V)

When we translate (11a) back into English, we get
(11b) Oil makes a great tasting salad dressing and vinegar makes a great tasting salad dressing.

Sentences (11) and (11b) do not have the same meaning. Nor do they necessarily have the same truth value. Sentence (11b) is an inadequate translation of (11). As it turns out, (11) is a very complicated sentence which cannot be adequately translated using the limited number and variety of symbols we have here. To do it justice, we would have to move into *Predicate Logic* (Ch. 8). Nonetheless, it is instructive to see that there are some sentences containing 'and' that are not straightforward conjunctions. Examples:

Oil and water don't mix.
Oxygen and hydrogen comprise breathable air.
Elaine, George and Kramer are three characters on *Seinfeld*.
"Penn and Teller" is a very witty comedy team.

There are other sentences which, with a little thought, can be seen to be conjunctions. For example, take the following sentence:

(12)   Stephanie and Tim are wife and husband.

With the proper translation dictionary, we will be able to translate this sentence quite easily. Let 'S' = 'Stephanie is the wife of Tim,' 'T' = 'Tim is the husband of Stephanie.' We derive

(12a) (S • T)

Other examples of these sorts of sentence are:

Hollie and Mark are siblings to one another.
Janice and David are sister and brother.
Michelangelo and Magellan were contemporaries.

Negations

To *negate*, or deny, any simple or compound sentence, we use the symbol known as the bar (-). The resulting sentence is called a *negation*. These are quite easily dealt with as long as it is kept in mind precisely what is being negated. There are numerous ways of negating sentences in English by merely placing the negative term in the correct position in the sentence. For example, to negate the sentence "Don will spend the summer in the Sierras," each of the following would suffice:

It is not the case that Don will spend the summer in the Sierras.
Don will not spend the summer in the Sierras.
Don won't spend the summer in the Sierras.
It is false that Don will spend the summer in the Sierras.
It is not true that Don will spend the summer in the Sierras.
Don isn't going to spend the summer in the Sierras.

If 'S' = 'Don will spend the summer in the Sierras,' then the sentences above would each be correctly translated as '-S.'

Now that we have a symbol for negation, it is important to observe that the dictionary may not contain any word or phrase that indicates a negation. That is, the translation dictionary must not contain any sentence that would be translated using the bar. In fact, as was said before, one's dictionary must not contain *any* word or phrase that indicates any of the truth functional connectives. The reason for this is simple: Translating is an attempt to capture as much of the logical structure of a sentence as is possible with the tools one has. If we include a "logical" word in the translation dictionary, such as 'not' or 'and,' then that word will not be given the proper logical symbol in the translation and the translation will *not* capture as much of the logical structure of the sentence as is possible.

To negate a compound sentence, groupers are needed, and it is vital that the bar be placed at the proper location. Consider, for example,

(13) Lon rented the tiller and Dustin paid for it.

This sentence may be translated as (L • D). To negate the entire sentence, we place the bar in front of the first parenthesis, thus ranging over the entire formula, yielding "-(L • D)." Translating back into English, we derive the following sentence:

(14) It is not the case that Lon rented the tiller and Dustin paid for it.

Below are five sentences, each with dictionary and translation.

(15) Rita and June will not both skate. [R = Rita will skate; J = June will skate] -(R • J)

(16) Both Ronnie and Lennie are not as casual in their dress as Hayward. [R = Ronnie is as casual in his dress as Hayward; L= Lennie is as casual in his dress as Hayward] (-R • -L)
[Note here the difference between 'not . . . both' and 'both . . . not,' as exhibited in the translations of (15) and (16). The term "both" indicates that a conjunction is present in each sentence. However, whereas (16) says that neither Ronnie nor Lennie is as casual in his dress as Hayward, (15) does not say that neither Rita nor June will skate. In effect, what (15) says is that either one or the other won't skate. We will see how to translate sentences containing 'or' directly below.]

(17) Training in the military can develop a sense of discipline as well as comradeship between trainees, but not a sense of egoism. [C = training in the military can develop a sense of comradeship between trainees; D = training in the military can develop a sense of discipline; E = training in the military can develop a sense of egoism] [(D • C) • -E]

(18) Sisley's paintings of reflections on water are good, but they're not as good as Monet's. [M = Sisley's paintings of reflections on water are

as good as Monet's paintings of reflections on water; S = Sisley's paintings of reflections on water are good] (S • -M)

(19) Tom, Kathy, Jantz and Veden went skiing together, and so did Dustin, Nathan, Greg, and Henry. [D = Dustin went skiing; Greg went skiing; . . .]{[(T • K) • (J • V)] • [(D • N) • (G • H)]}

The grouping of the *sentence letters* in the translation of (19) is arbitrary. Sentence letters are the letters we use to designate sentences in the translation of a sentence from English into symbolic notation. A different, and logically equivalent, translation of (19) might be:

{[((T • K) • J) • V] • [(D • N) • (G • H)]}

What matters here is that 'T,' 'K,' 'J,' and 'V' are located within the same grouping, and that 'D,' 'N,' 'G,' and 'H' are grouped together. This should be obvious from the presence of the word "together" in the sentence. There is usually some indication of which letters are to be grouped together, though there are instances where it is not clear. This is where actual punctuation is important. Note that every parenthesis has a matching parenthesis, every bracket a matching bracket, and every brace a matching brace.

Notice the care that has been taken above in making each entry in the translation dictionaries complete simple sentences. This is vital to making it clear just what is being translated. Consider the sentence:

Elves live in the forest, but witches don't.

The following translation dictionary is incorrect: E = elves; W = witches. The reason for its being incorrect is that 'E' is not to represent only the word "elves," which is not itself a complete simple sentence, but rather 'E' must stand for 'elves live in the forest,' which *is* a complete simple sentence. The same is true for 'W,' which is not to represent 'witches' but rather 'witches live in the forest.' The translation for the sentence, then, is: (E d -W).

Disjunctions

The third type of sentence to be treated here is called the *disjunction*. Disjunctions are sentences containing some form of the word "or," and are translated with the *wedge* (v), also known as the *vel* or the *vee*. As the sentence components in conjunctions are called "conjuncts," so the sentence components in disjunctions are called *disjuncts*. Consider the following disjunction:

(20) Either England or France imports the most rice.
(20a) (E v F)   The disjuncts are "E" and "F"

There are actually two sorts of disjunctions, one called *inclusive* and the other called *exclusive*. The inclusive sense has the meaning "either one or the other and perhaps both," while the exclusive sense has the meaning "either one or the other, but not both." Since England and France cannot both import the most rice at the same time, (20) is an example of an exclusive disjunction. A fuller, more precise translation of (20), as an exclusive disjunction, would be:

(20b) [(E v F) • -(E • F)]

The English sentence for (20b) would be:

(20c) Either England or France imports the most rice, and it is not the case that both England and France import the most rice.

In general, we take the disjunction as having the inclusive sense in sentential logic. The reasoning behind this practice will become apparent when we get to truth tables. Suffice it to say, at this point, that it is sometimes difficult to determine the intention of someone who utters a disjunction, whether it is to have the inclusive or exclusive sense. For example, in the following sentence, the intention is ambiguous.

(21) This policy covers you when you are ill or unemployed.

It seems clear that the policy covers you if you are get sick. And it seems that it covers you if you lose your job. The question is: Does the policy cover you if you are ill *and* unemployed? Sentence (21) is not clear on this question and it would be well to ask the insurance agent to provide a precise translation of the sentence before signing anything.

The word *unless* is at times troublesome. It can be translated in two different, though equivalent, ways. Consider (22):

(22) Unless it rains, we'll go to the beach.

We can reword this sentence in at least two ways:
(22a) If it doesn't rain, then we'll go to the beach.
(22b) It will either rain or we'll go to the beach.

Sentence (22a) is what we call a *conditional sentence*, because it contains the word 'if' (next on our list of sentences to be studied). (22b) is a disjunction. For the sake of simplicity and economy, we will adopt the convention of translating all sentences with 'unless' as disjunctions. Hence, where 'R' = 'it rains,' and 'B' = 'we'll go to the beach,' the translation of (22) will be:

(22c) (R v B)   The disjuncts are "R" and "B"

Below are further examples of disjunctions, with translations. Note the various forms in which disjuncts may appear.

Either the general will move the troops into position or retreat. (M v R)

Martha will vacation in either Vienna or Athens, or in both Florence and Naples. [(V v A) v (F • N)]

Murderers either have rights or they don't. (R v -R)

California will divide into two states, unless the issue of water resources isn't resolved and a Democrat is elected to the governorship. [C v (-W • D)]

Neither the owners nor the players have a good historical record of compromise. -(O v P)

Not either the National Hockey League or Major League Baseball will accept binding arbitration. -(N v M)

Either Colleen or John won't set up a river boat guide service on the Red River in Shreveport. (-C v -J)

Christian will go to either the University of Chicago or Fordham, but not Indiana University. [(C v F) • -I]

Mark will become a Senator and a Democrat, or a Libertarian Marxist. [(S • D) v L]

Eileen will donate huge amounts of money to the Georgetown University and become a trustee of the University, or, either move to Washington D.C. or not endow Rochester with a chair in economics. [(G • T) v (W v -R)]

James thought he would major in either Accounting or Finance, or either Wildlife Management or Biology. [(A v F) v (W v B)]

Shawn will either travel to the orient or open a bookstore in London, but not both. [(O v L) • -(O • L)]

Conditionals

As mentioned above, a *conditional sentence* is a sentence containing the word "if." However, there many variants of 'if,' i.e., words that involve the same sort of logical operation/function within a sentence. The symbol used for conditionals is the *right-hand arrow* (→), or simply the "arrow." The sentence components in a conditional are called the *antecedent* and the *consequent*. The antecedent is the component that appears *before* the arrow and is the sentence that "implies" the consequent, which appears *after* the arrow. Each of the following sentences is a conditional and is translated in the same way:

If Plato dealt with ethics, *then* Plato was a philosopher.
Plato was a philosopher, *provided that* he dealt with ethics.
Plato's dealing with ethics *implies that* he was a philosopher.
Plato's dealing with ethics *entails that* he was a philosopher.
Plato was a philosopher *if* he dealt with ethics.
Plato dealt with ethics *only if* he was a philosopher.
Plato's dealing with ethics is a *sufficient condition* for his being a philosopher.
Plato's being a philosopher is a *necessary condition* for his dealing with ethics.

Each of the *italicized* words and phrases above is known as a *conditional indicator*. To translate any sentence containing any one or more of these indicators, an arrow is used. For the translation of these sentences, let 'E' = 'Plato dealt with ethics,' and let 'P' = 'Plato was a philosopher.' The translation of each is:

$(E \rightarrow P)$ Antecedent = E; Consequent = P

It is vitally important to achieve the correct order of the antecedent and consequent in the translation. That is, '$(P \rightarrow E)$' would be an incorrect translation of the sentences above. To translate conditionals, always ask, "Which sentence is entailed by which sentence?" Or, Which sentence is doing the implying and which is the sentence being implied? Always place the entailed/implied sentence *after* the arrow. Contrariwise, place the entailing/implying sentence *before* the arrow. Further examples:

(23) If Oriel College hosts the conference and Cambridge sends a Dean, then Edinburgh will send its most renown mathematician. Dictionary: C = Cambridge will send a dean to the conference; E = Edinburgh will send its most renown mathematician to the conference; O = Oriel College will host the conference. Translation: $[(O \cdot C) \rightarrow E]$. Notice here that the antecedent is "$(O \cdot C)$" and the consequent is "E." There is no rule saying that the antecedent or consequent must be a simple sentence. In this case, the antecedent is a compound sentence, conjunction.

(24) Provided that either Illinois or Michigan agree to fund the expedition, then either the Gold Coast or the Cape of Good Hope will be the jumping off point. Dictionary: C = the Cape of Good Hope will be the jumping off point for the expedition; G = the Gold Coast will be the jumping off point for the expedition; I = Illinois will agree to fund the

expedition; M = Michigan will agree to fund the expedition. Translation: [(I v M) → (G v C)]. In this case both antecedent and consequent are disjunctions.

(25) The present condition of politics in Washington D.C. being so unstable is a sufficient condition for either the Speaker of the House and the Minority Whip or the Secretary Pro Tem and the Senator from Utah to resign. Dictionary: H = the Speaker of the House will resign; P = the present condition of politics in Washington D.C. is stable; M = the Minority Whip will resign; S = the Secretary Pro Tem will resign; U = the Senator from Utah will resign. Trans: {-P → [(H •d M) v (S • U)]}. In this sentence the antecedent is a negated simple sentence, while the consequent is a disjunction, each disjunct of which is a conjunction. Also note the entry for 'P' in the translation dictionary; it is positive.

(26) If the Democrats push the health care plan, then if the Independents don't side with the Republicans, then either unemployment or welfare clients will suffer. Dictionary: D = the Democrats will push the health care plan; I = the Independents will side with the Republicans; U = unemployment clients will suffer; W = welfare clients will suffer. Trans: {D → [-I → (U v W)]}. This is a conditional sentence, the antecedent of which is a simple sentence while the consequent is itself a conditional, of which the antecedent to this *sub*-conditional is a negated simple sentence, while the consequent is a disjunction.

(27) Human adults are moral persons only if they are capable of rationality, self-consciousness, and complex communication. Dictionary: C = human adults are capable of complex communication; P = human adults are moral persons; R = human adults are capable of rationality; S = human adults are capable of self-consciousness. The Translation here is: {P → [(R • S) • C]}. In this conditional, the antecedent is a simple sentence while the consequent is a conjunction in which one of the conjuncts is also a conjunction.

The above sentence (27) contains the conditional indicator "only if." It may be thought curious that when translating 'only if,' the consequent follows rather than precedes the 'if.' The standard way of explaining this is that 'only if' is another way of indicating a necessary condition. For example,

(28) The key will work only if it is clean.

After what has been said above, it may look as though this sentence should be translated as (C → W), where C = the key is clean and W = the key will work. This is incorrect, however. For a key to work, it is usually a necessary condition that it be clean. But being clean is not a sufficient condition for a key to work. It also has to be cut for the specific lock, it has to be cut correctly, i.e., with no rough spots or extra ridges, etc., the lock itself has to be clean, and so on. What (28) actually says is that if the key works, then the key is clean; it does not say that if the key is clean, then it works. Hence, the proper translation of (28) is

(28a) (W → C).

The following will be a useful rule to adopt: *When translating a conditional sentence containing the word "if," the antecedent follows directly after 'if,' except in the case of 'only if,' where the consequent follows 'if.'*

Another common conditional indicator phrase is "is entailed by." Consider these two sentences:

(29) Full civil rights entails having voting privileges.
(30) Having voting privileges is entailed by full civil rights.

Both (29) and (30) are translated as (R → P). (29) has the antecedent at the beginning of the sentence, while (30) has the consequent at the beginning. The order of antecedent and consequent in the English sentences makes no difference to the translation itself. What is important is that one under-stands the function of the phrases "entails" and "is entailed by," because these indicate the order of implication, and it is only where one can say what is doing the implying and what is being implied that one can translate conditional sentences correctly. The term "implies" acts in the same way as 'entails.' Hence, in (29) and (30), 'implies' and 'is implied by' can replace 'entails' and 'is entailed by' with no loss of meaning or truth value and without change of translation. A different example follows:

(29a) Natural selection implies diversity. (N → D)
(30a) Diversity is implied by natural selection. (N → D)

Biconditionals

The last class of sentence we will study is the *biconditional*. As the name implies, a biconditional is comprised of two conditionals. Since we already know how to translate conditionals, translating biconditionals will cause no problems. What must be remembered are the "biconditional indicator phrases." There are essentially three of them, as indicated in the following set of biconditional sentences:

(31) One enjoys reading *if, and only if*, one learns something.
(32) John will move *just in case that* the rent increases.
(33) Your being eighteen years old is a *sufficient and necessary condition* for your being able to vote.

Whereas in the conditional, the arrow is used as the connective sign, in the biconditional, since we have two conditionals, the sign is the *double arrow* ($\leftrightarrow$), indicating a two-way implication. (31)-(33) are translated as,

(31a) ($E \leftrightarrow L$)
(32a) ($M \leftrightarrow R$)
(33a) ($E \leftrightarrow V$)

What (31) is saying, in the long form, is this: If you are enjoying reading, then you are learning something, and if you are learning something, then you are enjoying reading. This English sentence would be translated as

$[(E \rightarrow L) \bullet (L \rightarrow E)]$.

You might think of the biconditional as a short-cut way of expressing two conditionals in a conjunction. The biconditional indicator phrases are each treated as different ways of expressing the same thing. And, though the standard phrase is "if, and only if," each of the others, including "necessary and sufficient condition," "entails, and is entailed by," and "implies, and is implied by" is translated in the same way, i.e., with the double arrow. Consider the following sentence.

(34) That the safari will be dangerous entails, and is entailed by, the fact that there will be wild animals along the way.

Let 'S' = 'the safari will be dangerous,' and let 'W' = 'there will be wild animals along the way.' Translation for (34) is ($S \leftrightarrow W$).

If one replaces the biconditional indicator phrase in (34), i.e., "entails, and is entailed by," with any of the other biconditional indicator phrases, the translation will *not* thereby be altered. This is because all biconditional indicator phrases operate in the same fashion in a sentence. The same may be said for *all* indicator terms and phrases. That is, all conjunction indicator terms and phrases "match" in the sense of being interchangeable whenever they occur.

As noted above, each of the compound sentences are made up of simple sentences. These simple sentences are said to be components of the compound sentences, and have a name, e.g., the components in a disjunction are called disjuncts. There is no formal name for the components of biconditionals.

Let us mention once again that an important point to remember about translation dictionaries is that they should never contain any occurrence of an indicator term, either conjunctive, disjunctive, negative, conditional or biconditional. Each sentence letter should represent a simple sentence, without a negation.

On the next page both the table of connectives and the table of indicator terms are given. These tables are designed to lay out explicitly exactly which symbols go with each type of sentence (e.g., the dot with conjunctions) and which terms are indicative of which types of sentences (e.g., 'only if' is conditional in nature).

Table of Connectives

Sentence name:	Components:	Symbol:	Example:
Conjunction	conjuncts	(•)	(p • q)
Negation	---------	(-)	-p
Disjunction	disjuncts	(v)	(p v p)
Conditional	antecedent/consequent	(→)	(p → q)
Biconditional	---------	(↔)	(p ↔ q)

Table of Indicator Terms

Conjunction: and, yet, but, since, moreover, nevertheless, however, although, also, as well as.

Negation: not, didn't, won't, haven't, it is false that.

Disjunction: or, unless, either . . . or, neither . . . nor.

Conditional: if . . . then, if, only if, implies that, entails, sufficient condition, necessary condition, provided that, on condition that.

Biconditional: if and only if, just in case that, necessary and sufficient condition, entails and is entailed by, implies and is implied by.

Exercise: Ch. 3.

A. Translate the following sentences into symbolic notation, providing your own translation dictionary for each sentence.

1.   Stubby cannot fail this class if he will practice.
2.   Either the St. Francis or the Mark Hopkins will prove unsuitable for the conference, although the Mark Hopkins is large enough to accommodate a party of 300.
3.   If the University expands, then, since it has to add two more departments and not just one, Russian and either Advertising or History of Science will be added.
4.   On the condition that the United Nations takes action in the Orkney Islands, Commander Johnson will get a ship.
5.* The Orkney Islands will become an independent state provided that Scotland is willing to grant independence and England sees no threat to its own economic security.
6.   If either England or Scotland has a long range plan to set up a nuclear research center in the Orkneys, then the Orkneys will remain a county of Scotland.
7.   If Carla doesn't score high on the Graduate Record Exam (GRE), but scores in the top 5% on the Law School Exam (LSAT), then either she will change her major to Pre-Law and cut back on the number of units she's taking, or she'll stay

with her present major and attempt to secure a position as a legal researcher for Thomson, Turner & Tutwell.

8.   Carla's scoring high on the LSAT is a necessary condition for her getting the assistantship next year, but it is not a sufficient condition.

9.   Carla will score high on the GRE if, and only if, Janet remembers to return Carla's notes before leaving for Berkeley.

10.* Janet won't remember to return Carla's notes, but she'll apologize profusely and never borrow Carla's notes again.

11. One either believes David Hume to be the most important philosopher to ever write in English and agrees with his reasoning concerning causality, or one criticizes Hume's redundancy and finds the arguments naive and uninteresting.

12. No one will believe what Hume said about the future being like the past unless one can show his arguments to be valid.

13. Journal publications should be a necessary and sufficient condition for any university teacher getting tenure.

14. It will either rain or shine today, but not both.

15.*It will rain tomorrow only if either a high pressure front or a cold front moves in with the jet stream tonight.

16. Anne Rice will either write one more vampire book or she won't; however, she won't both write another and not write another.

17. It is false that Ronald Reagan's administration will be judged by history as having been good to the poor.

18. If #17 is true, then if Thomas Jefferson's administration won't be so judged, then John Kennedy's administration will be.

19. Martin makes the finest acoustic guitars, while either Fender or Gibson makes the finest electric guitars.

20.* Understanding Einstein is a necessary condition for obtaining a PhD in physics, unless understanding Bohr is a sufficient condition and under-standing Einstein is not a necessary condition for understanding Bohr.

B. Use the dictionary below in translating the following sentences into standard English from the symbolic notation.

C = Brahe rejected the Copernican theory
D = Galileo's works are full of important philosophical insights
E = Kepler's Third Law is still in use today
F = Kepler was Brahe's assistant
G = Galileo contradicted himself
H = Ptolemy was contradicted by Copernicus
K = Kepler admired Brahe
L = Ptolemy was the father of astronomy
P = Shakespeare was born in 1564
R = Galileo was born in 1564
S = Galileo and Shakespeare were contemporaries/
T = Galileo proved Aristotle wrong about planetary motion
U = Copernicus held a heliocentric theory

Z = Copernicus was the father of astronomy

1. [(P • R) → S]   2. [L → (H → U)]
3. (L v Z)   4. -(G ↔ D)
5.* (C → -K)   6. [C • (U → -F)]
7. [(T v -T) • -(T • -T)]   8. [(Z v L) v H]
9. -[L • (U • H)]   10.* {Z → [U → (-L • -K)]}
11. (-H v -E)   12. -[(T • G) • D]
13. [(U → Z) • (T → -Z)]   14. -(F → E)
15.* [(C → U) → -H]

C. Which of the following sentences are true; which are false?

1. A sentence translated with a wedge is called a conditional.
2. No sentence translated with a dot can contain another sentence which is not translated with a dot.
3. The components of sentences translated with an arrow are called "disjuncts."
4. No false sentence can be translated into symbolic notation.
5.* One translates a sentence with a dot if, and only if, the sentence contains anyone of the conjunction indicator terms.
6. It is proper to include connective indicator terms and/or phrases in a translation dictionary.
7. It is impossible for a sentence to contain three or more disjuncts.
8. The consequent is always implied by the antecedent.
9. The proper translation of 'Patti Page sings like a bird only if Herb's opinion of Patti Page is correct,' where 'B' = 'Patti Page sings like a bird,' and 'H' = 'Herb's opinion of Patti Page is correct,' is: (H → B).
10.* The following sentences should be translated in the same way:
    a) Teresa's good mood implies that she bought a new car.
    b) Teresa's good mood is entailed by her having bought a new car.
11. One proper translation of 'the Governor of Alabama will not seek another term in office unless the Crimson Tide wins the national championship,' where 'G' = 'the Governor of Alabama will seek another term in office' and 'C' = 'the Crimson Tide will win the national championship,' is: (G → C).
12. There is no exception to the rule that the antecedent always follows the word "if" when one translates.
13. There is no exception to the rule that the necessary condition always follows the arrow in translations.
14. Let 'L' = '*Love and Death* is a Woody Allen film' and 'S' = '*Sleeper* is a Woody Allen film' and 'F' = 'Woody Allen is a funny guy.' '[(L • S) → F]' could be translated as 'If *Love and Death* and *Sleeper* are Woody Allen films, then Woody Allen is a funny guy.'
15.* Only conditional sentences can be translated with an arrow.

D. Create your own dictionary and translate the following sentences into standard English from the symbolic notation. Create sentences that make sense, and attempt, through the dictionary, to make each sentence true. Note any problems in constructing a consistent dictionary.

1. [(S → -I) → (E v -S)]
2. -[(-G • P) → -(B • P)]
3. -(-Y → -R)
4. {[(B • M) • -A] → -X}
5.* [(R ↔ L) → R]
6. [(G v -G) v -X]
7. ((J → -L) v I)
8. [A → -(P • -B)]
9. --(-D ↔ B)
10.* [(S → E) ↔ K]

4. Truth Tables: Sentences

4.1. Preliminaries

With this chapter we begin our study of techniques for determining both the truth value of sentences and the validity or invalidity of arguments. These techniques are made possible in part by the creation of the special logical symbols in the artificial language we have sketched in Chapter 3. The present chapter treats one specific technique, namely, *Truth Tables*. Chapter 5 will cover *Truth Trees*. Truth tables are mechanical devices for determining the truth value of sentences and the validity of arguments with a set of rules that must be learned through practice if one is to work efficiently and effectively within the system. The key, as always, is *practice*.

A further word is due on the subject of acceptability at this point. The primary goal in the next three chapters is the determination of the logical status of sentences and arguments. This is to say that we will be attempting to see which sentences are true, which are false, and which arguments are valid and which invalid by appealing to certain logical rules. This is part of the work of logic, but it is not sufficient in itself to determine that some sentence or argument is to be accepted by a given individual. It is clear that a sentence is acceptable if it is true, also if there is good evidence to believe that it is true. An argument is acceptable if there is good evidence to show that each premise is true *and* if the conclusion either follows from the set of premises with a high degree of probability or is guaranteed to be true by virtue of the premises being true, i.e., follows conclusively (is *valid*). In a vast number of cases, one cannot determine, by the systems of logic alone, whether a sentence is indeed true or false. We see, then, that the techniques we will study only go so far in assisting the individual in determining the acceptability of arguments. An important thing one *can* determine, via the techniques of logic alone, is whether some conclusion really does follow from the premises offered in its support. If someone tries to persuade you, say, to vote against a certain legislative proposition, that person will present an argument. Through applying your knowledge of logic, you will be able to tell whether the conclusion actually follows. If the conclusion does not follow from the premises presented, that does not mean that you should not vote against the proposition. What it means is that the arguer has not presented *decisive* evidence for the conclusion. There may still be a better argument, one that *will* be decisive. On the other hand, there may not be a better argument, in which case, it may well be that you should vote for the Proposition.

We may now proceed to the techniques of sentential logic, beginning with a study of the logical status of sentences, moving into a treatment of arguments themselves.

4.2. Truth Tables for Sentences

We will be concerned, in this section, with a method for determining the truth or falsity of sentences containing one or more occurrences of the truth functional connectives. We will use what is called *The Method of Truth Tables*.

To begin, recall The Law of Excluded Middle. This "law of thought" says that every sentence is either true or false, and is preeminent for the method of truth tables. While there are many facts about the world the truth of which we are ignorant, still, any sentence expressing a fact about the world is either true or false. This is to say that just because we may not know the actual height of, say, Mt. Shasta, it does not follow that the sentence "Mt. Shasta is 5,341 feet high" is neither true nor false. Mt. Shasta has height and it is either true or false that Mt. Shasta is 5,341 feet high. Another example will help. The sentence "Reuben Blades, the singer and actor, ran for the presidency of Panama some years back," is either true or false. We may not know which it is (true or false), but that is really irrelevant to whether the sentence is actually true or not.

We are working in a *two-valued logic*, the values being *truth* and *falsehood*, where every declarative sentence is said to have one or the other value. For example,

(1) Reuben Blades ran for the presidency of Panama.

is a simple sentence, translated as *P*. This sentence (*P*) is either true or false, and its full truth table is:

P
t
f

A truth table is essentially a diagram showing the truth value *possibilities* for any given sentence. If you have never heard of Reuben Blades, you will not know whether he ran for the presidency of Panama or not. Hence, you will not know the actual truth value of *P*. As the truth table for *P* shows, it may be either true or false, and it has to be one or the other. Similarly for,

(2) Reuben Blades ran for the presidency of Chile.

C
t
f

What one needs to do, to discover the truth values of P and C, is do some research on the recent political activities of both Panama and Chile. If you found, as I believe you would, that Blades ran for the presidency of Panama but not for the presidency of Chile, you would know that P is true but that C is false.

Since compound sentences are made up of simple sentences, to discover the truth value of any compound sentence, it suffices to lay out the possible truth value combinations of the component simple sentences and determine the truth functional nature of the connective occurring in the compound sentence. Consider the following sentence:

(3) Caillebotte was an Impressionist and lived in Paris.

Let 'I' = 'Caillebotte was an Impressionist' and 'P' = 'Caillebotte lived in Paris.' The occurrence of 'and' in (3) indicates that we have a conjunction here. Our translation of (3) is: (I • P). To construct a full truth table for the translated sentence, we need to consider the number of different combinations of truth values for I and P. That is, I and P could both be true; I could be true while P is false; I could be false while P is true; or I and P could both be false. Each combination of truth values is called a *row*, or an *interpretation*. We can construct the following partial table:

	(I • P)	
Row 1	t	t
Row 2	t	f
Row 3	f	t
Row 4	f	f

Every possible combination of the truth values for I and P are found in the above table. [We are not concerned, at this point, with the actual truth value of sentence 3 above.]

Whereas (2) is a simple sentence, and hence, requires only two possible truth values, (3) is a compound sentence, has two different components, and requires four possible combinations of truth value. If we were to add one more component, say, R, we would need eight possible combinations of truth value.

	(I •	P) •	R]
Interpretation 1	t	t	t
Interpretation 2	t	t	f
Interpretation 3	t	f	t
Interpretation 4	t	f	f
Interpretation 5	f	t	t
Interpretation 6	f	t	f
Interpretation 7	f	f	t
Interpretation 8	f	f	f

The number of truth value combinations (rows, interpretations) doubles with each added component. Hence, if there are 4 components, 16 interpretations are needed; 5 components, 32 interpretations; 6 components, 64, and so on.

A convention we shall adopt at this time is that when assigning truth values to components, begin with the component letter closest to the letter "Z" (in the alphabet) and assign 't' and 'f' alternating by one's; then proceed to the next component letter closest to 'Z' and assign 't' and 'f' alternating by two's; and so on. This is what was done in constructing the truth table directly above, where R is closest to 'Z,' P is next closest to 'Z,' and then I. Each component has the same number of "t's" and "f's," but R gets "t,f,t,f . . .," P gets "t,t,f,f . . .," and I gets "t,t,t,t,f,f,f,f," which is a long way of saying that the number is the same while the order is different.

Conjunctions

Now, with these preliminaries, we are in a position to construct a full truth table for '(I • P).' The crucial factor here is the truth functional nature of the dot (conjunction). That is, given that we have the interpretations under I and P, what remains is to assign a truth value, under the dot, for every interpretation, according to a rule. The rule here will be *the truth table for conjunctions*, and will be a guide for every occurrence of a conjunction in the method of truth tables. (Each of the five connectives has a truth table.)

The truth table for the conjunction is:

(p • q)
t t t
t f f
f f t
f f f

We shall be using the lower case letters 'p,' 'q,' 'r,' 's,' and 't' to designate simple *sentence forms*. Any string of these letters, in any combination, with one or more occurrences of the connectives, and the appropriate number and arrangement of groupers, will be designated a sentence form. Sentence forms are not sentences, because sentences are "about the world," i.e., have meaning. Sentence forms have no meaning because 'p,' 'q,' etc. are *variables* and have no meaning. Notice that the truth table for the conjunction is given for a sentence form. This is done to show that it does not matter what letters appear in the conjunction itself. We could easily substitute 'I' for 'p' and 'P' for 'q.' The point is that whereas 'p' has no meaning, 'I' means 'Caillebotte was an Impressionist.' This matters to the actual truth value of the sentence.

Given someone who does not know anything about the painter Gustave Caillebotte, that person would have to construct a full truth table for the sentence '(I • P),' which would be the following:

(I • P)
t t t
t f f
f f t
f f f

From the truth table alone, it is impossible to tell the actual truth value of the sentence "(I • P)." This is so because one cannot determine here which interpretation is the *actual* interpretation of the sentence. That is, we don't know the actual truth values of the simple sentences here. However, if you know that Caillebotte was an Impressionist, and if you also know that he lived in Arles and not in Paris, then one is able to determine, through consulting the truth table for the conjunction, the actual truth value of the sentence. So, where *I* is true and *P* is false, '(I • P)' is seen to be false. The actual values in the full table for '(I • P)' are in Interpretation 2. Here is the result:

(I • P)
t f f

In justifying the truth table for conjunctions, that is, why the truth table for conjunctions is as it is, consider what is really taking place in a sentence expressing a conjunction. A person who utters a conjunction is saying that both of the conjuncts are true. If I say, "I went downtown and bought ice cream," I am saying 1) that I went downtown *and* 2) that I bought ice cream. If it is true that I went downtown, and if it is true that I bought ice cream (both conjuncts being true), then what I have said is true (that is, the conjunction that I uttered is true). But what if I went downtown but didn't buy ice cream (the first conjunct being true, the second false)? Then what I have said is false. Or, what if I didn't go downtown but bought ice cream, say, from the ice cream truck (the first conjunct false, the second true)? Then, again, what I have said is false. Lastly, what if I neither went downtown nor bought ice cream (both conjuncts being false)? The result is a false sentence. The rule for conjunction is this: *A conjunction is true if, and only if, each of its conjuncts is true; a conjunction is false if, and only if, at least one of its conjuncts is false.*

Negations

Our next truth table is for negations. What is said here holds for both simple sentences and compound sentences being negated. The table for the "negation" is:

-p
f t
t f

This is as much as to say that the truth value of a negated sentence is the opposite to that of the non-negated sentence. Hence, where 'p' is true, '-p' is false, and conversely. For instance, if someone says that Abraham Lincoln is one of the presidents represented on Mt. Rushmore, which would be a simple sentence, and if this sentence were true, then whoever were to deny this, which is to *negate* it, would be saying something false.

This would also hold for compound sentences that are negated. Take, for example, the following sentence:

(4) Jackie and Clarence won't both run the Boston marathon.

(4) may be translated as: -(J • C). We lay out the partial truth table for this symbolic sentence as before, holding to the convention of beginning with the letter closest to Z. Thus,

```
-(J • C)
  t   t
  f   t
  t   f
  f   f
```

Now we can assign truth values to (under) the dot and then the bar. We must begin with the dot, because to determine the truth value of the negated sentence one must know the truth value of the sentence itself. Another way of saying this is to point to the bar as the *primary/major connective*, i.e., the connective with the largest scope, and observe that *the major connective is always the last connective to be assigned truth values*. The dot, in this case, is called the *subordinate/minor connective*. The two truth tables below show the two further steps in constructing a full truth table for (4):

```
      1                2
  -(J • C)         -(J • C)
   tt t             ft t t
   ff t             tf f t
   tf f             tt f f
   ff f             tf f f
```

Table (1) above is the penultimate stage in constructing the full truth table for sentence (4). It does not contain any assignment of truth values under the bar. Table (2) is the proper full truth table for '-(J • C).' Since we do not know whether it is true or false that Jackie will run in the marathon, and since we do not know whether it is true or false that Clarence will run in the marathon, we cannot determine the actual truth value of sentence (4) just by using the truth table method. At most, what we can say is this: Where *J* and *C* are both true, the sentence is false; in all other cases, the sentence is true.

But let's say that we *do* know that Jackie will but Clarence will not run in the marathon. We now know the truth value of the sentence, as all we have to do is consult the full truth table and check the 3rd interpretation, where *J* is true but *C* is false. This is so because the sentence says, essentially, that *one or the other of them will not run in the marathon*.

Consider a more complicated sentence now, and its corresponding series of truth tables. Let E = Eggers will sign a contract with the Canadian Football League; F = Farley will sign a contract with the Canadian Football League; G = Gustaf sign a contract with the Canadian Football League; H = Holbrook will sign a contract with the Canadian Football League. Sentence (5) is a negated conjunction. Note that the conjuncts of this conjunction are also conjunctions.

(5) It is false that both Eggers and Farley and both Gustaf and Holbrook will sign contracts with the Canadian Football League.
Translation = -[(E • F) • (G • H)]

Notice again here that the primary connective is the bar (as mentioned, (5) is a negated conjunction). Hence, the bar will be the last of the four occurrences of connectives to receive the assignment of truth values. Clearly, since there are four different letters in this negated conjunction, we will need sixteen different interpretations. The following series of tables shows a proper order for assigning the truth values to the various symbols in the sentence. (1a) begins by assigning values to just the letters themselves. The tables that follow assign values one symbol at a time, until the last table is completed with the assignment of values under the bar itself. Recall that the connective symbol that has the largest scope in the sentence is the symbol that is the last to have values placed under it.

1a					2a					
-[(E	•	F) • (G	•	H)]	-[(E	•	F) • (G	•	H)]	
t	t	t	t		t	t t		t	t	
t	t	t	f		t	t t		t	f	
t	t	f	t		t	t t		f	t	
t	t	f	f		t	t t		f	f	
t	f	t	t		t	f f		t	t	
t	f	t	f		t	f f		t	f	
t	f	f	t		t	f f		f	t	
t	f	f	f		t	f f		f	f	
f	t	t	t		f	f t		t	t	
f	t	t	f		f	f f		t	f	
f	t	f	t		f	f t		f	t	
f	t	f	f		f	f t		f	f	
f	f	t	t		f	f f		t	t	
f	f	t	f		f	f f		t	f	
f	f	f	t		f	f f		f	t	
f	f	f	f		f	f f		f	f	

```
                    3a
        -[(E • F) • (G • H)]
           t t t     t t t
           t t t     t f f
           t t t     f f t
           t t t     f f f
           t f f     t t t
           t f f     t f f
           t f f     f f t
           t f f     f f f
           f f t     t t t
           f f t     t f f
           f f t     f f t
           f f t     f f f
           f f f     t t t
           f f f     t f f
           f f f     f f t
           f f f     f f f
```

```
                4a                              5a
      -[(E • F) • (G • H)]              -[(E • F) • (G • H)]
        t tt t  t t t                    f t t t  t t t t
        t tt f  t ff                     t t t t  f t f f
        t tt f  f ft                     t t t t  f f f t
        t tt f  f ff                     t t t t  f f f f
        t ff f  t tt                     t t f f  f t t t
        t ff f  t ff                     t t f f  f t f f
        t ff f  f ft                     t t f f  f f f t
        t ff f  f ff                     t t f f  f f f f
        f ft f  t tt                     t f f t  f t t t
        f ft f  t ff                     t f f t  f t f f
        f ft f  f ft                     t f f t  f f f t
        f ft f  f ff                     t f f t  f f f f
        f ff f  t tt                     t f f f  f t t t
        f ff f  t ff                     t f f f  f t f f
        f ff f  f ft                     t f f f  f f f t
        f ff f  f ff                     t f f f  f f f f
```

When constructing a truth table for any sentence, after assigning truth values to the sentence components, begin to assign truth values under the connective with the smallest scope. Table (2a) above shows this. Since the dots have equal scope in '(E • F)' and '(G • H),' it does not matter which of these dots is assigned truth values first. When continuing with the truth table, assign truth values to formulas with connectives of ever-increasing scope. Finally, as in (5a), you will reach the primary connective, which will have the widest scope of all the connectives in the sentence. (5a) is the full truth table for the symbolized sentence (5).

At this point, it is well to point out once again that truth values are assigned to sentence components in accord with the adopted convention, and assigned to any sentence connective only in accord with the truth table for that connective. Hence, when assigning truth values to conjunctions, consult the truth table for the conjunction; when assigning truth values to negations, consult the truth table for the negation, and so on.

Disjunctions

As noted previously, disjunctions have two senses, i.e., the inclusive and the exclusive. However, there is only one truth table for the wedge. We use the truth table for the inclusive sense, which is:

```
(p v q)
 t t t
 t t f
 f t t
 f f f
```

We say that the truth table for disjunctions defines the wedge symbol in truth functional terms (as the truth table for conjunctions defines the dot). The reason one truth table is sufficient for all disjunctions is that all disjunctions have at least one thing in common, i.e., each asserts that at least one of its disjuncts is true (as all conjunctions have in common the assertion that both conjuncts are true). If you check the truth table for the wedge, you will see that whenever at least one of the disjuncts is true, the entire sentence is true. Consider the following sentence, dictionary, translation, and truth table.

(6) Either the Blackfoot tribe will continue its fight to save the ancient paintings and not attend the gathering in Tulsa, or they will learn that the paintings are of recent origin and they will not continue their fight for the paintings. [B = the Blackfoot tribe continues its fight to save the ancient paintings; L = they will learn that the paintings are of recent origin; T = the Blackfoot tribe will attend the gathering in Tulsa]. Translation: [(B • -T) v (L • -B)]

```
[(B • -T) v (L • -B)]
  t f ft  f  t f f ft
  t t tf  t  t t f ft
  t f ft  f  f f f ft
  t t tf  t  f f f ft
  f f ft  t  t t t tf
  f f tf  t  t t t tf
```

```
f f  ft   f  f f  tf
f f  tf   f  f f  tf
```

Here is a step by step explanation of this truth table.

1) Since there are three different sentence letters, viz., B, L, and T, eight rows in the table are needed to cover all the possible combinations of truth values. The truth values assigned to /these letters are determined by the relative proximity of each letter to the letter Z in the alphabet (recall our convention for assigning truth values to sentence letters). These letters are the smallest units to which truth values are assigned. Therefore, we start with them.

2) The next smallest units are the bars on 'T' and 'B.' This is to say that a bar ranges over the 'T' and over the 'B' and nothing else. Truth values are assigned under the bar in accord with the truth table for negations, but are determined by the truth values under 'T' and 'B.' Thus, for example, when 'B' is true, '-B' is false, and vice-versa.

3) The next smallest units are '(B • -T)' and '(L • -B).' Strictly, as with '-T' and '-B' above, it does not matter which formula you assign truth value to first here. What does matter is that you understand that the scope of these formulas is determined by the dots. The point here is to understand where the truth values under the dots come from. The truth values under the dot in '(B • -T)' come from the truth values under 'B' and the bar in '-T' in accord with the truth table for conjunctions. This is because '(B • -T)' is a conjunction. Hence, to find the truth value under the dot for this formula in, say, interpretation 5, one consults the truth table for conjunctions to determine what the truth value is of a conjunction when the conjuncts are both false. A conjunction is false when one or both of the conjuncts is false and true only when both conjuncts are true. Therefore, we assign 'f' to '(B • -T)' in row 5 of the above truth table.

It must be understood that the conjuncts in '(L • -B)' are 'L' and '-B.' 'B' is not a conjunct here; '-B' is a conjunct. This means that when assigning truth values to the dot in this formula, one looks at the truth values under 'L' and '-B' rather than at 'L' and 'B.' The same reasoning applies to the following conjunction: '(B • -T).' That is, the conjuncts in '(B • -T)' are 'B' and '-T.'

4) Since sentence (6) is a disjunction, the major connective is the wedge. It ranges from the left-hand bracket to the right-hand bracket, and over all formulas between the brackets. To determine the truth value assignments under the wedge, one looks at the truth values under the two dots of the conjunctions, assigning truth values under the wedge in accord with the truth table for disjunctions. Now, when you have determined the truth values under the major connective, you are in a position to say whether the sentence is true, false, or *indeterminate* (when one is not sure of the *actual* truth values of the components). Sentence (6) seems a sentence the components of which are of unknown truth value to us. That is, we cannot really say whether it is true or false that the Blackfoot tribe will continue to fight to save the paintings, or whether the tribe will attend the gathering or whether the paintings will prove to be of more recent origin than previously thought. Hence, sentence (6) is indeterminate. At most, then, we

can merely enumerate the various combinations of truth values in the different rows, as follows: Sentence (6) is *true* when B and L are true (row 2); when B is true and T and L are false (row 4); when B is false and T and L are true (row 5); and when B and T are false and L is true (row 6). Otherwise, it is *false.*

Conditionals

As there are different senses of disjunctions, so there are different sorts of conditional sentences. As examples, consider the following conditional sentences:

(7) If the match is struck, then the sulfur will ignite.
(8) If '(R • S)' is a true sentence, then 'S' is a true sentence.
(9) If Nip is a porpoise, then Nip is of the genus *Phocaena.*
(10) If the Mad River waters clear, then we'll go fishing.

We can name these different sorts of conditionals as follows: (7) is an example of a *causal conditional*, pointing to one event as the cause of another event; (8) is an example of an *inferential conditional*, stating that one sentence can be inferred from another sentence; (9) is an example of a *lexical conditional*, stating the definition of 'porpoise' as "of the genus *Phocaena;*" (10) is what is called a *material conditional*. In each of these conditionals there is a relation of implication between the antecedent and the consequent. In each of the first three, the relation seems to be as follows: if the antecedent is true, then the consequent is also true. The last, however, does not exhibit this sort of relation explicitly. If the Mad River waters do indeed clear, still, we might not go fishing; other things may intrude in our lives preventing our going fishing. There seems to be no definiteness, or necessity, about the implication relation from the antecedent to the consequent in *material* conditionals.

There is one commonality between each of these conditionals, however. This is that each expresses a relation of implication from the antecedent to the consequent. Just as a conjunction "says" that both conjuncts are true, the conditional "says" that the antecedent implies the consequent. If I say, "if the Sockeye Salmon isn't the most beautiful fish in the river, then I'm a monkey's uncle," no one seriously thinks that the Sockeye not being the most beautiful fish in the river implies that I'm a monkey's uncle. But, equally so, no one can doubt that *that* is precisely what the sentence expresses.

There is only one truth table for conditionals, and only one is needed, because the arrow is defined in truth functional terms for all conditionals in terms of what is common for all conditionals, which is, again, that each expresses a relation of implication from antecedent to consequent. From this consideration, it follows that all conditionals have a second thing in common, and that is that there is only one interpretation under which a conditional is false, i.e., when the antecedent is true and the consequent is false. Look at it this way: what a conditional says is that if the antecedent is true, then the consequent is true. Now, when it turns out that the antecedent is true but the consequent is false, this goes against what the conditional itself expresses. In other words, where the antecedent is true and the consequent is false, what the conditional expresses is false. Hence, the following truth table:

(p → q)
t t t
t f f
f t t
f t f

Another way of understanding why the truth table for the conditional is the way it is might be to think of the arrow as an abbreviation for a specific sort of negated conjunction. Consider the following:

1	2
-(p • -q)	(p → q)
t t f ft	t t t
f tt tf	t f f
t ff ft	f t t
t ff tf	f t f

Since the truth values in (1) and (2) are identical under the primary connectives, and have the same sentence components, (1) and (2) express the same thing. (1) expresses something such as: "not both p and not q," which is as much as to say "if p, then q." Other examples of tables using conditionals are below:

[(R → E) • (E → R)]	[(R → E) v -R]
t tt t tt t	t tt t ft
t ff fft t	t f ff ft
f tt f tf f	f tt t tf
f tf t ft f	f tf t tf

Note that the left-hand table directly above is for a conjunction in which both conjuncts are conditionals. The right-hand table is a disjunction with one disjunct being a conditional.

[(C v -D) → (E • -C)]	{[(G → J) v -G] → -B}
t t ft f t f ft	t t t t ft f ft
t t ft f f f ft	t f f f ft t ft
t t tf f t f ft	f tt t tf f ft
t t tf f f f ft	f t f t tf f ft
f f ft t t t tf	t t t t ft t tf
f f ft t f f tf	t f f f ft t tf
f t tf t t t tf	f t t t tf t tf
f t tf f f f tf	f t f t tf t tf

```
     [L • -(-K → M)]
       t f f ft  t t
       t f f ft  t f
       f f f ft  t t
       f f f ft  t f
       t f f tf  t t
       t t t tf  f f
       f f f tf  t t
       f f t tf  f f
```

Biconditionals

The last of the five truth functional connectives is the biconditional. Its truth table is deducible from the truth tables for the conditional and the conjunction, because the biconditional is simply two conditionals conjoined.

```
            1                    2
  [(p → q) • (q → p)]        (p ↔ q)
    t  t t  t  t t t          t t t
    t  f f f  f t t           t f f
    f  t t f  t f f           f f t
    f  t f t  f t f           f t f
```

A biconditional is true whenever the components have the same truth value, and is false otherwise. Sentence (2) directly above *is* the truth table for the bi-conditional. The double arrow symbol may be understood as defined by the truth table. Sentence (2) may also be understood as an abbreviation of sentence (1). Notice that the truth values under the dot in (1) are the same as the truth values under the double arrow in (2). This means that (1) and (2) are logically equivalent.

For another way of explaining how to assign truth values to the various units in a symbolized sentence, consider the truth table below. Each column is numbered, but this is only for purposes of explanation.

```
  1 2 3 4  5 6 78
  [(B • P) v (L • -B)]
    t t t  t  t f ft
    t f f  ft  f f ft
    t t t  t  f f ft
    t f f  f f f ft
    f f t  t t t  tf
    f f f  t t t  tf
    f f t  f ff  tf
    f f f  f ff  tf
```

Truth values for the units under numbers 1, 3, 5, and 8 are determined by the convention of beginning with the letter closest to Z and alternating truth values by one's, then by two's, and so on. The truth values under 7 are determined by the truth values under 8, in accord with the truth table for negation. The truth values under 2 are determined by the truth values under 1 and 3 in accord with the truth table for conjunctions. The truth values under 6 are determined by the truth values under 5 and 7 in accord with the truth table for conjunctions. The truth values under 4 are determined by the truth values under 2 and 6 in accord with the truth table for disjunctions.

Exercise: Ch. 4, Sect. 4.2.

A. Identify each of the following symbolized sentences as conjunctions, negations, conditionals, disjunctions, or biconditionals? If any sentence is a negation, say what kind of negation it is, e.g., negated disjunction.

1. -(-L v -K)
2. ((D → N) → E)
3. [-(B • -H) v -J]
4. {[-(C ↔ F) → W] v Y}
5.* [(W v -D) v (-A → -W)]
6. (-T • -(U • -O))
7. -[-(-C v -U) → -T]
8. --[K ↔ (-L • -D)]
9. [-(-S → -M) → -S]
10.* [-(Ar ↔ Si) ↔ -Bp]
11. -{[G v (-X → -I)] → I}
12. -(Ljm • -Lmj)
13. [(F • R) v (-R v -F)]
14. -(-(-R → R) v --R)
15.* (E → (-H → -O))
16. [-(I v O) v U]
17. {[(T → -G) • (R ↔ G)] → G}
18. {[(-H → I) → -J] v (-I v J)}
19. [(E ↔ -D) → (D ↔ -Q)]
20.* -{[(V v K) → -V] ↔ O}

B. In this section, let the truth value of A, B, and H be known to be true; let O, J, and K be known to be false; and let the truth value of L, M, and N be unknown. Can the values of the following sentences be determined? If so, indicate the truth values. If not, explain why not.

1. (B → -M)
2. [L → (-A • M)]
3. [L ↔ -(B → H)]
4. (M v -K) v (M ↔ -N)
5.* [(-M • M) v (H • -H)]
6. [(J → K) ↔ -B]
7. (-(-(N → -M) v L) • --M)
8. [J v (O v -H]
9. [(-L ↔ N) → (B ↔ L)]
10.* [(A → -K) • (J → -K)]
11. [(-O v J) ↔ (-J → -O]
12. [(-B • -J) v -(J v B)]
13. [(-H v B) ↔ (-B v -H)]
14. [-(-M v N) ↔ (-N ↔ -M)]
15.* -{[M • (-N → -M)] → N}
16. {H ↔ [H • (H → -B)]}
17. {[O • (L v A)] ↔ (O • -D)}
18. --[(O • -O) • (-O • O)]
19. [(A → -J) v (J → -A)]
20.* -{[(-K ↔ L) • -N] • -H}
21. (-((B → (-L → O)) v -K) → B)
22. [(-A v A) • (N v -N)]

23. $\{[-((A \rightarrow -M) \leftrightarrow (-A \vee K)) \bullet -B] \rightarrow A\}$
24. $-\{(M \rightarrow L) \leftrightarrow [(L \rightarrow M) \bullet (-L \bullet -M)]\}$
25. $\{[(A \rightarrow -K) \bullet (J \rightarrow -O)] \rightarrow [J \vee (H \vee -O]\}$

4.3. Truth Functional Classes of Sentences

As we have said, sentences, i.e., assertions about the world, are either true or false (exclusive "or"). The method of truth tables allows us to determine the truth value of a compound sentence, given that we know the truth values of the simple sentences making up the compound sentence. However, if the truth values of the simple sentences are *un*known, then usually the truth value of the compound sentence is also unknown. I say *usually* here because there are two cases in which the truth value of the compound sentence can be known even when the values of the simple sentences remain unknown. These cases are when a sentence is either *logically true* or *logically false*.

A sentence is logically true (*L-true*) if it is true under every interpretation. These sorts of sentences are also called *tautologies*. For example, '(p v -p)' is L-true. This is to say that '(p v -p)' is true no matter what the truth value of 'p' happens to be. Notice that it is the *form* of the sentence that determines its classification here. In the examples below, all values under the primary connectives are 't,' which shows that each sentence form is "true under every interpretation." So, each sentence form below is L-true.

$(-p \rightarrow -p)$	$(p \leftrightarrow --p)$	$[p \rightarrow (p \vee q)]$
ft t ft	t t tft	t t t t
tf t tf	f t ftf	t t t f
		f t f t t
		f t f f f

$$\{[(p \rightarrow q) \bullet (q \rightarrow r)] \rightarrow (p \rightarrow r)\}$$

```
t t t t  t t t  t t  t t t
t t t f  t f f  t t  f f
t f f f  f t t  t t  t t
t f f f  f t f  t t  f f
f t t t  t t t  t f  t t
f t t f  t f f  t f  t f
f t f t  f t t  t f  t t
f t f t  f t f  t f  t f
```

A sentence is logically false (*L-false*) if it is true under no interpretation. These sentences are also called *self-contradictions*. For example, '(p • -p)' is L-false. Again, it is the *form* of the sentence that determines the class of the sentence. Denying (placing a bar in front of) an L-true sentence yields an L-false sentence, and *vice-versa*. Each of the following is an example of an L-false sentence form, i.e., true under no interpretation.

```
-(-p → -p)              -[(p → q) ·· (-p v q)]
f ft t ft               f t  t t  t  ft t t
f tf t  tf              f t  f f  t  ft f f
                        f f  t t  t  tf t t
                        f f  t f  t  tf t f


      {(p → q) • -[-q → (p → -r)]}
        t t t ff ft t  t f ft
        t t t ff ft t  t t tf
        t f f f t tf f  t f ft
        t f f ff tf t  t t tf
        f t t ff ft t  f t ft
        f t t ff ft t  f t tf
        f t f ff tf t  f t ft
        f t f ff tf t  f t tf
```

A sentence which is neither logically true nor logically false is termed logically indeterminate (*L-indeterminate*). These sentences are also called *contingent*. A sentence is logically indeterminate if the sentence is true under some, but not all, interpretations. For example, all simple sentences, as well as their negations, are L-indeterminate. What 'logically indeterminate' means is that one cannot determine the truth value by using the methods of logic alone; it does not mean that the sentence is neither true nor false, or that it has no truth value. As stipulated, all sentences are either true or false. Each of the sentence forms below is L-indeterminate.

```
p    -q    (p v q)    -[(r • -p) → r]    (q → -q)
t    ft    t t t      f tf ft t t        t f ft
f    tf    t t f      f ff ft t f        f t tf
           f t t      t t t tf f f
           f f f      f f f tf t f
```

In each of the above sentence forms, there is at least one occurrence of 't' under the primary connective and at least one occurrence of 'f' under the primary connective. The simple sentence form 'p,' of course, has no connective. Hence, under 'p' itself, 't' and 'f' each occur once. Since each of these sentence forms is true under at least one interpretation and false under at least one interpretation, each is L-indeterminate.

Now, if one substitutes 'B' for 'p' and 'C' for 'q' in the sentence form '(p v q),' one gets the following sentence: (B v C). Let B = the Boston Red Sox used to be called the Boston Americans' and let C = the Chicago Cubs used to be called the Chicago Blues. Since B and C stand for actual sentences, which make assertions about the world and are either true or false, the sentence (B v C) has a determinable truth value. In accord with the table for disjunctions, we see that the sentence is true, since one of its disjuncts is true, viz., the first disjunct. The truth value of this sentence, that is, (B v C), cannot be determined simply by the methods of logic. Rather, one needs to know the truth values of the components, i.e., B and/or C. And, when one knows the truth values of the components of *any* given sentence, one can determine the truth value of that sentence.

There is another set of characteristics sentences have. These are relations sentences have with respect to one another. If any two or more sentences with the same components have the same truth values under each interpretation, these sentences are said to be *equivalent*. For example,

(p v -q)	(-q v p)	(q → p)
t t ft	ft t t	t t t
t t tf	tf t t	f t t
f f ft	ft f f	t f f
f t tf	tf t f	f t f

Since these three sentence forms are all true under the first, second, and fourth interpretations, and all false under the third interpretation, these three sentence forms are equivalent. (If one makes a biconditional of any two of these sentence forms, one will derive a sentence form that is L-true.)

Any two sentences with the same components having opposite truth values under every interpretation are said to be *contradictory*.

1	2
(p v -q)	-(p v -q)
t t ft	f t t ft
t t tf	f t t tf
f f ft	t f f ft
f t tf	f f t tf

Since (1) is true under every interpretation under which (2) is false, and false under every interpretation under which (2) is true, (1) and (2) are contradictory sentence forms.

Sentences with the same components which are neither equivalent nor contradictory are *incompatible*. These sentences will have the same truth values under some interpretations and different truth values under other interpretations. Examples are:

1	2
(p ↔ r)	(r → p)
t t t	t t t
t f f	f t t
f f t	t f f
f t f	f t f

Here we have both sentence forms true in the first and last interpretations and both false in the third interpretation. Under the second interpretation, (1) is false while (2) is true. So, these sentences forms are neither logically equivalent nor logically contradictory. Since they have at least one interpretation under which they differ in truth value and at least one interpretation in which they have the same truth value, they are incompatible.

Below you will find the truth tables for the five connectives represented in both schematic form as well as explained in English. These will be helpful references as you work through the exercises throughout. Following the truth tables you will find the table of truth functional classes. These will also be useful for reference while working exercises.

Table of Truth Tables

Conjunction
True when both conjuncts are true; false otherwise.

$$(p \bullet q)$$
t t t
t f f
f f t
f f f

Disjunction
True when at least one disjunct is true, false otherwise.

$$(p \lor q)$$
t t t
t t f
f t t
f f f

Conditional
False when antecedent is true and consequent is false; true otherwise.

$$(p \rightarrow q)$$
t t t
t f f
f t t
f t f

Biconditional
True when components have same truth values; false otherwise.

$$(p \leftrightarrow q)$$
t t t
t f f
f f t
f t f

Negation
True when non-negated sentence is false; false otherwise.

$$-p$$
ft
tf

Table of Truth Functional Classes

Logically True Sentence
True under every interpretation.

Logically False Sentence
True under no interpretation.

Logically Indeterminate Sentence
True under some, but not all, interpretations.

Equivalent Sentences
True under the same interpretations.
False under the same interpretations.

Contradictory Sentences
Opposite truth values under every interpretation.

Incompatible Sentences
Same truth values under some interpretations.
Different truth values under some interpretations.

Exercise: Ch. 4, Sect. 4.3.

A. Determine whether the following sentences are L-true, L-false, or L-indeterminate using the method of truth tables.

1. (-L v -L)
2. (-L → -L)
3. [R • (G v -R)]
4. [(J ↔ O) → -J]
5.* [A → (A → --A)]
6. -[-(--S → S) → S]
7. [(D v C) v (D → C)]
8. [(K → M) → (M v -K)]
9. -[(B ↔ L) → (-B v L)]
10.* {P • [(E → W) • -P]}
11. [(L → R) • -(R → L)]
12. {[E • (-I v E)] ↔ [-I v (E → E)]}
13. {[S → (G → W)] ↔ [-(-W → -G) → -S]}
14. [(-D v -C) ↔ --(C • D)]
15.* {[[(K → G) v (P ↔ G)] • (K • P)] → (G → G)}
16. -{[(R → S) ↔ (S v -R)] ↔ [(R → S) ↔ (-S → -R)]}
17. {[(-X v Y) ↔ (X → Y)] → [-(X • -Y) → -(-Y • X)]}
18. -{{[(L • A) v D] → [-A v (D → -L)]} v (L → L)}
19. {[(-B v B) → (B → B)] v (B v -B)}
20.* -{[(Hrr → -Hrg) • (Hrr → Hrg)] → [(Hrr → Hrs) • -Hsr]}

B. Determine whether the following pairs of sentences are equivalent, contradictory, or incompatible using truth tables.

1. H   (J • -H)
2. (S → L)   (-L → -S)
3. (G • -I)   (I ↔ -G)
4. (D v P)   (-D v -P)
5.* (C → -C)   (-C v M)
6. (R ↔ O)   [(R v O) → R]
7. -(Z → X)   -(-X • Z)
8. (W • -A)   -(A ↔ --W)
9. [(E • L) v (B • E)]   [B v L) • E]
10.* [E → (J → G)]   [-(J • E) v G]
11. [(I • M) → D]   [D v -(M • I)]
12. [Q v (D v V)]   [-Q v (-D v -V)]
13. [(W → W) v -W]   (W v -W)
14. [(O ↔ C) → R]   [-R → (-C → O)]
15.* -(N • J)   -(-N v -J)
16. [H → (Y v H)]   [-H v -(-Y • -H)]
17. [(G • P) • E]   [G • (-P v E)]
18. {L v -[((J → I) • (-J → -I)) v -S]}   {[S → (J ↔ I)] → L}
19. [(Lii • Kup) → Frj]   -[Frj v (Kup → -Lii)]
20.* {[Bt v (Ie → Cc)] v [Ie • (Bt → Cc)]}   [(-Cc • -Ie) • -Bt]

C. Which of the following are true, which are false?

1. Two sentences are incompatible only if the truth values under the primary connectives in each sentence are opposite.
2. It is false that the negation of a self-contradiction is a tautology.
3. Equivalent sentences imply one another.
4. '(p v -p)' entails '(p • p).'
5* If any sentence is true under some, but not all, interpretations, then that sentence is L-indeterminate.
6. A valid argument is one for which it is impossible to assign 't' to all the premises and 'f' to the consequent under any interpretation.
7. A necessary and sufficient condition for any sentence to be L-true is that it be true under at least one interpretation.
8. No two sentences are contradictory unless the truth values under the primary connectives of each sentence are opposite.
9. No two sentences are contradictory if one sentence is L-true and the other is L-indeterminate.
10.* Given any three sentences, if the first sentence affirms exactly what the third sentence affirms and denies exactly what the third denies, and if the second sentence affirms exactly what the third denies while denying exactly what the third affirms, then the first and second sentences are contradictory.

5. Truth Tables: Arguments

5.1. Truth Tables for Arguments

We may now begin to analyze arguments by the method of truth tables. In this section, we will study full truth tables for arguments in sentential logic. In the next section we will outline the indirect method, a short-cut method. Here, of course, we are interested in *validity* rather than truth value, though to determine the validity of an argument via truth tables, we use the truth values in accord with the truth tables. To that extent, truth values, and therefore the tables, are essential.

To construct a truth table for an argument, we simply construct a table for each of the sentences in the argument. The *first step* is to lay the argument out in horizontal form, as such:

$(E \rightarrow D)$ -D $\vdash$ -E

Here we have '$(E \rightarrow D)$' as the first premise, '-D' as the second premise, and '-E' as the conclusion.

The *second step* is to give each of the letters in the argument its set of truth values. In doing this, recall that we want to start with the letter that is closest to 'Z' and give it truth values alternating by ones, then on to the next letter, etc. So, for the above argument, 'E' gets "t,f,t,f." We need four rows (interpretations) here because we have two *different* letters ('E' and 'D'). Then, 'D' will get "t,t,f,f." As so:

$(E \rightarrow D)$	-D	$\vdash$	-E
t	t	t	t
f	t	t	f
t	f	f	t
f	f	f	f

Note that there will *not* be any column of truth values under the conclusion indicator sign ('$\vdash$').

The *third step* in constructing this truth table will be to assign the truth values to the connective symbols (we have two here, namely, the arrow and the bar). We do this in accord with the truth tables for the individual connectives. So, when assigning the truth values under the arrow in our first premise, we consult the truth table for the arrow. And, when assigning the values under the two bars in our argument, we consult the truth table for the bar.

100

sult the truth table for the arrow. And, when assigning the values under the two bars in our argument, we consult the truth table for the bar.

(E → D)	-D	⊢	-E
t t t	f t		f t
f t t	f t		t f
t f f	t f		f t
f t f	t f		t f

This a finished truth table for this argument. Strictly speaking, it does not matter where we start the third step. We can start with the first premise, or the second premise, or the conclusion. In the end, however, all letters and all connectives must have the required number of truth values under them in a column. Also, it is vital that we maintain consistency in our assignment of truth values. That is, 'D' is true in the first and second interpretations and it must be assigned 't' at all occurrences in the first and third interpretations. 'D' is false in the third and fourth interpretations and must be assigned 'f' at all occurrences in those interpretations. Likewise for 'E' at its occurrences in its interpretations.

Recall, once again, our definition of *validity*: *An argument is valid if, and only if, it is impossible for the premises to be true while the conclusion is false.* For our purposes, we can add to this definition the phrase "under any interpretation," and capture the sense of validity required by the method of truth tables. Below is an example of an invalid argument. Its two premises are '(G v B)' and '-B'; its conclusion is 'G.' Here is the full truth table for this argument:

(G v B)	B	⊢	-G
t t t	t		f t
f t t	t		t f
t t f	f		f t
f f f	f		t f

Notice that in Interpretation 1, there is a 't' under the wedge in the first premise, a 't' under the 'B' that is the second premise, and an 'f' under the bar in the conclusion. In this interpretation, then, we see that the premises are both true, but the conclusion is false. This shows that it is possible for this argument to have true premises and a false conclusion under at least one interpretation. [Note again: there are no truth values under the conclusion sign ('⊢'). This sign is not a truth functional connective and there is no truth table for this sign. It is therefore only one reason, which is to note that the sentence that follows it is the conclusion to the argument.] Other arguments may have more than one interpretation under which the premises are true and the conclusion false, but one is enough to show the invalidity of any argument. Since there are no degrees of validity or invalidity, one argument is not more invalid because it may have all true premises and a false conclusion under two interpretations while another has all true premises and a false conclusion under just one. Both arguments would be equally invalid. Likewise with arguments that have true premises and a false conclusion under no interpretation. They are equally valid. Consider the following argument:

```
(E ↔ G)    -G    ⊢    -E
 t t t     f t         ft
 t f f     t f         ft
 f f t     f t         tf
 f t f     t f         tf
```

In this argument, there is no interpretation under which all of the premises are true while the conclusion is false. Hence, the argument is valid.

And that is all there is to it. The arguments may be long or short, with as many components in the sentences making up the premises and conclusion as you please. As long as every combination of truth values has been exhibited, one cannot fail to determine the validity of the argument. The reason this is so is because the concept of validity is like a grading system for *forms* of sentences purporting to entail a further sentence form. It does not matter which letters are present, whether capital letters from A to Z, or p, q, r, and so on.

Take the form of the argument directly above, "plug in" any letters designating any sentences whatever, and it is guaranteed that *if* the premises of the argument are true, the conclusion will also be true. Further examples of valid and invalid arguments, analyzed via the method of truth tables, are:

```
(B • C)   ⊢ C                     (K ↔ I)   I   ⊢   K
 t t t      t                      t t t    t       t
 t f f      f    Valid             f f t    t       f    Valid
 f f t      t                      t f f    f       t
 f f f      f                      f t f    f       f
```

```
(S → B)   (W v -B)   ⊢   (-W → -S)
 t t t     t t ft        ft  t ft
 t t t     f f ft        tf  f ft
 f t t     t t ft        ft  t tf
 f t t     f f ft        tf  t tf       Valid
 t f f     t t tf        ft  t ft
 t f f     f t tf        tf  f ft
 f t f     t t tf        ft  t tf
 f t f     f t tf        tf  t tf
```

```
[(-P v -O) → M]     -P    ⊢    M
 ft f ft  t t        ft         t
 tf t ft  t t        tf         t
 ft t tf  t t        ft         t    Valid
 tf t tf  t t        tf         t
```

```
ft f ft   t f      ft          f
tf t ft   f f      t f         f
ft t tf   f f      ft          f
tf t tf   f f      t f         f
```

(B → F)	(-B → U)	⊢	(U • -F)	
t t t	ft t t		t f f t	
t t t	ft t f		f f f t	
t f f	ft t t		t t t f	
t f f	ft t f		f f t f	
f t t	tf t t		t f f t	Invalid
f t t	tf f f		f f f t	
f t f	tf t t		t t t f	
f t f	tf f f		f f t f	

-(N → D)	(-D v P)	⊢	--D	
f t t t	ft t t		tft	
f t t t	ft f f		tft	
f f t t	ft t t		tft	
f f t t	ft f f		tft	
t t f f	tf t t		ftf	Invalid
t t f f	tf t f		ftf	
f f t f	tf t t		ftf	
f f t f	tf t f		ftf	

(J • E)	⊢	[(J v M) • E]		
t t t		t t t	t t	
t t t		t t f	t t	
f f t		f t t	t t	Valid
f f t		f f f	f t	
t f f		t t t	f f	
t f f		t t f	f f	
f f f		f t t	f f	
f f f		f f f	f f	

-(A → Z)	(A v V)	(-V • -W)	⊢	Z	
f t t t	t t t	ft f ft		t	
t t f f	t t t	ft f ft		f	
f t t t	t t t	ft f tf		t	
t t f f	t t t	ft f tf		f	
f t t t	t t f	tf f ft		t	
t t f f	t t f	tf f ft		f	
f t t t	t t f	tf t tf		t	
t t f f	t t f	tf t tf		f	Invalid
f f t t	f t t	ft f ft		t	
```
```

```
f f t  f      f t t       f t  f  f t        f
f f t  t      f t t       f t  f t f         t
f f t  f      f t t       f t  f t f         f
f f t  t      f f f       t f  f  f t        t
f f t  f      f f f       t f  f  f t        f
f f t  t      f f f       t f t  t f         t
f f t  f      f f f       t f t  t f         f
```

Exercise: Ch. 5, Sect. 5.1.

A. Which of the following are true and which are false?

1. Equivalent sentences are always true under the same interpretations.
2. Incompatible sentences have differing truth values under all interpretations.
3. To analyze '[-(R v L) ⟷ G]' using the truth table method will require eight interpretations.
4. It is never proper to write two negation signs in a row since they would cancel each other out.
5.* Disjunctions are false in one case only, that is, when both disjuncts are false.
6. It is false that an argument with five sentence components, to be analyzed via truth tables, needs thirty-two different interpretations.
7. To show an argument to be invalid using truth tables, one needs to locate at least two interpretations under which at least one of the premises is false while the conclusion is true.
8. Two arguments, one valid and one invalid, are said to be incompatible.
9. It is not true that a conditional is true when either the antecedent is false or the consequent is true.
10.* A conditional is true whenever the antecedent is false.
11. A sentence form differs from a sentence in that the former is made up of component letters having no meaning while the latter contains only component letters designating sentences in natural language.
12. If 'A' = 'Alice is on the hill' and 'B' = 'Bill is on the hill,' then the proper translation of 'Not both Bill and Alice are on the hill' would be: -(B v A).
13. In #12, if 'B' is known to be false but the value of 'A' is unknown, then it is impossible to logically determine the truth value of '-(B v A).'
14. The one thing all conjunctions have in common is that they are true when at least one of the conjuncts is true.
15.* One thing all self-contradictory sentences have in common is that when they when they are denied (negated), they become L-true.
16. '-(S v W)' is logically equivalent to '(-S • -W).'
17. '(-D v -K)' is logically incompatible with '-(D • K).'
18. '(A → Y)' and '-(-Y → -A)' contradictory.
19. The following argument is invalid: (X v -Z) (Z → R)   ⊢ (R → X)
20.* The following argument is valid: (Q • E) (L • B) (P • C) ⊢ [E • (B • C)]

B. Show which of the following arguments are valid, which invalid, by the method of truth tables.

1. (-R • R) ⊢ G
2. (-R v R) ⊢ G
3. (E • -W) -(S ↔ -E) (W v -E) ⊢ S
4. {[(A → Q) • -(M → J)] → -Q} ⊢ (J → A)
5.* [(D → F) → O] (D • -O) ⊢ (F • -F)
6. (L → K) (B v L) (-B v P) ⊢ -(-P • -K)
7. {(C → C) v [(C → C) • (C → C)]} ⊢ -C
8. -G W -U -(W → U) ⊢ (-G v -U)
9. (B → -Y) (-Y → H) (H → B) -(Y → -B) ⊢ (H v -B)
10.* [(E → J) • (I → I)] E [(J v -J) → (I → E)] ⊢ [(E v -I) v -J]
11. [(D • X) ↔ -N] (-X v -D) ⊢ -N
12. [(E v G) • (E v F)] ⊢ -[E • (G v F)]
13. (Z → -P) [P → (K • Z)] ⊢ (K v -Z)
14. (M → -I) -(R v M) [-R → (-M v I)] ⊢ -I
15.* {(B → A) → [B → (B • C)]} -(-B → -B) ⊢ (A v C)
16. [(D v R) → (R • E)] [-(R v D) • E] ⊢ -(E • R)
17. {[(K v W) v Z] v (-W • -Z)} Z ⊢ [W v (K v Z)]
18. -[(Y → U) • (U → Y)] ⊢ [(Y • U) v (-U • -Y)]
19. (T → H) (F → -H) ⊢ [(F → T) → -H]
20.* [(Gj → Gp) v (-Gj v Gg)] --(-Gp • Gj) ⊢ [(Gg v Gp) v -Gj]

C. Translate the following passages into symbolic notation. Each contains an argument. Determine which arguments are valid, which are invalid. Provide your own dictionary.

1.   University fees will increase only if the Governor decides to reduce funds for welfare programs. The Governor will make that decision if crime increases in San Diego. Hence, university fees won't increase unless crime increases in San Diego.

2.   It is false that big waves hitting the North Shore implies and is implied by high winds coming from the direction of Japan. So, the waves will be small on the North Shore just in case there are no high winds coming from Japan.

3.   Voting a Democratic ticket does not imply that one is a member of the pro-choice campaign. Being a member of the pro-choice campaign does not imply that one believes abortion is morally permissible in all cases. Hence, voting a democratic ticket does not imply that one believes abortion is morally permissible in all cases.

4.   If one gives money to beggars, then the beggars will be encouraged to beg; and if one does not give money to beggars, then the beggars will not eat. It is better that beggars eat than not eat. Therefore, it is all right to give money to beggars.

5.* If truth is impossible to obtain, then we should give up the search and concentrate on more down to earth matters. But, if it is possible to secure the truth, and if securing the truth would help us solve many "down to earth" matters, then we should pay people to search for the truth. It is possible to know the truth and it is the job of the philosopher to seek it. Hence, we should pay philosophers to search for the truth.

6. If Colleen enrolls in Romantic Literature, Renaissance Philosophy, and Survey of World War II, then she will not enroll in History of Science. And since we know she will not enroll in the World War II course, it follows that she will enroll in the History of Science course.

7. Either Jane or Susan is in the warehouse. But, they are not both in the warehouse. If Susan is in the warehouse, then Chris is also in the ware-house. If Jane is not in the warehouse, then neither is Chris. We know that Jane is not in the warehouse, and so we can conclude that Susan is, though Chris is not.

8. The sun will rise tomorrow just in case the earth continues to rotate on it axis. The sun will not rise tomorrow only if the sun novas during the next twenty-four hour period. The earth will continue on its axis and the sun will not nova. Hence, the sun will rise tomorrow.

9. No artist will agree to show her/his work unless he/she can be assured that a suitable number of critics will be invited and asked to comment on the showing in the next issue of some popular magazine. It is a sufficient condition, to get any critic to show up at an art exhibit, to provide free wine and cheese. Therefore, if any artist agrees to show his/her work, he/she also agrees to provide free wine and cheese.

10.* Provided that the cost of the hotel in London is not too expensive and that the British Rail pass is good for eleven days, we will take our vacation in mid-October. If we cannot get away in October, then if the London hotel is too expensive, then we will just stay in Edinburgh. We will not stay in Edinburgh unless we can visit Hume's birthplace. But, since no one knows exactly where Hume was born, we will not visit his birthplace. Hence, we will take our vacation in October.

11. Jack and Art both believe there are ghosts. They are right if there really are ghosts. Now, neither Jack nor Art has ever seen a ghost, since ghosts, if they do exist, aren't the sorts of things that can be seen. Ghosts do exist, and hence, though Jack and Art are right about this, they believe without seeing.

12. A fetus conceived from human parents is a not a person but it is a human being, because a fetus conceived from human parents having a human genetic code is a sufficient condition for its being human and its being self-conscious is a necessary condition for its being a person. A fetus conceived from human parents is not self-conscious, although it does have a human genetic code.

13. Carmen is one of the best staff persons at the university. We know this is so since if Carmen is one of the best, she can type well, file well, can answer important questions about who to contact about special problems, and can inform the professors about curriculum deadlines; and Carmen can do all of these things.

14. If Jerry takes Intermediate Logic, and gets an "A," then if Pat takes Beginning Logic, then Jerry will tutor Pat. If Jerry spends a lot of time with Pat, then Jerry and Pat will fall in love. Jerry will take Intermediate Logic and Pat will take Beginning Logic, and both will get "A's." Now, Jerry will tutor, and spend a lot of time with, Pat. Thus, Jerry and Pat will fall in love.

15.* Either a conditional sentence is true when the consequent is true, or our truth table is incorrect. No reputable publisher of a logic book would let the truth table for the conditional be incorrect; the truth table is not incorrect. This leads to the conclusion that a conditional is true when the consequent is true.

5.2. Truth Tables: The Short-Cut Method

As we have seen, the method of truth tables can be quite effective for determining validity of arguments. This is especially so when the arguments we are working with are fairly simple, i.e., if the arguments contain, say, five components or less. But, as the number of components increases, the number of interpretations increases. If, for example, there were ten different components in an argument, the number of interpretations needed would be 1,024. Consider the following argument:

$[(M \lor N) \lor (O \lor P)]$
$[(I \cdot J) \cdot (K \to L)]$
$[(U \cdot -V) \lor W]$
$[(E \lor F) \cdot (G \cdot H)]$ ⊢ $[(U \lor W) \to -J]$

If we were to attempt to determine the validity of this argument using full truth tables, we would have to employ literally thousands of interpretations. We need a method of proving its validity, or invalidity, that will allow us to accomplish the task in a reasonable length of time. Gladly, there is such a method.

Since all methods of using truth tables for determining validity rely on our conception of validity itself, let me state the principle of validity we have been using: *An argument is valid if, and only if, it is impossible for the premises to be true (under any given interpretation) while the conclusion is false (under the same interpretation).* The truth table short-cut method makes use of this principle, and no other.

The short-cut method is this: Attempt to assign truth values to the components in such a way which shows the argument to be *in*valid. That is, when we use the short-cut method, we are going to try to make all the premises true and the conclusion false.

First, assign truth values to the components in the conclusion which render the conclusion false. Second, assign consistent truth values to the components of the premises in an attempt to render each premise true. If there is any interpretation under which all the premises are true and the conclusion false, the argument is invalid. Conversely, if there is no interpretation under which all of the premises are true and the conclusion false, the argument is valid. In short, 1) show all the possible ways the conclusion is false, and 2) attempt to make each premise true. If you succeed for any interpretation, the argument is invalid. If not, the argument is valid.

Regarding the argument above, the conclusion is false under the following assignments of truth values to J, U, and W:

$$[(U \lor W) \to -J]$$
$$\begin{array}{ccc} t & t & t \\ f & t & t \\ t & f & t \end{array}$$

Notice that only premises (2) and (3) contain components found in the conclusion. Premise (2) can be rendered true by assigning 't' to each of the components as follows:

$$[(I \bullet J) \bullet (K \to L)]$$
$$\begin{array}{cccc} t & t & t & t \end{array}$$

Premise (3) is rendered true by assigning 't' to W, since if one disjunct in a disjunction is true, the disjunction is true. Here we see that the third interpretation in the conclusion above cannot now be used, since one must be consistent in the assignment of truth values and W is assigned 'f' in that interpretation. At this point, as they say, it's academic. You simply assign 't' to each of the components found in each of the other premises.

On the assignment of the truth values that I have suggested for this complex argument, the argument is shown to be invalid. This is to say that we've found an interpretation in which each of the premises is true and the conclusion is false. Directly below are the four premises with an assignment of truth values that makes each true:

$$[(M \lor N) \lor (O \lor P)] \quad [(I \bullet J) \bullet (K \to L)] \quad [(U \bullet -V) \lor W] \quad [(E \lor F) \bullet (G \bullet H)]$$
$$\begin{array}{ll} t\ t\ t\ t\ t\ t\ t & t\ t\ t\ t\ t\ t\ t \quad\quad t\ t\ f t\ t\ t \quad\quad t\ t\ t\ t\ t\ t\ t \end{array}$$

Now, here is a set of truth values that makes the conclusion false, which is consistent with the truth values present in the set of premises above:

$$[(U \lor W) \to -J]$$
$$\begin{array}{ccc} t\ \ t\ \ t\ \ f\ \ ft \end{array}$$

This table shows that the "short-cut method" really can be short. We have proven this argument to be invalid with only one interpretation of truth values. We don't have to know the result of assigning truth values to the letters in any other interpretation because only one is needed to show that any given argument is invalid.

Let's work through an argument one step at a time, using the short-cut method. Recall now that what we are doing, using the short-cut method, is trying to make each of the premises true and the conclusion false. Given this, all the interpretations in which the conclusion is true are of no concern to us. Also, all the cases where one or more of the premises is false are of no concern to us. We are working toward "all truth premises and a false conclusion in any one interpretation."

First, the argument is stated with the possible way(s) in which the conclusion is false. The conclusion is false in only one case, i.e., where R is true.

$$[(R \rightarrow S) \vee -G] \quad (-S \vee G) \quad \vdash \quad -R$$
$$ft$$

Now, we must assign 't' to 'R' wherever it occurs in the set of premises because it is assigned 't' in the conclusion. 'R' occurs only once in the set of premises, so we give it 't,' like so:

$$[(R \rightarrow S) \vee -G] \quad (-S \vee G) \quad \vdash \quad -R$$
$$tft$$

At this point, we have a choice. We can 1) try to make the first premise true or 2) try to make the second premise true. It does not matter which premise we deal with first. Let's do the first premise first. Recall once again that we are now trying to make the premises true. There are three ways to make premise #1 true when 'R' is also true, like so:

$$[(R \rightarrow S) \vee -G] \quad (-S \vee G) \quad \vdash \quad -R$$
t f f t ft		ft
t t t t tf		ft
t f f t tf		ft

We now plug in the truth values for 'S' and 'G' in the second premise in accord with the values we have for these letters in the first premise.

$$[(R \rightarrow S) \vee -G] \quad (-S \vee G) \quad \vdash \quad -R$$
t f f t ft	f t	ft
t t t t tf	t f	ft
t f f t tf	f f	ft

At this point, we can assign the values under both the bar and the wedge in premise #2, like so:

$$[(R \rightarrow S) \vee -G] \quad (-S \vee G) \quad \vdash \quad -R$$
| t f f *t* ft | tf *t* t | *f* t |
| t t t t tf | ft f f | ft |

t f f *t* tf   tf *t* f   *f* t

Directly above is the finished truth table for this argument. As we can see, there are two rows/interpretations in which both premises are true and the conclusion false, viz., the first and third. Either one of these is enough to prove the argument invalid. The argument is proven invalid.

If we take the same argument, but replace the wedge in the second premise with a dot, we have a valid argument.

$$[(R \rightarrow S) v -G] \quad (-S \bullet G) \quad \vdash \quad -R$$
t f f f ft   tf t t   ft

Notice that there is only one assignment of truth values that will render the second premise true. That assignment of truth values necessitates a consistent assignment of truth values to the first premise, rendering it false. Hence, there is no interpretation under which the argument has all true premises and a false conclusion. Hence, the argument is valid.

Let us look at another valid argument and analyze it step by step. In the following argument, there is only one assignment of truth values to the conclusion that makes the conclusion false:

$$(E \rightarrow H) \ (H \rightarrow A) \quad \vdash \quad (E \rightarrow A)$$
t f f

That is, '(E → A)' is false only when 'E' is true and 'A' is false. The next thing to do is to assign 't' to 'E' and 'f' to 'A' in the premises:

$$(E \rightarrow H) \ (H \rightarrow A) \quad \vdash \quad (E \rightarrow A)$$
t   f   t f f

It remains only to try to assign a truth value to 'H' in the premises that makes both premises true. Now, if we assign 't' to 'H' in the first premise, thus making that premise true, we then have to assign 't' to 'H' in the second premise, making it false. Here is how that would look:

$$(E \rightarrow H) \ (H \rightarrow A) \quad \vdash \quad (E \rightarrow A)$$
t t t   t *f* f   t f f

Notice the *Italicized* 'f' under the arrow in the second premises. This indicates that when making 'H' true in the first premise, then the second premise was rendered false.

Here is the table we would get if we were to assign 'f' to 'H' in the second premise, thus making the second premise true.

$$(E \rightarrow H) \ (H \rightarrow A) \quad \vdash \quad (E \rightarrow A)$$
$$t \ f \ f \quad f \ t \ f \qquad t \ f \ f$$

Notice the *Italicized* 'f' in the first premise under the arrow. That 'f' indicates that it was impossible to make the first premise true since when assigning 'f' to 'H' in the second premise.

What we have here is exactly what will happen *every* time we do a short-cut method truth table on a valid argument, namely, that it will be impossible for us to make all the premises true when we first make the conclusion false.

It would be well to stress, once again, the concept of *a consistent assignment of truth values*. To assign the same truth value to a letter at each occurrence of that letter in a single interpretation is to *assign consistently*. See the argument below and its assignment of truth values to the letters:

$$(R \rightarrow S) \quad -(S \ v \ -K) \quad \vdash \quad -R$$
$$f \ t \ f \qquad t \ tf \ ft \qquad f \ t$$

You will notice that R has been given 'f' in the first premise, but 't' in the conclusion. *This is an inconsistent assignment of truth values to R* and defeats the entire enterprise of the short-cut method (and the "long-cut" method as well, for that matter). The result is that we would judge this argument to be invalid (since each of the premises is shown to be true and the conclusion is shown to be false). However, the argument is actually valid, as shown here in the correct table:

$$(R \rightarrow S) \quad -(S \ v \ -K) \quad \vdash \quad -R$$
$$t \ t \ t \qquad f \ t \ t \ tf \qquad ft$$

Since 'R' is given 't' in the conclusion (to make the conclusion false), it must be given 't' in the first premise. But when it is given 't' in the first premise, then 'S' must be given 't' as well, otherwise the first premise will be rendered false (recall that our goal with the short-cut method is to see whether we can make all the premises true while the conclusion is false). Now, when 'S' is given 't' in the first premise, it must also be given 't' in the second premise (that, in a nutshell, is what the consistent assignment of truth values is all about). But, when 'S' is given 't' in the second premise, that automatically renders the disjunction of the second premise true, shown by the 't' under the wedge, rendering the second premise itself (which is a negated disjunction) false. Thus, it was not possible to make both premises true while the conclusion is false. Hence, the argument is shown to be valid.

Consider the following argument:

$$(U \rightarrow W) \quad (P \leftrightarrow W) \quad -P \quad \vdash \quad (-U \bullet P)$$

The normal way of going about doing the short-cut method is to go to the conclusion first, make it false in all the possible ways, then proceed to the premises and try to make them true. However, we *can* start with the premises, if we want, try to make them true and see whether we can then make the conclusion false. This sometimes works a bit better, especially as in the above argument where there is three ways to make the conclusion false. What we can do, then, is begin with premise #3 and make it true:

$$(U \rightarrow W) \quad (P \leftrightarrow W) \quad -P \quad \vdash \quad (-U \bullet P)$$
$$ tf$$

To make the third premise true, we have to give 'f' to 'P.' The next step would be to give 'f' to 'P' at all other occurrences, like so:

$$(U \rightarrow W) \quad (P \leftrightarrow W) \quad -P \quad \vdash \quad (-U \bullet P)$$
$$ f tf f$$

If we now go to the second premise, we see that the only way to make it true would be to give 'f' to 'W' there, like so:

$$(U \rightarrow W) \quad (P \leftrightarrow W) \quad -P \quad \vdash \quad (-U \bullet P)$$
$$ f \ t \ f \quad tf f$$

So we now have two true premises. Note also that with 'P' being false in the conclusion, the conclusion is also false, no matter whether 'U' is true or false. Now, since 'W' got 'f' in premise #2, we have to give it 'f' in premise #1 as well, like so:

$$(U \rightarrow W) \quad (P \leftrightarrow W) \quad -P \quad \vdash \quad (-U \bullet P)$$
$$ f f \ t \ f \quad tf f$$

Okay, so since 'W' has 'f' in the first premise, to make that premise true, we have to give 'f' to 'U' there also, like so:

$$(U \rightarrow W) \quad (P \leftrightarrow W) \quad -P \quad \vdash \quad (-U \bullet P)$$
$$ f \ t \ f f \ t \ f \quad tf f$$

To finish up this table, we have to give 'U' 'f' in the conclusion, thus making '-U' true, which then necessitates an 'f' under the dot in the conclusion:

$$(U \rightarrow W) \quad (P \leftrightarrow W) \quad -P \quad \vdash \quad (-U \bullet P)$$
$$ f \ t \ f f \ t \ f \quad tf tf \ f \ f$$

This is an invalid argument, as we can see, because all the premises are true and the conclusion is false in this interpretation. Instead of eight interpretations, we have merely one.

Exercise: Ch. 5, Sect. 5.2.

Determine whether the following arguments are valid or invalid using the truth table short-cut method.

1. (R v -D) D ⊢ R
2. (C → H) ⊢ (H v -C)
3. (B • -N) ⊢ (B → N)
4. [(S • Y) v (-S • X)] ⊢ (Y • X)
5.* (O • K) ⊢ (O ↔ K)
6. (O ↔ K) ⊢ (O • K)
7. (L → G) (G → I) ⊢ (-L v I)
8. (K ↔ A) ⊢ [(K → A) v C]
9. [(E v W) → -W] ⊢ [E v (W → -W)]
10.* [M → (D • -S)] -M ⊢ -(D • -S)
11. (K ↔ W) -(-C → W) ⊢ -K
12. [-(L → Q) • -(N → Q)] -(-L • -N) ⊢ (-Q v N)
13. [(-Z v -E) • -P] (J → P) (J v E) ⊢ (Z • -J)
14. (F → Y) [Y → (N → -U)] [-(D • R) → U] ⊢ [-Q • (U • L)]
15.* (A → B) [B → (C → E)] ⊢ [(F ↔ C) → (I → E)]
16. [(G → R) • (U → H)] (N → U) [(R → N) • -H] ⊢ -G
17. {[F → (T → F)] v [-F • (T → F)]} ⊢ [(T • F) • (-T v -F)]
18. [(I ↔ J) ↔ (L ↔ P)] ⊢ {-[(I → J) • (-I → -J)] ↔ (-L → -P)}
19. (C → J) [(J • E) → (L → P)] (-E • -U) ⊢ -C
20.* (Sa → Se) (Sc → Sr) [(Se • Sr) → (Sg → Sn)] -Sn ⊢ [-Sc v (Se → -Sg)]

6. Truth Trees

In Chapter 5, we examined one method of testing arguments for validity, namely, truth tables. This way of testing for validity concerned truth-functional sentences, connectives, and sentence components. The tables allowed us to determine whether it is possible, for any given argument in Sentential Logic, to have true premises and a false conclusion under at least one interpretation.

We saw, however, that while the truth table method is a purely mechanical and an effective device, it can be laborious when the number of sentence letters contained in an argument is large. Even the truth table short-cut method could involve the quite lengthy process of examining each interpretation in which the conclusion is false. While the short-cut method of tables greatly diminishes the number of interpretation one needs to finish a proof, tables themselves are limited in their scope and application in the study of Logic generally.

As we move into studying *truth trees*, we note that the method of trees makes use of an ancient method of proof, called *Reductio ad Absurdum*. This method works like this: You assume the denial of the conclusion and work to produce contradictions; if you generate a contradiction on every "branch" of the tree, then you know the original argument is valid.

The method of truth trees, for testing validity, works according to the same principle as all truth-functional methods for proving validity of arguments. The principle is this: *An argument is valid if, and only if, it is not possible for the premise(s) and the denial of the conclusion to be true at the same time (or under the same interpretation, in the same row . . .)*. This is another way of saying that the premises cannot be true while the conclusion is false, or, that the conclusion is logically necessitated by the premise(s). Note, however, that we have introduced a new concept here, that being the denial of the conclusion.

As mentioned, the tree method uses the ancient device of assuming the premises of an argument to be true, assuming the conclusion to be false, and then attempting to derive a contradiction from these. The idea behind it is that in a valid argument, the premises lead to the conclusion with some sort of logical necessity whereby if the premises are true, the conclusion could not be false. Now, if we assume the premises to be true and the conclusion false, then if the argument is valid, contradictions (at least one) should arise.

The sort of contradiction we are attempting to derive is quite simple, taking the form of a conjunction of any sentence and the negation of that same sentence. Example: '(S • -S).' This sentence says that 'S' is both true and false,

$$[(G \rightarrow J) \bullet -(G \rightarrow J)]$$

This sentence "says" that '(G → J)' is both true and not true. That is, it is affirmed as well as denied. That is a contradiction.

In working truth trees, then, it suffices to deny the conclusion and work for (try to derive) a contradiction, which will assert that both conjuncts in a conjunction are true, which is impossible. (Recall that contradictions are false under all interpretations.) For truth trees, specifically, the objective is to derive a contradiction on *each and every branch* of the tree, according to the rules. If, after denying the conclusion, this can be accomplished, the original argument is said to be *proven valid*. If, after denying the conclusion, there is at least one "branch" of the tree that has no contradiction, the argument is thereby shown to be *invalid*, which means that it is possible, on at least one interpretation, for each of the premises to be true while the conclusion is false.

To construct a truth tree, the premises and conclusion are listed in a single column. This column may be thought of as the "trunk" of the tree, from which the "branches" will grow. The growth of the tree is determined by the nine rules below. Notice that there is but one rule for each type of sentence, i.e., the conjunction, the conditional, etc. *The rules require only a single application to any given sentence found in an argument.* Never apply a rule to a sentence more than one time. To remind yourself that a sentence has had a rule applied to it, and to avoid unnecessary duplication, put a check mark [√] beside each sentence to which you apply a rule.

It should be noted that each sentence presented in an argument is given as true, i.e., is assumed to be true for the purpose of attempting to determine the validity of the argument itself. This is to say that there is never a question about a premise being true or false in actuality, but rather one is to keep in mind the definition of *validity* and ask: could the premises be true while the conclusion is false? If so, the argument is invalid.

Here is how we set up the arguments for the tree method:

$$(D \vee -S)$$
$$-H$$
$$(-H \rightarrow -D)$$
$$\text{-----------------}$$
$$-S$$

The line separating '-S' and '(-H → -D)' is our conclusion indicator. All sentences above the line are premises; the sentence directly below is the conclusion.

6.2. The Truth Tree Rules

There are nine truth tree rules. There is one rule for every type of sentence (e.g., conjunctions) as well as for the negation of every type of sentence (e.g., negative conjunctions). There is no rule for simple sentences or their negations.

Below you will find the truth tree rules stated in English. The schemata for the rules follow directly below.

Conjunction: If a conjunction [•] appears on a branch of the tree, put both conjuncts, in a line, on that branch.

Disjunction: If a disjunction [v] appears on a branch of the tree, divide the branch into two branches; put one disjunct on one branch and the other disjunct on the other branch.

Conditional: If a conditional [→] appears on a branch of the tree, divide the branch into two branches and put the negation of the conditional's antecedent on one branch and the consequent on the other branch.

Biconditional: If a biconditional [↔] appears on a branch of a tree, divide the branch into two branches, putting both components of the biconditional on one branch and their negations on the other branch.

Double Negation: If a double negation [--] appears on a branch of a tree, put the sentence that is doubly negated on that branch.

Negated Conjunction: If a negated conjunction [- •] appears on a branch of a tree, divide the branch into two branches and put the negation of one conjunct on one branch and the negation of the other conjunct on the other branch.

Negated Disjunction: If a negated disjunction [-v] appears on a branch of a tree, put the negations of both disjuncts on that branch.

Negated Conditional: If a negated conditional [-→] appears on a branch of a tree, put both its antecedent and the negation of its consequent on that branch.

Negated Biconditional: If a negated biconditional [-↔] appears on a branch of a tree, divide the branch into two branches and put the first component together with the negation of the second component on one branch and put the negation of the first component together with the second component on the other branch.

Schemata for, and justification of, the rules

Conjunction:

$$(p \cdot q)$$
$$p$$
$$q$$

There is only one case where a conjunction is true, viz., when *both* of its conjuncts are true. Hence, where '(p • q)' is true on any branch, 'p' is true and 'q' is true on that branch. Hence, we put them on the same branch.

Notice the correspondence between the truth tree rule for conjunction and the truth table for the conjunction. Recall the table:

$$(p \bullet q)$$
t t t
t f f
f f t
f f f

When a conjunction appears on a branch, it is given as constituting a true sentence. That is, the conjunction itself is presumed to be true and hence both conjuncts are presumed true. Again, there is only one instance where the conjunction itself is true, and that is shown in row #1 in the table above. Since both conjuncts must be true for the conjunction itself to be true, the truth tree rule records each conjunct as true on the same branch.

Negated conjunction:

A conjunction is false whenever at least one of its conjuncts is false. Note that in the truth table for conjunction above, there are three instances wherein the conjunction itself is false. Since in truth trees we are not assigning truth values to the components of our sentences, we cannot say which component is true, which is false. For a negated conjunction, dividing the branch into two branches is as much as to say that at least one of the components *is* false. Where '-(p • q)' is true, either '-p' or '-q' is false, and perhaps both are false.

Disjunction:

A disjunction is true whenever at least one of its disjuncts is true. For the disjunction, dividing the branch into two branches is as much as to say that at least one, if not both, of its disjuncts is true. Where '(p v q)' is true, either 'p' or 'q' is true, and perhaps both. Recall the truth table:

$$(p \; v \; q)$$
t t t
t t f
f t t
f f f

Note the correspondence between the truth tree rule for disjunction and the truth table above. The table shows the disjunction to be true in three instances, i.e., rows #1, #2, and #3. In trees, dividing the branch into two branches tokens each of the three possible interpretations under which the disjunction may be true.

Negated disjunction:

$$-(p \vee q)$$
$$-p$$
$$-q$$

There is only one case where a negated disjunction is true, namely, when both disjuncts are false. A negated disjunction is true in the one instance where the disjunction itself is false. Where '-(p v q)' is true on any branch, '-p' and '-q' are both true on that branch and hence should be written on the branch.

It is worth repeating that the appearance of '-(p v q)' on the branch of a tree is to be construed as a true occurrence of '-(p v q).' This is so for each occurrence of any sentence appearing in a tree.

Conditional:

$$(p \rightarrow q)$$

-p   q

A conditional is true just in case its antecedent is false or its consequent is true. Compare the truth tree rule above with the table below. For a conditional, dividing the branch into two branches, putting the negation of the antecedent on one branch and the consequent on another branch, is as much as to say that either the antecedent 'p' is false *or* the consequent 'q' is true, and perhaps the antecedent is false *and* the consequent is true, as in row #3 of the table for the conditional.

$$(p \rightarrow q)$$
t	t	t
t	f	f
f	t	t
f	t	f

Negated conditional:

$$-(p \rightarrow q)$$
$$p$$
$$-q$$

As we know, there is only one instance where a conditional is false, viz., when the antecedent is true and the consequent is false. Note row #2 in the truth table for the conditional on the previous page. Hence, where '-(p → q)' is true on any branch, 'p' and '-q' will both be true on that branch.

Biconditional:

A biconditional is true when the components have the same truth values. Note the table below. In rows #1 and #4, 'p' and 'q' have the same truth values, as do rows #2 and #3. Dividing the branch into two branches is as much as to say that either both components are true or both components are false. Where '(p ↔ q)' is true, then, either 'p' *and* 'q' are both true, or '-p' *and* '-q' are both true.

$$(p \leftrightarrow q)$$
$$t \; t \; t$$
$$t \; f \; f$$
$$f \; f \; t$$
$$f \; t \; f$$

Negated biconditional:

A biconditional is false just in case the components have opposing truth values. Note the table above. In rows #2 and #3, 'p' and 'q' have opposite truth values, rendering the biconditional itself false. Where a biconditional is false, the negated biconditional is true. Dividing the branch into two branches is as much to say that where '-(p ↔ q)' is true, either 'p' *and* '-q' are true, or '-p' *and* 'q' are true.

Double Negation:

$$--p$$
$$p$$

As the truth table for the double negation shows on the following page, the truth value of the original simple sentence is reversed with each addition of a single negation sign (the bar):

```
- - p
t f t
f t f
```

Where '- -p' is true, 'p' is also true, and where '- -p' is false, 'p' is also false. The rule for double negation is very convenient although in some cases it is, strictly speaking, unnecessary. Take the following example:
'(- - -D → - -E).' Since this sentence is a conditional, applying the rule for the conditional here yields:

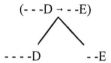

You will note that '---D' contradicts '--D' and is contradicted by '----D.' So, if '- - -D' were to occur by itself under some interpretation connected with '----D,' where '----D' appears on the branch *by itself*, that branch can be closed. If there *is* reason to reduce '----D' to 'D,' the rule for double negation applies to '----D' in the following way:

```
- - - -D
- -D
D
```

One further point of form is important. In the tree method, it is illicit to remove double negation signs from any sentence that is not itself a double negation, such as moving from '(---D → --E)' to '(-D → --E)' or to '(---D → E)' or to '(-D → E).' This is because '(---D → --E)' is a conditional, and only the rule for the conditional may be applied to it. We will see that in Natural Deduction (Chapter 7) there will be a rule, actually called "Double Negation," where we may add or delete two negation signs in a row.

It may be convenient to think of a divided branch as indicating that there is more than one instance (case, interpretation) in which the given sentence is true (or false, where applicable). When a branch extends undivided, the indication is that a given sentence is true (or false) in one case only. The two trees below illustrate this.

```
[(P • A) • -N] √₁
     -P        D.C.
   (P • A)     √₂
     -N
     P
     A
     X        Valid
```

There is only one premise in the above argument. It is '[(P • A) • -N].' The conclusion is 'P.' The letters "D.C." indicate that the conclusion has been denied. Hence, while it may look as though '-P' is the conclusion, what has happened here is that the conclusion has been denied, yielding '-P' on that line. Now go back to the first line of the tree, to the check mark with the number 1 beside it. This means that the rule for conjunction has been applied to the premise. Directly below '-P' there is '(P • A)' and '-N.' These two sentences are the result of applying the rule for the conjunction to the premise. The checkmark with the number 1 indicates that the sentence to its left has had a rule applied to it and also that it is the first time a rule has been applied to a sentence in this tree. The next sentence to have a rule applied to it is '(P • A).' Hence, the checkmark and number 2 is beside this sentence. What you get when you apply the rule for conjunction to this sentence is 'P' and 'A' in a line directly under the sentence. Now, since every sentence that can have a rule applied to it has had a rule applied to it, it is time to look to see whether there are any contradictions in this tree. There is indeed a contradiction here, namely, 'P' and '-P' both appear on the same branch (or trunk in this case since there has been no branching). The 'X' directly below 'A' there indicates that there is a contradiction here. The trunk is said to be *closed*. When all branches close (when the trunk itself closes), we know the argument is valid.

Let us now go through a truth tree for an argument one step at a time. Here is the argument itself:

$$-(R \to G)$$
$$\underline{-[(L \bullet O) \to J]}$$
$$O$$

This argument has two premises, each of which is a negated conditional. The conclusion is simply 'O.' The next step is to deny the conclusion, like so:

$$-(R \to G)$$
$$\underline{-[(L \bullet O) \to J]}$$
$$-O \qquad \text{D.C.}$$

It is important to always note that the conclusion has been denied. Anyone looking at your tree will be able to see clearly what the conclusion is. The next step is to apply a rule to one of the premises. Let's begin with the first premise, though, strictly speaking, it does not matter where we begin:

$$-(R \to G) \qquad \checkmark_1$$
$$\underline{-[(L \bullet O) \to J]}$$
$$-O \qquad \text{D.C.}$$
$$R$$
$$-G$$

Consult the rule for "negated conditional." It says to bring down, in a line, the antecedent to the conditional along with the negation of the consequent, as has been done here. Note that there is a checkmark and a number beside the first premise. This indicates the first premise has had a rule applied to it and also that it is the first sentence to have a rule applied to it.

At this point, we want to check to see whether there are contradictions present in the tree. Recall that we are looking for any sentence, sitting alone on a line, and its denial, sitting alone on another line. There are no contradictions at present. Since there are no contradictions yet, and since there is still one sentence that can be checked that has not been checked, we continue to apply the rules.

The next step is to apply the rule for "negated conditional" to the second premise, like so:

$$
\begin{array}{ll}
\text{-(R → G)} & \checkmark_1 \\
\text{-[(L • O) → J]} & \checkmark_2 \\
\text{-O} & \text{D.C.} \\
\text{R} & \\
\text{-G} & \\
\text{(L • O)} & \\
\text{-J} &
\end{array}
$$

The application of the rule for the second premise tells us to bring down the antecedent ('(L • O)') on a line by itself and also bring down the negation of the consequent ('-J') on a line by itself. This has been done. Note that premise #2 has been checked and numbered.

Any contradictions? No contradictions yet. We continue, and since there is another sentence in the tree, that is, '(L • O),' that can be checked that has not been checked, we now apply a rule to this sentence, like so:

$$
\begin{array}{ll}
\text{-(R → G)} & \checkmark_1 \\
\text{-[(L • O) → J]} & \checkmark_2 \\
\text{-O} & \text{D.C.} \\
\text{R} & \\
\text{-G} & \\
\text{(L • O)} & \checkmark_3 \\
\text{-J} & \\
\text{L} & \\
\text{O} & \\
\text{X} &
\end{array}
$$

What we did here is to bring down 'L' and 'O' in a line, in accord with the rule for "conjunction." Note that '(L • O)' has been checked and numbered.

Contradictions? Yes. The sentences 'O' and '-O' contradict each other and appear on the same branch (trunk, in this case). Since there is a contradiction on this branch, we close it by putting an 'X' at the bottom of the branch, indicating that it is *closed*. All the branches have closed. This means that the argument is valid.

There will be some trees that are quite complicated with many branches. There is no exception to the following fact: When the conclusion of an argument is denied and rules applied to the sentences of the argument, the argument is valid if, and only if, all branches are closed.

Now let us walk through a more detailed truth tree.

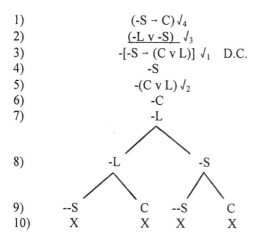

The above steps have been numbered solely for convenience of explanation. The premises are located in (1) and (2).

As indicated by 'D.C.' to the far right in (3), the conclusion, which is has been denied. It is important to note that it would not suffice to deny the conclusion by writing '[--S → (C v L)],' because the conclusion is a conditional. Denying '-S' would simply be denying the antecedent to the conclusion. A conditional denied becomes a negated conditional.

As mentioned, it does not matter which sentence you apply the rules to first, second, third, etc. I have chosen to work with the denial of the conclusion first because, upon examining the argument, I saw that I could extend the trunk of the tree rather than make new branches by doing so. (A rule of thumb that can makes trees shorter is this: *first apply rules to sentences that **don't** branch, then apply rules to sentences that do branch.*) The end result, i.e., our discovery of the validity or the invalidity of the argument, is independent of the order in which the rules are applied. The correctness of our applications is primary.

Lines (4) and (5) are the result of one step, i.e., the rule for negated conditional was applied to the denial of the conclusion (3). Since a negated conditional is true only when the conditional's antecedent is true and its consequent false, I continued the "trunk" of the tree by writing the antecedent, which is '-S,' on line (4), and by also writing the denial of the consequent, which is '-(C v L),' on line (5). At this point, since the sentence in line (3) has had a rule applied to it, a check (√) was written beside the sentence.

Again, when a sentence is checked, assign the appropriate numerical subscript to the checkmark. Since the denied conclusion is the first sentence to which a rule was applied, it is checked with the number '1,' i.e., $[\sqrt{}_1]$.

Questions: Does a contradiction appear on any branch? No. Are there sentences to which rules have yet to be applied, that is, sentences which can be checked but which have not been checked? Yes. Then continue to apply the rules.

Lines (6) and (7) have resulted, again, from one step, viz., the rule for negated disjunction has been applied to the sentence on line (5). Since a disjunction is false only when both disjuncts are false, the trunk has been once again extended, but this time by denying each disjunct in the negated disjunction. Line (5) was checked, with the appropriate number, since a rule was applied to it. It was the second sentence to which a rule was applied, so the subscript on the checkmark is "2."

Are there any contradictions yet? No. Have all sentences containing connectives been checked? No. Then continue.

Line (8) is the result of applying the rule for disjunction to line (2). Since a disjunction is true if at least one of its disjuncts is true, we divide the branch into two branches and write one disjunct, '-L,' on one branch, and the other disjunct, '-S,' on the other branch. Line (2) is now checked and numbered.

Are there any contradictions on any branch? No. Are all sentences checked that can be checked? No. Then continue.

Line (9) is the result of applying the rule for the conditional to line (1). [It is important to note that any result of applying a rule must extend to *every open branch* of the tree under the interpretation with which you are working.] Since a conditional is true when either the antecedent is false or the consequent is true, (9) consists in four branches which stem from the two branches in (8), with each set of two branches in (9) consisting in the negation of the antecedent of line (1), '--S,' and with consequent of (1), i.e., 'C.' The sentence on line (1) is checked and numbered.

There are now contradictions on the tree. In (9), 'C' appears on two branches, albeit in different interpretations. But '-C' appears in (6), which is *common to* both occurrences of 'C' on line (9). Since 'C' and '-C' are contradictories [cannot both be true at the same time *and* cannot both be false at the same time], we can *close* both branches in (9) where 'C' appears alone. *To close a branch, place an 'X' directly below the last sentence appearing on that branch.* That indicates *closure.* When a branch is closed, no further work will occur on that branch.

Since '-S' in (4) contradicts both occurrences of '--S' in line (9), we can close both branches on line (9) containing '--S.'

We see that there are now no open branches in the tree. Hence. the original argument is *valid.*

Let us now work a tree for an invalid argument. We will see that, after all sentences in the argument that can be checked have been checked, there will be at least one *open branch*, that is, a branch that does not have a contradiction on it. The lines of this tree will be numbered for convenience of the explanation below.

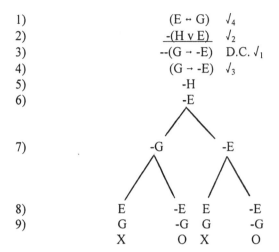

1) $\quad$ (E ↔ G) $\quad \checkmark_4$
2) $\quad$ -(H v E) $\quad \checkmark_2$
3) $\quad$ --(G → -E) $\quad$ D.C. $\checkmark_1$
4) $\quad$ (G → -E) $\quad \checkmark_3$
5) $\quad$ -H
6) $\quad$ -E

7) $\quad$ -G $\qquad$ -E

8) $\quad$ E $\quad$ -E $\quad$ E $\quad$ -E
9) $\quad$ G $\quad$ -G $\quad$ G $\quad$ -G
$\qquad$ X $\qquad$ O $\quad$ X $\qquad$ O

The tree for this argument is instructive in a number of ways. Lines (1), (2), and (3) state the argument itself, although the conclusion ("-(G → -E)") has already denied in line (3), as can be seen by the entry of 'D.C.' to the right of the denied conclusion in line (3). Note that the conclusion was denied by adding one negation sign (the bar) to the conclusion itself. Line (4) is the result of applying the rule of Double Negation to line (3). Notice that this using this rule extends the trunk rather than branching. Lines (5) and (6) are the result of applying the rule for negated disjunctions to the sentence on line (2). No branching occurs here either. There are no contradictions in the tree up to this point. Line (7) is the result of applying the rule for conditionals to the sentence on line (4). The trunk/branch has been split, creating two branches, with the negation of the antecedent on the left branch and the consequent on the right branch.

To check for contradictions at this point, we look up from '-G' on line (7) to the first sentence of the argument. If there were a 'G' appearing by itself on any line *above* '-G,' we would have a contradiction and would close that branch. We also have '-E' and '-H' on the same branch as '-G' and if either (or both) 'E' or 'H' were to appear on that branch, we would have a contradiction and the branch would be closed. So there are no contradictions on the left branch. Next, go to the right branch and look up from '-E' to the top of the tree. No contradictions here either; hence, we have two open branches at this point. Hence we proceed.

Lines (8) and (9) are the result of applying the rule for biconditionals to the first premise of the argument. It is vital that we apply this rule for each open branch. Hence, the split branches below '-G' on line (7) *and* the split branches below '-E' on line (7).

There are now contradictions on this tree. On the extreme left hand branch, notice that 'E' exists on line (8) and '-E' exists on line (5). Line (5) is common with all lines and branches below it. Also, the extreme left branch has 'G.' And line (7) has '-G.' This is a contradiction. Hence, the extreme left hand branch of this tree is closed.

The branch directly to the right of the extreme left hand branch does not close, however. Look up from the very bottom '-G' on that branch. There is no 'G' above it. We would need 'E' above the '-E' on that branch, or 'H,' for contradictions. There are no contradictions on this branch. It is very important to designate a branch as *open* if, and only if, there are no sentences on that branch that can be checked that haven't been checked. We see that there are no sentences on this branch that can be checked which have not been checked. All checkable sentences have been checked. The branch is, indeed, open. Since all it takes is one open branch to show that an argument is invalid, we can say with certainty that this argument is invalid.

The steps to follow in constructing truth trees are as follows:

1. List sentences in order, premises and conclusion.
2. Deny the conclusion.
3. Search for trunk extension (optional).
4. Apply a rule to a sentence with any of the connectives (except simple sentences that are negated).
5. Check and number the sentence.
6. Search for contradictions.
7. If no contradictions are found, *and* if there are one or more sentences unchecked, return to #4 and proceed.
8. If one or more contradictions is/are found, close each branch on which one *is* found.
9. For each remaining open branch, return to #4 and proceed.
10. When all sentences are checked and numbered, search for open branches.
11. If there are no open branches, designate the argument valid.
12. If there is at least one open branch, write a ring under the last letter appearing on the branch and designate the argument invalid.

Further examples of truth trees are below. It is easier to "read" a tree if you will go by the numbers by the check marks. As indicated above, check 1 ($\checkmark_1$) marks the place where the first rule was applied to a sentence in the tree.

Below are numerous examples of trees, fully worked.

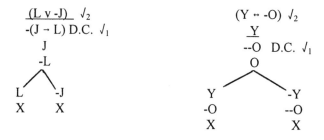

The right hand tree above has 'Y' as the second premise. Note that '-Y' is its contradiction. Hence the right hand branch is closed. We see, then, that though the last sentence on the right hand branch ('- -O') does not contradict anything on its branch, there is a contradiction (i.e., 'Y' and '-Y') on that branch. Any contradiction on a branch closes the branch.

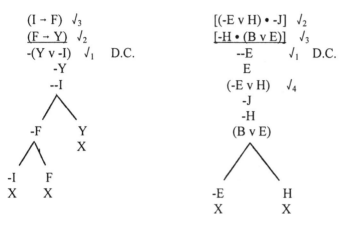

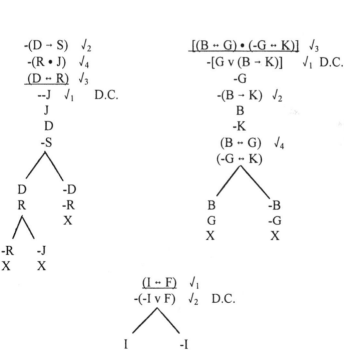

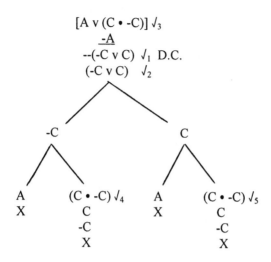

$[A \lor (C \bullet -C)]$ √₃
-A
--(-C ∨ C) √₁ D.C.
(-C ∨ C) √₂

-C   C

A   (C • -C) √₄   A   (C • -C) √₅
X   C   X   C
             -C   -C
             X   X

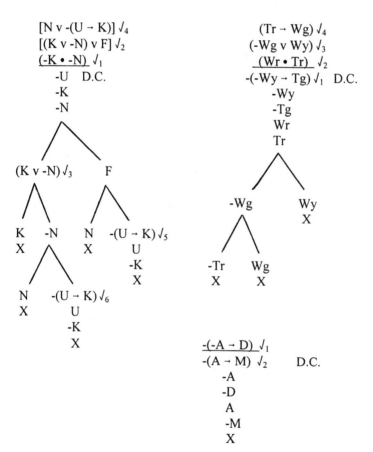

$[N \lor -(U \rightarrow K)]$ √₄
$[(K \lor -N) \lor F]$ √₂
(-K • -N) √₁
-U   D.C.
-K
-N

(K ∨ -N) √₃   F

K   -N   N   -(U → K) √₅
X   X   U
                      -K
                      X

N   -(U → K) √₆
X   U
         -K
         X

(Tr → Wg) √₄
(-Wg ∨ Wy) √₃
(Wr • Tr) √₂
-(-Wy → Tg) √₁ D.C.
-Wy
-Tg
Wr
Tr

-Wg   Wy
                 X

-Tr   Wg
X   X

-(-A → D) √₁
-(A → M) √₂   D.C.
-A
-D
A
-M
X

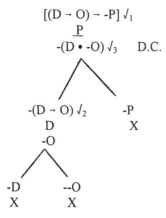

The truth tree on the following page shows the argument to be invalid. At least one branch fails to close. Please note that all sentences that *can* be checked *have been* checked on the branch that is open (on the extreme left). It is important to never designate a branch as open as long as there is one or more sentences on that branch that is unchecked (which can be checked).

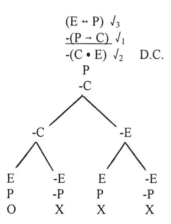

The result of applying the truth tree rule for the biconditional to the first premise led to four branches (interpretations) in the last two lines. Three of these branches are closed. The other branch is open because all the rules that *can* be applied to the sentences *have* been applied and no contradiction is found on that branch. Invalid argument.

As discussed, we count an argument to be *invalid* just in case at least one branch remains open when all sentences containing connectives have been checked. It does not matter how many branches close in any given tree; if one is open, the argument is invalid.

Further examples of truth trees follow:

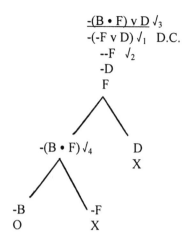

-(B • F) v D √₃
-(-F v D) √₁   D.C.
--F √₂
-D
F

-(B • F) √₄   D
                   X

-B   -F
O   X

(R → J) √₁
R
(J → N) √₃
(N → H) √₂
-H   D.C.

-R   J
X

-N   H
          X

-J   N
X   X

(Yg ↔ Ya) √₁
-(-Yy v -Yg) √₂
(Ya → -Ya)
-Ya   D.C.

Yg   -Yg
Ya   -Ya
X   --Yy
          --Yg
          X

{[-L → (S v E)] • [(-L • -E) → -S]}
[(L v S) • -(S • -E)] √₂
-[(E v S) v (E v L)] √₁   D.C.
-(E v S) √₃
-(E v L) √₄
(L v S) √₅
-(S • -E)

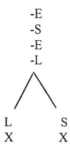

-E
-S
-E
-L

L   S
X   X

Note here that not all sentences that can be checked have been checked. This is all right, since all the branches close. What this amounts to, or tells us, is that some of the premises in the above argument are not required to establish the validity of the argument.

6.3. The Logical Status of Sentences

As noted in Chapter 4, sentences are either logically true, or logically false, or logically indeterminate. This section is designed to show you how to determine, via truth trees, the logical status of sentences. To determine that a given sentence is a truth of logic, i.e., L-true, construct a tree for the negation of the sentence. The sentence is L-true just in case the tree closes (each of its branches closes). 'S.D.' indicates that the sentence has been denied. Examples:

<u>Zero premises</u>
-(-R → -R) $\checkmark_1$ S.D.
   -R
   --R $\checkmark_2$
   R
   X   L-true

<u>Zero premises</u>
-{T → [(T → F) → F]} $\checkmark_1$ S.D.
      T
  -[(T → F) → F] $\checkmark_2$
    (T → F) $\checkmark_3$
     -F

L-true

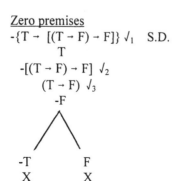

-T   F
X   X

The above tree is sufficient to show that '{T → [(T → F) → F]}' is a logical truth, or tautology. The writing of 'zero premises' is merely a convention used to augment the formality of the proof.

The vital first move in the proof is the denying of the sentence to be shown to be tautologous. The essential reasoning is this: If some sentence, 'S,' is L-true, then if 'S' is denied, then '-S' will always prove to be self-contradictory. A tree for a self-contradictory sentence will close (that is, all branches will close). This is precisely what has been achieved in the above tree, since all (in this case, both) branches close.

Consider the following tautology, i.e., -[(-A v B) • -(-B → -A)].

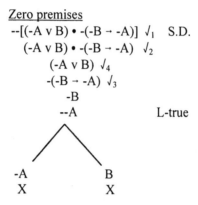

To determine whether a given sentence is L-false, construct a tree for the sentence itself. That is, do a tree without denying the sentence. It is L-false just in case the tree closes, i.e., all branches close. Example:

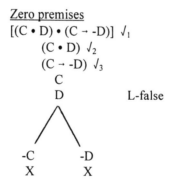

The above tree shows that '[(C • D) • (C → -D)]' is self-contradictory and, therefore, logically false, since contradictions have been found on all branches without denying the sentence itself.

To show that some sentence, 'S,' is *neither* logically true *nor* logically false, construct two trees, one for 'S' and one for '-S.' If neither tree closes, 'S' is said to be *L-indeterminate*. What this means in literal terms is that one cannot determine the truth value of the sentence ('*S*') through logical analysis alone. The following two truth trees, taken together, show that '[(P • Q) ↔ (Q v P)]' is neither L-true nor L-false. The first tree proves it to be not L-true, while the latter proves it to be not L-false. If a sentence is neither L-true nor L-false, then it is L-indeterminate.

<u>Zero premises</u>

-[(P • Q) ↔ (Q v P)] √₁ S.D.

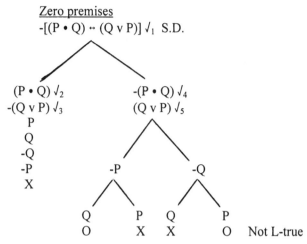

The major connective in the sentence '[(P • Q) ↔ (Q v P)]' is the double arrow, so the sentence is a biconditional. In the first tree, the sentence was denied, rendering the sentence a negated biconditional. The rule for the negated biconditional must be applied as the first move.

In the second tree, below, the sentence is not denied. Hence, the first move of the second tree is to apply the rule for the biconditional to the sentence itself. Note that 'S.D.' does not appear to the right of the sentence in the second tree. This is because to show a sentence L-false, which is the goal of the second tree, we do not deny the object sentence. Here is that tree. It is a curiosity that, in fact, no branches close for this sentence.

<u>Zero premises</u>

[(P • Q) ↔ (Q v P)] √₁

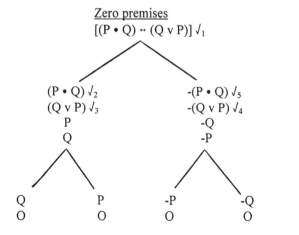

To repeat, then, when you are working to discover whether some sentence is L-true, L-false, or L-indeterminate, begin by denying the sentence and working a tree for it. If the tree closes, you know the sentence is indeed L-true. If the tree doesn't close, you know the sentence is not L-true, but you do not know, yet, whether it is L-false. Next, do a tree for the sentence itself (not denied). If the tree closes, then you know the sentence is L-false. If the tree does not close, then, you have just proven that it is not L-false. Since you already know it is not L-true, it follows that the sentence is L-indeterminate.

Further examples of truth trees are below.

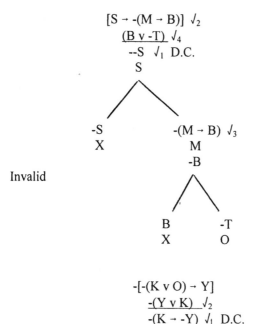

$$[S \rightarrow -(M \rightarrow B)] \; \sqrt{_2}$$
$$\underline{(B \vee -T)} \; \sqrt{_4}$$
$$--S \; \sqrt{_1} \; D.C.$$
$$S$$

-S
X

-(M → B) $\sqrt{_3}$
M
-B

Invalid

B   -T
X   O

Valid

$$-[-(K \vee O) \rightarrow Y]$$
$$\underline{-(Y \vee K)} \; \sqrt{_2}$$
$$-(K \rightarrow -Y) \; \sqrt{_1} \; D.C.$$
$$K$$
$$--Y$$
$$-Y$$
$$-K$$
$$X$$

Note here once again that the tree above closes without all of the sentences being checked that can be checked. If we were to apply the tree rules to the first premise here, the tree would still close (that is, each branch would close).

$$[(J \leftrightarrow F) \rightarrow E] \; \sqrt{_3}$$
$$-(E \vee J) \; \sqrt{_2}$$
$$\underline{(-E \rightarrow -N)} \; \sqrt{_5}$$
$$-(N \rightarrow J) \; \sqrt{_1} \; D.C.$$
$$N$$

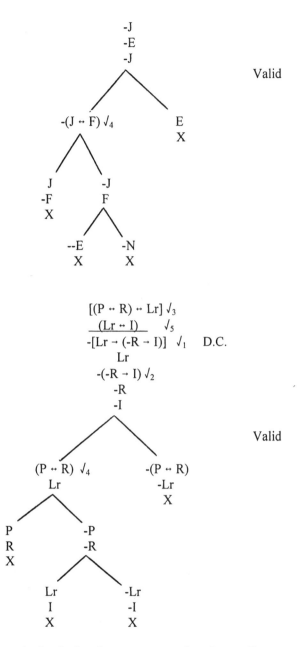

Note here again that in the above tree, even though not all sentences that can be checked have been checked, such as '-(P ↔ R)' on the middle right hand branch, that sentence doesn't need to be checked because the branch closes (there is a contradiction) without checking that sentence. When a branch closes, nothing more is added to the branch.

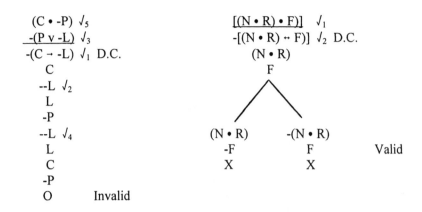

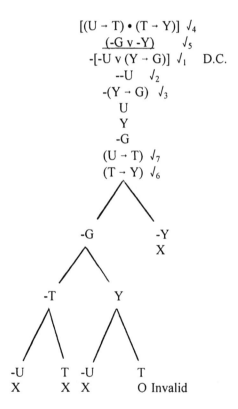

The tree above is a good example showing that if even one branch is open, then the argument is invalid. To reiterate, the conclusion was denied and contradictions were not found on *every* branch. Hence, it is possible that the premises may be true and the conclusion false, as seen by the fact that the conclusion was denied (rendered false) in the beginning.

Exercise: Ch. 6.

A. Use truth trees to determine whether the following arguments are valid or invalid.

1. (R v T)
   (-R → T)

2. (L • -U)
   (U → I)

3. (-F → C)
   (C → F)

4. (J → E)
   (-E → -J)

5.* (D • O)
   (D v O)

6. (A ↔ W)
   (A → W)

7. (K ↔ L)
   (K v L)
   (L • K)

8. (B • T) → Y
   (-B → M)
   L → (M v N)

9. S • (-F v G)
   (-F → -S)
   (F → F)
   F

10.*(U → C)
   (C v P)
   (-U → P)
   (-P → -C) v U

11. (R v S) → Z
   (Z v R)

12. O v (Y • G)
   (-G v -Y)
   O

13. (B ↔ D)
   -D
   B → (C v -E)

14. -(K → -L) → M
   -L v (M v -K)

15.* (I → F)
   (P → -Q)
   (Q v -I)
   -(U ↔ P)
   -[(P • -Q) ↔ (-U • P)]

16. -[(V • N) v T] → -S
   (V • N) → -S
   (E → -T)
   -(S → -E)

17. (A v B) → (C • D)
   (D v F) → G
   (A ↔ G)

18. (C → J)
   J → [(L → --L) → K]
   --C → --K

19. -Rc
   Rd → (Ra v Re)
   Ra → (Rb • Rc)
   (Rd → Rb)

20.*(-Raa → Rcg) v -Rc
   (Rc → Rd) v Rcg
   (Rcg → -Rd) ↔ -Raa
   (-Rc v Raa)

B. Use truth trees to determine the logical status of the following sentences. Some are L-true, some are L-false and some are L-indeterminate.

1. N → -(C → -N)
2. S → (-S → S)
3. ((S → -S) → S)
4. (H v -H) • (-H • A)
5.* -(M ↔ T) ↔ (-M ↔T)
6. (F → -T) → (-T → -F)
7. (-T → F) • (-F v -T)
8. [W v (W • Z)] ↔ W
9. -[(-P → P) • -(P → -P)]
10.* -[-(E • E) → -E]
11. {[(R → U) • R] ↔ U}
12. (K → -B) ↔ (B • K)
13. (J ↔ -D) ↔ [-D ↔ (J v -W)]
14. -{(O → F) → [-F → (O → -Y)]}
15.* (J v -C) → (C → -J)
16. -{[(-S → E) • -Z] → (Z → -E)}
17. -[-(W v Y) v -(Y → -W)]
18. (Hr → Vw) → [(Hr • Vn) → (Vw • Vn)]
19. [B → (D • F)] → {[(F v G) → K] → (B → K)}
20.* (A ↔ (-Z v -N)) ↔ (-Z → (N • -A))
21. ((E ↔ T) • -M) → (M → (T • -E))
22. (Q → (P → L)) → ((Q → P) → (Q → L))
23. (J • -J) → ((T → J) → (-T → -J))
24. (-(Y → I) • (D • -A)) • ((I v -Y) v ((D • R) → A)))
25. -[(-M → -N) v O] ↔ {[(O → -N) → (M → O)] → -M}
26. (((G v S) • (I v -G)) • ((-I • -C) • -C) • -S))
27. {(B → -E) • [E → (T • B)]} → (T v -B)
28. -((--K ↔ --J) → {[-Q v (-K → -J)] • (K → J)})
29. [(Cy v Cc) → Rn] ↔ [(Rn • -Ws) v -Cy]
30.* (Rs ↔ -Sr) ↔ [Rs ↔ (Sr ↔ Ri)]

C. Provide a dictionary for each of the following arguments and translate the arguments into symbolic notation. Use the method of truth trees to determine validity or invalidity.

1. Oahu's North Shore attracts the world's best surfers if, and only if, the North Shore has the world's biggest rideable waves. The waves on the North Shore are definitely the biggest rideable waves in the world. Hence, if the North Shore attracts the world's best surfers, then the best surfers in the world are also attracted to the surf in California.

2. If compact discs provide the best possible listening enjoyment, then cassettes will slowly lose market shares. If cassettes lose market shares, then the car

stereo business will be turned on its head. Therefore, either the car stereo business will be turned on its head or compact discs do not provide the best possible listening enjoyment.

3. Taylor Payne's seeking another term in office entails that a Republican won't be elected. But if another Democrat wants to be Senator of California, then it certainly won't be Rick Arno. If no other Democrat seeks office, Payne will seek another term. It follows that a Republican being elected implies Arno's not wanting to be Senator.

4. Either Sisley was a great artist or half of the art critics in the Western world aren't very critical. If R.C. Gorman isn't a great artist, then Sisley wasn't a great artist. Hence, Gorman is a great artist provided that half of the critics are critical.

5.* The physics major learns much about the ultimate constituents of matter and the literature major learns much about the constituents of fine poetry and prose, unless the physics and literature teachers are unhappy with their jobs. If a physics teacher is happy at work, then the physics teacher's colleagues will be happy and the physics majors will learn much. If the college president is neither a physics teacher nor a literature teacher, then both the physics and literature teachers are happy. The president is a physics teacher. Hence, the literature majors learn much.

6. If Jed Towne retires next year and Ernie Semeck completes over 43% of his passes, the Cossacks will lose in the championship game. The Cossacks winning is implied by Semeck's completing less than 43% of his passes. Semeck never completes 43% of his passes. So, Semeck won't complete 43% and Towne won't retire.

7. Hindu mystics believe either in God or in a nonpersonal Unity. If the Hindu mystic has had a religious mystical experience, then the mystic believes in God; however, if the mystic has never had a religious mystical experience, then the mystic won't believe in God but a nonpersonal Unity. No Hindu mystic has ever had a religious mystical experience. We can conclude that no Hindu mystic believes in God.

8. If Rodin's "Balzac" is the most beautiful statue in existence, then Rodin was the greatest sculptor who ever lived. Its not being the case that both Rodin was the greatest sculptor and that Michelangelo wasn't the greatest sculptor who ever lived implies that "Balzac" is indeed the most beautiful statue in existence. It follows that Rodin was the greatest sculptor.

9. One's being an ethical relativist entails one's believing that any ethical theory is as good as any other. One's being an ethical absolutist implies that one believes there are actions which are right independent of how anybody perceives the world. If anyone views the world from a moral perspective, then that person is a relativist or an absolutist. Everyone views the world from a moral perspective. Hence, everyone believes either that any theory is as good as any other, or that there are no actions which are right no matter how anyone perceives the world.

10.* If Fredrica is either a Republican or a Libertarian, then if Fredrica is a feminist, then she is a liberal. If she is not a feminist or is a socialist, then if she is Republican, she is either a moderate or a conservative. Fredrica is either a feminist or a Republican. But, she isn't a feminist. Thus, Fredrica is a liberal, and either a moderate or a conservative.

11. If Jess has much leisure time and likes to watch game shows on T.V., then Jess is either unproductive or is a fast worker. If Jess is productive or independently wealthy, she has much leisure time. If Jess is productive or has a very limited taste for fine entertainment, then she likes to watch game shows. Jess is not only productive, but the best judge of her own entertain-ments. It follows from the above that Jess is a fast worker.

12. If London continues to sink one-half inch per year, then by the year 2050, Picadilly Circus will be under water. If the River Thames continues to rise, London will continue to sink. If something is done about the blockages at the mouth of the Thames, London won't continue to sink. If Picadilly goes under water, tourism in London will be destroyed. But we know that tourism in London will never be destroyed. Thus, London will not continue to sink.

13. If the antecedent to this conditional is false, the conditional is true. The conditional's being true implies that language is paradoxical. But language is not paradoxical. The antecedent to this conditional is false provided that it is true that English is whimsical. Either English is whimsical or the antecedent to this conditional is false. Therefore, either language is paradoxical or language is paradoxical.

14. If it rains for more than three days, Highway 299 will be closed. If a high pressure ridge rolls in and the wind blows from the southwest, then it will rain for more than three days. If 299 closes, Highway 101 will close. But Highway 101 won't close. Hence, either no high pressure ridge will come in or the wind won't blow from the southwest.

15. Either the U.S. Ambassador to Ireland won't both reside in Dublin and import British goods for use at the embassy, or will win the hearts of the Irish people. If she wins the hearts of the Irish people, then if the ambassador does import British goods, the Irish Republican Army will demand her removal as ambassador. If the ambassador doesn't care what the IRA thinks, she will live in Dublin and buy British goods. She really doesn't care what the IRA thinks. Thus, the IRA will demand her removal.

16. If logic is necessary for adequate thinking, then good thinkers use logic. If good thinkers use logic, then logic is useful. Either logic is necessary or good thinkers use logic. Therefore, not only is logic necessary or useful, but if it is necessary, then it is also useful.

17. If the laws of science are merely probable, then the safety of home appliances is doubtful, since appliances have arisen from technology based on sets of laws of science. If science is progressive or always changing, then the laws of science are only probable. Science *is* always changing, but some things never change. We can conclude that the safety of home appliances is doubtful.

18. The President will go to Congress and praise them or the President will go to Congress and scold them. If the President goes to Congress or proposes a "*New* New Deal," Congress will laugh at the President. Therefore, Congress will laugh at the President.

19. Either California's secession from the Union implies that its leaders believe it to be financially equipped for such a move, or California's movie moguls will continue their lobbying in Sacramento and will finally win the battle for lower taxes for film companies. The moguls won't both continue their lobbying and win the battle for lower taxes. However, California leaders do not believe California is financially stable enough to leave the Union. Hence, California won't secede from the Union.

20.* Being morally responsible for one's actions implies both that one is rational and that one has free will. If one's not being rational implies that one is a nonperson, then one will certainly have no moral rights. Therefore, one has no moral rights only if one is not morally responsible for one's actions.

7. Natural Deduction

7.1. Preliminaries

The final method for showing arguments to be valid is known as the method of Natural Deduction. This method involves deriving a conclusion on the last line of a proof, from a specified finite set of premises, using a stipulated number of rules.

We have used various schema to set up arguments up to this point. In working out truth tables, the format was:

$$(R \rightarrow E) \quad (-E \lor S) \quad (R \lor S) \quad \vdash \quad -R$$
$$\uparrow \qquad \uparrow \qquad \uparrow \qquad \uparrow$$
Premise Premise Premise $\vdash$ Conclusion.

For truth trees, we set up arguments in this fashion:

$$(-D \lor -G) \quad \leftarrow \qquad \text{Premise}$$
$$\underline{(G \bullet --D)} \quad \leftarrow \qquad \text{Premise}$$
$$K \qquad \leftarrow \qquad \text{Conclusion}$$

In natural deduction our schema is:

1. Premise
2. Premise $\vdash$ Conclusion.

Each premise is numbered. The conclusion appears in two places in a proof in natural deduction, namely, once on the same line as the last premise of the argument, and once as the sentence/formula appearing on the last line of the proof itself. The following symbolized valid argument is represented in the method of natural deduction:

1. $(R \lor -G)$
2. $[R \rightarrow (K \rightarrow U)]$
3. $[(R \bullet K) \rightarrow U]$ $\vdash$ $[(G \bullet K) \rightarrow U]$

142

One of the seemingly curious things about the method of natural deduction is that it does not allow one to show any argument to be invalid. Since one is trying to derive a conclusion from a set of premises using some rules, and since the rules do not allow for drawing an illegitimate inference by their use, it follows that, using the rules correctly, one could never make an illegitimate inference, which is what an invalid argument does. The practical moral here is that if one spends a great deal of time attempting to prove some argument to be valid using natural deduction, and if one is having trouble showing it to be valid, it may be wise to check its validity via some other method, e.g., truth tables or truth trees. The person who tries to show that some invalid argument is valid is engaged in a task that cannot be completed. Natural deduction is a method for showing arguments to be valid, it is not a method for showing arguments to be invalid. For all that, however, one must not count as wasted the time one worked on the invalid argument trying to show it to be valid. At very least, one will have been attempting to use the rules to derive the conclusion, and to that extent will have become just that much more acquainted with the rules themselves and their possible uses. To work well in natural deduction, it is requisite that one have a ready apprehension of and an ability to apply the rules to the formulas presented. To that end, practice is indispensable.

7.2. The Rules of Inference

The primary rules are typically called "rules of inference." We will follow this practice. The rules of inference are stated first in English, then in schematic form.

The rule *Modus Ponens* states that 1) when a conditional sentence exists on a separate line and 2) when the antecedent to the conditional exists alone on a separate line, then 3) the consequent may be written on a further line.

The rule *Modus Tollens* states that 1) when a conditional sentence exists on a separate line, and 2) when the negated consequent to that conditional exists alone on a separate line, then 3) the negated antecedent may be written on a further line.

The rule *Hypothetical Syllogism* states that 1) when two conditionals each exist on separate lines and 2) when identical statements comprise the antecedent of one of the conditionals and the consequent of the other conditional, then 3) a third conditional statement may be written on a further line comprised of the two components in the original conditionals which are not the original identical components, the antecedent of the third conditional being the antecedent in one of the original conditionals and the consequent of the third conditional being the consequent of the other original conditional.

The rule *Disjunctive Syllogism* states that 1) when a disjunction exists on a separate line, and 2) when the negation of the first disjunct exists on a line by itself, then 3) the second disjunct may be written on a further line.

The rule *Constructive Dilemma* states that 1) when a conjunction, having as its conjuncts conditional statements, exists on a separate line and 2) when a disjunction, the disjuncts of which are identical to the antecedents of the conditionals in the conjunction, exists on a separate line, then 3) another disjunction may be written on a further line, the disjuncts of which are identical to the consequents of the conditionals in the conjunction.

The rule *Addition* states that when any sentence (simple or compound, negated or not) exists on a line, then a further statement may be written, on a separate line, in the form of a disjunction in which the original sentence appears as the first disjunct and the "added" sentence the second disjunct.

The rule *Simplification* states that when a conjunction exists on a separate line, then the first conjunct may be written on a further line.

The rule *Conjunction* states that when any two sentences exist, each on separate lines, then a further sentence may be written, on a separate line, in the form of a conjunction in which the original two sentences appear as the conjuncts.

In schematic form, the primary rules of inference are as follows. The rules in schematic form use 'p,' 'q,' 'r' and 's' as variables.

Modus Ponens (MP):
$(p \rightarrow q)$
$p \vdash q$

Modus Tollens (MT):
$(p \rightarrow q)$
$-q \vdash -p$

Hypothetical Syllogism (HS):
$(p \rightarrow q)$
$(q \rightarrow r) \vdash (p \rightarrow r)$

Disjunctive Syllogism (DS):
$(p \lor q)$
$-p \vdash q$

Constructive Dilemma (CD):
$[(p \rightarrow q) \cdot (r \rightarrow s)]$
$(p \lor r) \vdash (q \lor s)$

Addition (Ad):
$p \vdash (p \lor q)$

Simplification (Si):
$(p \cdot q) \vdash p$

Conjunction (Con):
p
$q \vdash (p \cdot q)$

The first rule of natural deduction is usually said to be *modus ponens*. The following four arguments each have the form of MP. The arguments are stated in English first; then their symbolic form is represented.

Matthew will graduate with a degree in Music Theory from the University of California at Santa Barbara provided that he writes a composition that uses at least nine of the traditional orchestral instruments. Matthew will write a musical composition using twelve traditional orchestral instruments. So, Matthew will graduate from UC Santa Barbara in Music Theory.

$(W \rightarrow U)$
$W \vdash U$

Anna will be happy only if she studies French or Art History. Anna will be happy. Hence, she will study French or Art History.

$$[A \rightarrow (F \lor H)]$$
$$A \vdash (F \lor H)$$

Jay's traveling through the Milky Way only if he becomes an astronaut implies that he does not get space-sickness very easily. Jay will travel through the Milky Way only if he becomes an astronaut. It follows that Jay does not get space-sick easily.

$$[(M \rightarrow A) \rightarrow \text{-}S]$$
$$(M \rightarrow A) \vdash \text{-}S$$

That Moira will not both become a Supreme Court Justice and President of the American Civil Liberties Union (ACLU) is implied by the fact that being a Supreme Court Justice and being President of the ACLU each takes all of one's time and energy. Being a Supreme Court Justice and being President of the ACLU does take all of one's time and energy. We can conclude that Moira won't both become a Supreme Court Justice and President of the ACLU.

$$[(Ti \bullet En) \rightarrow \text{-}(Scj \bullet Pac)]$$
$$(Ti \bullet En) \vdash \text{-}(Scj \bullet Pac)$$

The above four examples are to show that *modus ponens* is really an *argument form* with many instances that don't look *exactly* like *modus ponens*. The same is true for each of the other rules of inference as well. The symbolized argument directly above can be seen to have the same *form* as *modus ponens*; treat '(Ti • En)' as 'p' and '-(Scj • Pac)' as 'q.' It will be helpful for you to attempt to construct a few complex arguments with the forms of each of the other rules of inference. This will not prove difficult if you begin with the *forms* of the inferences; for example, the rule for simplification: $(p \bullet q) \vdash p$.

7.3. Incorrect Applications

If one follows the rules as shown in schematic form above, one will, for the most part, have little trouble applying such rules as *Modus Ponens*, *Modus Tollens*, Hypothetical Syllogism, and so on. However, it is worthwhile, at this point, to note some fairly common mistakes.

One of the canons of working in natural deduction is that when attempting to derive a certain formula on a given line by the rules, the formulas one uses to derive the further formula must "match" or "fit" the form of the formulas *exactly* as found in the rules to be used. For example, the following set of formulas matches the set of formulas of the rule *modus tollens* precisely:

1. (F → G)	Except for the fact that 'F' and 'G' have
2. -G	replaced 'p' and 'q' in this case, the form
3. -F	matches *modus tollens*, and is, hence, a
	valid inference. 3 follows from 1 and 2.

Compare now the following incorrect application of the rule Simplification on the left with the actual rule, as schematized on the right.

1. [D → (B • N)]	(p • q)
2. B	p

As can readily be seen, these two sets of formulas do *not* match. It follows that the first set is not an instance of Simplification and cannot have that rule cited as part of the justification of the inference. It is, in fact, an invalid inference. While it is true that '(B • N)' is a conjunction, in order to "simplify" out of a conjunction, the conjunction must appear on a line by itself, which '(B • N)' does not, since it appears as the consequent to the conditional in line 1.

Each of the following six inferences is either invalid or incorrect, owing to a misuse of one of the rules. The last sentence in each set is the sentence that was inferred from the other(s).

1. [(R → J) ↔ S]	It may appear that 'J' has been derived from 'R' on
2. R	line 2 and '(R → J)' on line 1 from *modus ponens*.
3. J	This is an error, since '(R → J)' does not exist on a
	separate line, as *modus ponens* requires.

1. (H • I)	This is an incorrect use of the rule Addition,
2. H • (I v C)	as the inferred proposition is not a disjunction,
	as is required by Addition.

1. (A → K)	As noted above, Addition requires that the line
2. [(A → K) • P]	inferred be a disjunction. So, 'P' cannot simply
	be "added." A correct use Addition from line 1 here
	would be '[(A → K) v P].'

1. (L v W)	While line 3 does follow from 1 and 2, this is not an
2. -W	instance of DS, because DS says it is the *right-hand*
3. L	disjunct which is to be inferred.

1. (F • Q)	'Q' cannot be got from line 1 by Simplification, as
2. Q	it isn't the *left-hand* conjunct. This argument *is* valid,
	however. We will see how to derive line 2 from line
	1 here when the axioms of replacement are used.

7.4. Proofs

As with many other things, perhaps it is best if we simply launch into a sufficiently detailed argument, work the proof, and then explain the details. Recall that when one attempts to prove the validity of any argument in natural deduction, the conclusion is to appear in two places, viz., once on the same line as the last premise, and once as the last line of the proof itself. Consider the following valid argument and proof.

1. $[D \rightarrow (L \rightarrow X)]$
2. $(X \rightarrow E)$
3. $D \qquad \vdash (L \rightarrow E)$
4. $(L \rightarrow X) \qquad$ 1,3, MP
5. $(L \rightarrow E) \qquad$ 2,4, HS

Lines 1, 2, and 3 are what we can call the *argument lines*. Each consists of the line number, and one or more formulae/sentences (e.g., '$(X \rightarrow E)$' in line 2 is a formula/sentence). Line 3 contains two formulae; the first is a premise and the second is the conclusion of the argument, as will be noted by the symbolic conclusion indicator ($\vdash$). The existence of the conclusion in this position is nothing more than an indication of what sentence we are trying to derive, or prove. The conclusion must not be used in the proof itself, however, as that would amount to begging the question. Lines 4 and 5 we can call *proof lines*. They contain the formulae and justifications of the inferences drawn. For example, line 4 contains the formula derived from lines 1 and 3 by the rule *Modus Ponens*, and the justification itself (i.e., 1,3, MP). Consider another argument and proof:

1. $(O \vee R) \rightarrow -T$
2. $G \rightarrow (O \vee R)$
3. $T \vee -F$
4. $G \qquad \vdash \qquad -F$
5. $(G \rightarrow -T) \qquad$ 1,2, HS
6. $-T \qquad$ 4,5, MP
7. $-F \qquad$ 3,6, DS

Quite as important as the formulas on each line of the proof are the justifications themselves, in this case those appearing on lines 5, 6, and 7.

Each justification must include the number(s) of the previous line(s) used as well as the rule from which the present formula was derived. For example, line 5 can be read as saying that '$(G \rightarrow -T)$' was derived from lines 1 and 2 using the rule Hypothetical Syllogism. Line 6 is read as saying that '$-T$' was derived from lines 4 and 5 by the rule Modus Ponens. And line 7 may be read as saying that '$-F$' was derived from lines 3 and 6 by the rule Disjunctive Syllogism. It is important to remember that *a justification is required for each and every proof line*.

The method of constructing a proof in natural deduction involves at once a creative process and a mechanical process. It is mechanical, like the method of truth trees, insofar as there are a certain number of specific rules one uses. The *form* of each rule never changes, though the formulas to which the rules may be applied can be ever so much more complicated than the bare rules themselves. The creative aspect of the method of natural deduction has to do with one's ability to manipulate the symbols according to the rules in such a way as to derive the desired formula(s). It is the creative aspect that makes natural deduction a time consuming and sometimes difficult system with which to prove the validity of arguments in sentential logic.

Constructing a proof in natural deduction is, in a way, like playing a game of chess. You know that you have a number of options as to which chess pieces you can move, and from and to which squares. You think, "Well, if I move my knight here, then I'm in position to check my opponent's king. On the other hand, if I move my rook here, I can take my opponent's queen." These are both conditional statements. If one is really concentrating on a game, and if there are a great many options that look plausible/promising, one keeps a notepad to remind one of the various possibilities. In constructing a proof in natural deduction, it is quite helpful to keep a notepad as well. This is how it works. Consider the following argument:

Notepad

1. -P
2. (S v R) | (S → T)
3. (S → P) | (S → P)
4. R → (P → T) ⊢ (S → T) | (P → T)
                                  | R
                                  | -S
                                  | -P

Beginning from the top of the notepad, I see that what I am looking for is the conclusion, which is '(S → T).' I can derive the conclusion from the rule Hypothetical Syllogism *if* I could get the formulas '(S → P)' and '(P → T)' each on lines by themselves. The first of those formulas is on line 3 of the argument. So, it remains for me to find '(P → T).' This formula can be derived by Modus Ponens from line 4, *if* 'R' can be derived on a line by itself. 'R' can be derived by Disjunctive Syllogism from line 2, *if* '-S' is derived on a line by itself. To get '-S,' it suffices to get '-P' on a line by itself and to use that line with line 3 and the rule Modus Tollens. '-P' already appears on a line by itself, i.e., line 1. Below is the full proof, showing the validity of the argument above.

1. -P   Notice that each of the justifications
2. (S v R)   cite 2 lines from which the line that
3. (S → P)   is justified is derived. This is
4. R → (P → T) ⊢ (S → T)   critically important, for each of the

5.	-S	1,3, MT	rules used in this proof requires 2
6.	R	2,5, DS	formulas to derive the third. Some of
7.	(P → T)	4,6, MP	the rules require only 1 line.
8.	(S → T)	3,7, HS	

In the following example, the rule MP is used four times successively to derive the conclusion. See the notepad to the right of the proof.

1.	(F → G)		Notepad
2.	(D → E)		
3.	(E → J)		G
4.	(J → F)		F
5.	D ⊢ G		J
6.	E	2,5, MP	E
7.	J	3,6, MP	D
8.	F	4,7, MP	
9.	G	1,8, MP	

Note how the entries in the Notepad are in reverse order of the last five lines of the proof. I reasoned this way: *if* I could get 'F,' then from 'F' and line 1, I could get 'G'; *if* I got 'J,' then I could get 'F' using line 4; *if* I got 'E,' the I could get 'J' using line 3, and so forth.

To see how MT, DS, Si, and CD are used to show the validity of more complicated arguments, the following may help.

A.

1. [(X → Y) → (-L ↔ C)]
2. [-(-L ↔ C) • (L → X)] ⊢ -(X → Y)
3. -(-L ↔ C)   2, Si
4. -(X → Y)   1,3, MT

In argument (A) above, in order to see how line 3 was derived from line 2 by Simplification, recall the rule Simplification. Treat '-(-L ↔ C),' which is one of the conjuncts of the conjunction on line 2, as 'p,' and treat '(L → X)' as 'q.' The rule Simplification says that if we have '(p • q)' on a line by itself, then we can get 'p' on a further line. So, line 2, '[-(-L ↔ C) • (L → X)],' is simply treated as '(p • q)' here. To see how line 4 was obtained from lines 1 and 3 by Modus Tollens, recall Modus Tollens and treat '(X → Y)' in line 1 as 'p' and '(-L ↔ C)' in line 1 as 'q.'

This is a good time to reiterate that 'p' and 'q' are variables and can stand for any symbolic sentence whatever. So, for example, 'p' may be represent a simple sentence on one line and a triple conjunction on another.

B.

1. [(B • Q) → U] • (-I → -Q)

2. $(U \to A) \lor [(B \cdot Q) \lor \text{-}I]$
3. $\text{-}(U \to A)$ $\vdash$ $(U \lor \text{-}Q)$
4. $(B \cdot Q) \lor \text{-}I$ 2,3, DS
5. $(U \lor \text{-}Q)$ 1,4, CD

In argument (B), in order to see how line 4 was derived from lines 2 and 3 by Disjunctive Syllogism, recall the rule and treat the formula '$(U \to A)$' as 'p' and treat '$[(B \cdot Q) \lor \text{-}I]$' as 'q.' To see how line 5 was derived from lines 1 and 4 by Constructive Dilemma, recall the rule and treat '$(B \cdot Q)$' as 'p,' treat 'U' as 'q,' treat '-I' as 'r,' and treat '-Q' as 's.'

It is instructive to note early on that many arguments can be proven to be valid in more than one way, i.e., using either a different sequence or a different combination of the rules. Proof (C) below uses HS, Ad, CD, Si and Con, whereas proof (D) uses Si, MP, and Ad twice. Note also that since each proof shows the argument to be valid using correct applications of the rules of inference, both proofs are correct. Neither proof is "better" than the other except insofar as one counts it preferable to prove an argument valid in as few steps as possible. Proof (D) does, however, have a further point in its favor, i.e., it shows that premises 3 and 4 are, strictly, unnecessary for the validity of the argument. This can be seen by the fact that neither premise is noted in the set of justifications in (D). These two considerations would lead many logicians to say that proof (D) is "elegant" in comparison with proof (C).

C.		
1.	$(H \to R)$	
2.	$(H \cdot V)$	
3.	$(N \to O)$	
4.	$(V \to N)$ $\vdash$ $(R \lor O) \lor H$	
5.	$(V \to O)$	3,4, HS
6.	$(H \to R) \cdot (V \to O)$	1,5, Con
7.	H	2, Si
8.	$(H \lor V)$	7, Ad
9.	$(R \lor O)$	6,8, CD
10	$(R \lor O) \lor H$	9, Ad

D.		
1.	$(H \to R)$	
2.	$(H \cdot V)$	
3.	$(N \to O)$	
4.	$(V \to N)$ $\vdash$ $(R \lor O) \lor H$	
5.	H	2, Si
6.	R	1,5, MP
7.	$(R \lor O)$	6, Ad
8.	$(R \lor O) \lor H$	7, Ad

To get a clearer picture of how the rules were used in (C), it is useful to run through the lines and justifications of the proof. Line 5 was derived from lines 3 and 4 by Hypothetical Syllogism by (recall the rule) treating 'V' as 'p,' 'N' as 'q,' and 'O' as 'r.' Line 6 of the proof was derived from lines 1 and 5 by Conjunction by treating '$(H \to R)$' as 'p' and by treating '$(V \to O)$' as 'q.' Line 7 is a Simplification where 'H' is treated as 'p' and 'V' is treated as 'q.' Line 8 was derived from line 7 by Addition with the same treatment of 'H' and 'V' as was used to derive line 7. Line 9 was derived from lines 6 and 8 by Constructive Dilemma by treating 'H' as 'p,' 'R' as 'q,' 'V' as 'r,' and 'O' as 's.' Line 10 was derived from line 9 by Addition by treating '(R v O)' as 'p' and by treating 'H' as 'q.'

Proof (D) runs as follows. Line 5 was derived in precisely the same manner as line 7 was derived in proof (C). Line 6 is a straight Modus Ponens from lines 1 and 5, treating 'H' as 'p' and 'R' as 'q.' Line 7 is derived by the rule of Addition from line 6 by treating 'R' as 'p' and 'O' as 'q.' The rule of Addition is used, once again, to derive line 8 from line 7, this time by treating '(R v O)' as 'p' and 'H' as 'q,' which is precisely the manner in which line 10 was obtained in proof (C).

Further examples of proofs are below.

1. (P → E)
2. (P • L)   ⊢ E
3. P   2, Si
4. E   1,3 MP

1. [(R → S) • U]
2. (S → U)   ⊢ (R → U)
3. (R → S)   1, Si
4. (R → U)   2,3 HS

1. D v (T → -E)
2. -D • (-E → F)
3. --E   ⊢ (-T v E)
4. -D   2, Si
5. (T → -E)   1,4, DS
6. -T   3,5, MT
7. (-T v E)   6, Ad

1. (C → G)
2. (S • C)
3. (S → C)   ⊢ G
4. (S → G)   1,3, HS
5. S   2, Si
6. G   4,5, MP

1. [(J → K) • L]
2. [(J → K) → (J → W)]
3. J   ⊢ (K v W)
4. (J → K)   1, Si
5. (J → W)   2,4, MP
6. [(J → K) • (J → W)]   4,5, Com
7. (J v J)   3, Ad
8. (K v W)   6,7, CD

1. [(O → F) • P]
2. [(O → F) → (O → J)]
3. O   ⊢ (F v J)
4. (O v O)   3, Ad
5. (F v J)   2,4, CD

1. [-L → (M → A)]
2. (H v A) • (-L v -K)
3. [(H v A) → R]   ⊢   [R v (M → A)]
4. [(H v A) → R] • [-L → (M → A)]   1,3, Con
5. (H v A)   2, Si
6. [(H v A) v -L]   5, Ad
7. [R v (M → A)   4,6, CD

1. (-L → --Y)
2. (-C → --Y)
3. -C   ⊢   (--Y v --Y)
4. (-C v -L)   3, Ad

5. [(-C → --Y) • (-L → --Y)]   1,2, Con
6. (--Y v --Y)   4,5, CD

1. (S → L)   1. (F → E)
2. (D → S)   2. [(A v N • (D v I)]
3. (L → G)   3. (N → F)
4. (A → D) ⊢ (A → G)   4. (A → K)   ⊢ (K v E)
5. (A → S)   2,4, HS   5. (A v N)   2, Si
6. (S → G)   1,3, HS   6. (N → E)   1,3, HS
7. (A → G)   5,6, HS   7. (A → K) • (N → E)   4,6, Con
                                  8. (K v E)   5,7, CD

1. -C → (W → U)   1. [P → -(V → Y)
2. (--C → -R)   2. (V → H)
3. -(W → U) ⊢ (-R v R)   3. --(V → Y)
4. --C   1,3, MT   4. -P → (H → M) ⊢ (V → M)
5. -R   2,4, MP   5. -P   1,3, MT
6. (-R v R)   5, Ad   6. (H → M)   4,5, MP
                                  7. (V → M)   2,6, HS

Exercise: Ch. 7, Sect. 7.4.

A. Fill in the blanks with the correct formula, as called for by the justification
appearing to the right of the blank.

1. 1. (V → L)   2. 1. (F v N) → P
    2. (V • U) ⊢ L   2. F   ⊢ P
    3.   2, Si   3.   2, Ad
    4.   1,3 MP   4.   1,3 MP

3. 1. (E • R)   4. 1. (B → S)
    2. (T • D) ⊢ (T • E)   2. (C → S) → L
    3.   1, Si   3. (C → B) ⊢ L
    4.   2, Si   4.   1,3 HS
    5.   3,4 Con   5.   2,4 MP

5.* 1. (D ↔ E) → S   6. 1. (H → -B)
    2. (D ↔ E) ⊢ (S v Q)   2. (-B → P)
    3.   1,2 MP   3. (P → A)   ⊢ (H → A)
    4.   3, Ad   4.   1,2 HS
                                 5.   3,4 HS

7. 1. (F → J) → (-F v -D)   8. 1. (S v R) → (B → C)
    2. -(-F v -D)   2. (R → S)

3.	(F → J) v F	
4.	J • (F v -F) ⊢ (F • J)	
5.	1,2, MT	
6.	3,5, DS	
7.	4, Si	
8.	6,7, Con	

3.	(R • B) • S ⊢ (B → C)	
4.	3, Si	
5.	4, Si	
6.	2,5, MP	
7.	6, Ad	
8.	1,7, MP	

9.
1. A → (A → E)
2. I v (L → P)
3. (-I • L)
4. A ⊢ (E v P)
5. 1,4, MP
6. 3, Si
7. 2,6, DS
8. 4, Ad
9. 5,7, Con
10 8,9, CD

10.*1. [H v (G ↔ L)] → (I → R)
2. R v [H v (G ↔ L)]
3. (-R • -H)
4. (H → I) ⊢ -I
5. 3, Si
6. 2,5, DS
7. 1,6, MP
8. 5,7, MT

11.
1. (-T • D) → (-T → -P)
2. [(-T • D) • -P] • [(P → N) v T]
3. (-N → N) ⊢ (-P v N)
4. 2, Si
5. 4, Si
6. 1,5, MP
7. 5, Si
8. 3,6, Con
9. 7, Ad
10 8,9, CD

12.
1. (Q v -I) → E
2. (-H v G) → W
3. Q ⊢ (E v W) v -Q
4. 3, Ad
5. 4, Ad
6. 1,2, Con
7. 5,6, CD
8. 7, Ad

B. Supply the correct justifications in the following proofs.

1.
1. [(V → G) • (L → O]
2. V ⊢ (G v O)
3. (V v L)
4. (G v O)

2.
1. (-F • G)
2. (H → F) ⊢ (-H v K)
3. -F
4. -H
5. (-H v K)

3. 1. [(-V → V) • (L → O)]   4. 1. [(-B v P) v S]
    2. -V   ⊢ (O v G)   2. [(S → O) • -(B v S)]
    3. (-V v L)   3. -(-B v P)   ⊢ O
    4. (V v O)   4. S
    5. O   5. (S → O)
    6. (O v G)   6. O

5* 1. (A → W)   6. 1. (Q → D) • (J → U)
    2. (Y v A)   2. (Q • D) • U ⊢ (D v U)
    3. (-Y • -Z) ⊢ W   3. (Q • D)
    4. -Y   4. Q
    5. A   5. (Q v J)
    6. W   6. (D v U)

7. 1. (R → F) • (I → D)   8. 1. (X • -T)
    2. R   2. (-Q • X) → Z
    3. (F v -D) → (I → -L)   3. (-Q • S)   ⊢ [(X • Z) v X]
    4. F   ⊢   (F v -L)   4. X
    5. (R → F)   5. -Q
    6. (R v I)   6. (-Q • X)
    7. (F v -D)   7. Z
    8. (I → -L)   8. (X • Z)
    9. (R → F) • (I → -L)   9. [(X • Z) v X]
    10. (F v -L)

C. Show the following arguments to be valid using any of the first eight rules
in the method of natural deduction.

1. 1. ((I • J) • L) ⊢ (I • (I • J))   2. 1. (-Q v -J) → U
                                             2. -Q   ⊢ U

3. 1. (R • A) ⊢ (R v (A v -A))   4. 1. (F → H)
                                       2. (F → O)
                                       3. F   ⊢   (O • H)

5.* 1. (-L • J) • -{(S ↔ I) v [-I ↔ (S • S)]}
    2. [-L → --(S → I)]   ⊢   --(S → I)

6. 1. (S v D) → (T → I)   7. 1. (F → Y)
    2. (T → I) → (-E • L)   2. (Y • S)
    3. (C v I) → S   3. Y → -(K → J)
    4. (C • I)   ⊢   -E   4. (K → J) v (Z → S)
                                       5. (J → Z) ⊢   (J → S)

8. 1. [(A → B) → (C → D)]   9. 1. (A → C)
    2. [-(A → B) → -C]   2. (B → A)
    3. -(C → D) ⊢ (-C v -B)   3. (C → D)
                                         4. -D ⊢ [(-B • -A) • -C]

10.*1. R → (S • T)   11. 1. (M → I)
    2. S → (U • V)   2. -I
    3. (R • S) ⊢ (S • T) • (U • V)   3. (-M → W) ⊢ (W • -I)

12. 1. [(-H v -Q) → -L]
    2. {[(Q v H) v -D] → (-H • -L)}
    3. (Q • -D)   ⊢   [-L • (Q • -D)]

13. 1. (-X • U)   14. 1. T → (-A • W)
    2. (-X → S)   2. O → (N v F)
    3. (S → U)   3. T
    4. (U → --E)   4. (N v F) → A ⊢   -O
    5. (-E v J) ⊢ J

15.*1. [(R → C) → (B → K)]   16. 1. (C → L)
    2. [R v (R → C)]   2. C
    3. (R → C) ⊢ [C v (B → K)]   3. (L → N)
                                         4. (N → -S) ⊢   -S

17. 1. (O → Q) • {(G ↔ O) → [(P → -R) v K]}
    2. {[(P → R) → (K → G)] → [(O → K) v -P]}
    3. {(O → Q) → [(P → R) → (K → G)]} ⊢ [(O → K) v -P]

18. 1. (-N → -M)
    2. (-M → -N)
    3. (-M v -M)   ⊢   (-N v -M)

19. 1. (-M → N)
    2. (-M v N)
    3. (N → N) ⊢ (N v N) v -M

20.*1. {[D → (G ↔ S)] • (G ↔ R)}
    2. (D v S)
    3. -(G ↔ S) ⊢   (S v R)

7.5. The Principle of Replacement

Many valid truth-functional arguments cannot be shown to be valid merely by using the rules of inference. Example:

$$-(N \lor W) \lor -S$$
$$-(S \rightarrow E) \vdash -N$$

To prove the validity of these sorts of arguments via natural deduction, an additional rule is necessary. The rule is called *The Principle of Replacement*, and is stated as follows: *Any sentence S, appearing on a line of a proof, may be replaced by any sentence, S', that is logically equivalent to S.* For example, if '(F → G)' were to appear on a line, then '(-F ∨ G)' could replace '(F → G)' on a further line of the proof, because the two sentences, '(-F ∨ G)' and '(F → G),' are logically equivalent. In fact, this particular replacement instance is an example of the replacement rule/axiom called Material Implication.

Each of the *Axioms of Replacement* (i.e. replacement instances, such as Distribution) is a logical equivalence. The symbol '↔' will function as denoting logical equivalence. Each of the ten axioms is schematized on the following page.

The Axioms of Replacement

De Morgan's Theorems (DM)
$$[-(p \lor q) \leftrightarrow (-p \bullet -q)]$$
$$[-(p \bullet q) \leftrightarrow (-p \lor -q)]$$

Commutation (Com)
$$[(p \lor q) \leftrightarrow (q \lor p)]$$
$$[(p \bullet q) \leftrightarrow (q \bullet p)]$$

Distribution (Di)
$$[p \bullet (q \lor r)] \leftrightarrow [(p \bullet q) \lor (p \bullet r)]$$
$$[p \lor (q \bullet r)] \leftrightarrow [(p \lor q) \bullet (p \lor r)]$$

Association (As)
$$[p \bullet (q \bullet r)] \leftrightarrow [(p \bullet q) \bullet r]$$
$$[p \lor (q \lor r)] \leftrightarrow [(p \lor q) \lor r]$$

Material Implication (MI)
$$(p \rightarrow q) \leftrightarrow (-p \lor q)$$

Contraposition (Cp)
$$(p \rightarrow q) \leftrightarrow (-q \rightarrow -p)$$

Material Equivalence (ME)
$$(p \leftrightarrow q) \leftrightarrow [(p \rightarrow q) \bullet (q \rightarrow p)]$$
$$(p \leftrightarrow q) \leftrightarrow [(p \bullet q) \lor (-p \bullet -q)]$$

Exportation (Exp)
$$[(p \bullet q) \rightarrow r] \leftrightarrow [(p \rightarrow (q \rightarrow r)]$$

Double Negation (DN)
p ⇔ --p

Replication (Re)
[(p • p) ⇔ p]
[(p v p) ⇔ p]

The symbol '⇔' will function as denoting logical equivalence, and will be called the "hollow double arrow." This symbol is metalogical in that it is used to refer to sentences themselves. The logical equivalence referred to here is limited to denoting sentences that are true under the same interpretations *and* false under the same interpretations. The system of natural deduction adopted here makes use of the ten specific axioms of replacement only, along with the rules of inference.

It is possible to view the axioms of replacement outlined above as replacement *rules*, though in fact there is but one replacement rule as such. Viewing the *axioms* as *rules*, however, can be helpful from an activity-directed perspective. The activity referred to here is that of working proofs. In working proofs, then, when making use of the axioms, since the formula on one side of the hollow double arrow is logically equivalent to the formula on the other side of the hollow double arrow, one formula may replace the other formula whenever it occurs in a proof. For example, consider the proof below.

1.	(M v -T)		Here, a combination of the rules of
2.	(T • R)	⊢ M	inference *and* axioms has been used.
3.	T	2, Si	As you will notice, some proofs may be
4.	(-T v M)	1, Com	worked using only the rules of inference
5.	(T → M)	4, MI	and some using only axioms.
6.	M	3,5, MP	

Concentrating on lines 4 and 5 in the above argument, as the justifications for those lines each involve an axiom, we see that line 1 has been replaced by line 4 and line 4 by line 5. Recalling Commutation, to see how line 4 was obtained, treat 'M' in line 1 as 'p' and '-T' in 1 as 'q.' Similarly, recall Material Implication and see that line 5 was obtained from line 4 by treating '-T' in 4 as 'p' and 'M' in 4 as 'q.'

The following proof shows one important feature of axioms not shared by rules of inference. The axioms can be applied to parts of lines, whereas the rules of inference cannot. [Recall that it is invalid to go from '[G → (M • E)]' to 'M' by Simplification, because '(M • E)' must appear on a line by itself to simplify to 'M.' The crucial reasoning here is that '[G → (M • E)]' does not assert that the conjunction of 'M' and 'E' is true, but only that *if* 'G' is true, then '(M • E)' is true, whereas '(M • E)' on a separate line *would* assert that the conjunction is true and, hence, that 'M' is true. Therefore, where '(M • E)' is asserted as true, i.e., appears on a line by itself, 'M' follows by Simplification.]

1.	(-F → H) → C ⊢ (F → C)	
2.	(-H → --F) → C	1, Cp
3.	(-H → F) → C	2. DN
4.	-(-H → F) v C	3, MI
5.	-(--H v F) v C	4, MI
6.	(---H • -F) v C	5, DM
7.	(-H • -F) v C	6, DN
8.	C v (-H • -F)	7, Com
9.	(C v -H) • (C v -F)	8, Di
10	(C v -F) • (C v -H)	9, Com
11	(C v -F)	10, Si
12	(-F v C)	11, Com
13	(F → C)	12, MI

It is interesting to note here that each line of the proof was derived from the line directly above it. Of course, this will not always be the case, as in the preceding example. Also, the only rule of inference used here is Simplification, on line 11.

The explication of the proof is as follows: Line 2 was obtained from line 1 and Contraposition by treating '-F' as 'p' and 'H' as 'q.' Accordingly, 'H' and '-F' have switched places and each has been negated. Note that 'C,' the consequent to the major conditional in line 1, is left untouched. This is as much as to say that the major conditional is not being treated at all in terms of applying Contraposition to line 1. Rather, the antecedent to the major conditional in line 1, which is '(-F → H),' is treated *as if* it appears on a separate line. This is legitimate insofar as we are replacing an occurrence of one formula with an occurrence of another, the result being a logically equivalent formula. When applying the rules of inference, however, one does not replace one formula with another; rather one draws an inference. Analogically, one might say inferences are one-way streets, whereas replacements are two-way streets.

Line 3 replaces '--F' in line 2 with 'F,' via Double Negation, leaving all other connectives and formulas in place. This is a perfect example how the axioms of replacement may be applied to parts of lines.

In line 4 we see that the second arrow has been changed into a wedge and that a negation sign has been inserted before the first disjunct. This has been done by treating '(-H → F)' as 'p' and 'C' as 'q,' in accord with Material Implication.

Line 5 has also been obtained by MI, but this time '-H' in 4 is treated as 'p' and 'F' in 4 as 'q.'

In line 6, 'C' again remains untouched, as in lines 2, 3, and 5. ['C' was not untouched in line 4, since when MI was applied to line 3, 'C' went from being the consequent to the conditional in line 3 to being a disjunct in 4.] Line 6 is the result of replacing '(---H • -F)' in line 5 with '-(--H v F).' This is done (recall DeMorgan's) by treating '--H' as 'p' and 'F' as 'q.' This version of De Morgan's changes a negated disjunction into a conjunction, negating each conjunct.

Line 7 is a straight Double Negation of '---H.' Again, not only is 'C' not affected by the replacement, neither are the other connectives, nor is '-F.'

Line 8 uses the axiom Commutation, treating '(-H • -F)' in line 7 as 'p'' and 'C' as 'q.'

Line 9 is an instance of Distribution, applied to line 8. To see this, teat 'C' in 8 as 'p,' '-H' as 'q,' and '-F' as 'r.' In effect, this version of Distribution changes a disjunction into a conjunction wherein each conjunct is itself a disjunction.

Line 10 uses Commutation on line 9, where '(C v -H)' is treated as 'p' and '(C v -F)' as 'q.'

Line 11 is a straight Simplification of '(C v -F)' from line 10.

Line 12 commutes 'C' and '-F' from line 10, treating the former as 'p' and the latter as 'q.'

Line 13 is the result of applying Material Implication to line 11, treating '-F' in 11 as 'p' and 'C' as 'q.'

Note that in line 4 Material Implication was applied to a conditional (arrow), changing it to a disjunction (wedge), with the first disjunct being negated. Line 13 is different in that it moves from a wedge in 12 (with the first disjunct negated) to an arrow in 13 (with the antecedent not being negated). Both are quite legitimate uses of MI. To make this point, though we can think of the axioms of replacement as replacement *rules*, some logicians schematize the axioms as biconditionals. Doing so makes it possible to talk about them as axioms of equivalence. To make this clearer, take, for instance, the axiom Exportation, $\{[(p \cdot q) \to r] \leftrightarrow [p \to (q \to r)]\}$. If we replace the double hollow arrow here with the double arrow, we would see that the truth table for the sentence would have 't' under the double arrow in all interpretations. This could only happen when the primary connectives on both sides of the double arrow have exactly the same truth values under the exact same interpretations. Here is that table:

$$\{[(p \cdot q) \to r] \leftrightarrow [p \to (q \to r)]\}$$

```
t t t t  t  t  t t  t tt
t t t f  f  t  t f  t ff
t f f t  t  t  t t  f tt
t f f t  f  t  t t  f tf
f f t t  t  t  f t  t tt
f f t t  f  t  f t  t ff
f f f t  t  t  f t  f tt
f f f t  f  t  f t  f tf
```

The fact that the truth values are identical under the primary connectives indicates that these sentences are logically equivalent, which means that the sentence forms have the same truth values in all possible worlds, or under every interpretation.

There is also a relation of implication from each of the statement forms to the other, as can be expressed by a biconditional. Consider the following formula:

$$\{[(p \cdot q) \to r] \to [p \to (q \to r)]\} \cdot \{[p \to (q \to r)] \to [(p \cdot q) \to r]\}$$

This is one version of Material Equivalence applied to Exportation. The same procedure can be applied to each of the axioms of replacement. Another way to show the equivalence of Exportation is to show that each side of the hollow double arrow follows from the other, derived by some of the other axioms of replacement. Below are two arguments, the first of which has one side of Exportation as the premise and the other side as the conclusion, the second of which has those formulas reversed. The symmetry of the justifications is something that would occur in all proofs of this nature.

1.	$(p \cdot q) \rightarrow r \vdash p \rightarrow (q \rightarrow r)$			1.	$p \rightarrow (q \rightarrow r) \vdash (p \cdot q) \rightarrow r$	
2.	$-(p \cdot q) \vee r$	1, MI		2.	$-p \vee (q \rightarrow r)$	1, MI
3.	$(-p \vee -q) \vee r$	2, DM		3.	$-p \vee (-q \vee r)$	2, MI
4.	$-p \vee (-q \vee r)$	3, As		4.	$(-p \vee -q) \vee r$	3, As
5.	$p \rightarrow (-q \vee r)$	4, MI		5.	$-(p \cdot q) \vee r$	4, DM
6.	$p \rightarrow (q \rightarrow r)$	5, MI		6.	$(p \cdot q) \rightarrow r$	5, MI

As you become more proficient at working proofs, you will naturally begin to see two or three or more moves ahead. There will be a tendency to use two rules/axioms at once. This is perfectly all right where it is clear what one is doing. In the following proof, Commutation and Simplification are used together to get line 7. What this amounts to is simply bypassing making the Commutation explicit on a line by itself.

1.	$(E \leftrightarrow G)$	
2.	$(-G \vee -E)$ $\vdash$ $-G$	
3.	$[(E \cdot G) \vee (-E \cdot -G)]$	1, ME
4.	$-(G \cdot E)$	2, DM
5.	$-(E \cdot G)$	4, Com
6.	$(-E \cdot -G)$	3,5 DS
7.	$-G$	6, Com, Si

In the proofs that follow, only Double Negation, Commutation, Addition, and Simplification will be used in tandem. The reason for this is that these four rules are perhaps the simplest of them all and one can save time by using them in conjunction. So, for example, one could use Double Negation twice, or Addition with Double Negation, or Commutation with Double Negation, and so on. Also, of course, it is not necessary for one to use them together. I do recommend these four rules *only* be used in tandem, but never three at once, as this becomes increasingly complicated. It is important, when using two rules at a time, to list each rule used. Below, for example, in line 4, you will see that the justification line reads, '3, DN, DN.' This indicates that Double Negation was used twice to derive line 4.

It will be useful to show examples of how each of the various replacement instances is used in proofs. Uncommon uses will be noted and explained.

1.	-(-O v -I) v (O v F)	
2.	-F ⊢ O	
3.	(--O • --I) v (O v F)	1, DM
4.	(O • I) v (O v F)	3, DN, DN
5.	[(O • I) v O] v F	4, As
6.	[O v (O • I)] v F	5, Com
7.	[(O v O) • (O v I)] v F	6, Di
8.	[O • (O v I)] v F	7, Re
9.	F v [O • (O v I)]	8, Com
10.	O • (O v I)	2,9, DS
11.	O	10, Si

It may be suspected that the use of Association in line 5 is not a precise fit with the schematized axiom. However, one can see that it is a legitimate use of that axiom by treating (line 4) '(O • I)' as 'p,' 'O' as 'q,' and 'F' as 'r.'

Another apparently uncommon use of a principle occurs in line 8 with the use of Replication from line 7. To obtain line 8, the first conjunct in the conjunction of line 7 was treated as '(p v p)' in the rule of Replication. It was replaced, in line 8, with 'O,' which is there treated as 'p.' This is one more prime example of how a principle can be applied to a *part* of a line.

Consider the more complicated argument below.

1.	-(B v -C) v (-B v C)	
2.	-B → -(D v -B) ⊢ (C ↔ B)	
3.	--B v -(D v -B)	2, MI
4.	B v -(D v -B)	3, DN
5.	B v (-D • --B)	4, DM
6.	B v (-D • B)	5, DN
7.	B v (B • -D)	6, Com
8.	(B v B) • (B v -D)	7, Di
9.	(B v B)	8, Si
10.	B	9, Re
11.	(B v -C)	10, Ad
12.	(-C v B)	11, Com
13.	(C → B)	12, MI
14.	(B v -C) → (-B v C)	1, MI
15.	(-C v B) → (-B v C)	14, Com
16.	(C → B) → (-B v C)	15, MI
17.	(-B v C)	13,16, MP
18.	(B → C)	17, MI
19.	(C → B) • (B → C)	13,18, Con
20.	(C ↔ B)	19, ME

It occurs that this proof is, though long, not one in which any principle is used in a way that should give trouble. The crucial insights here are 1) that the premises could be altered in such a way as to yield arrows, suggesting that the first version of ME may be used to obtain the conclusion, and 2) that 'B' could be obtained on a line by itself, and then '-C' Added to it to yield, ultimately, the first conjunct in line 19.

The further proofs below have some examples of various uses of the rules of inference and axioms of replacement.

1.	$(P \rightarrow -Q)$			1.	$(L \lor T)$ ⊢ $-(-T \cdot -L) \lor L$	
2.	$-(Q \cdot P) \rightarrow -M$ ⊢ $-M$			2.	$(T \lor L)$	1, Com
3.	$(--Q \rightarrow -P)$	1, Cp		3.	$(--T \lor L)$	2, DN
4.	$(---Q \lor -P)$	3, MI		4.	$(--T \lor --L)$	3, DN
5.	$(-Q \lor -P)$	4, DN		5.	$-(-T \cdot -L)$	4, DM
6.	$-(Q \cdot P)$	5, DM		6.	$-(-T \cdot -L) \lor L$	5, Ad
7.	$-M$	2,6 MP				

1.	$-S \rightarrow (G \rightarrow W)$			1.	$(H \lor -G)$	
2.	$-(G \rightarrow -H)$ ⊢ $(S \lor W)$			2.	$(G \lor -D)$	
3.	$(-S \cdot G) \rightarrow W$	1, Exp		3.	$-(G \rightarrow H)$ ⊢ W	
4.	$-(-S \cdot G) \lor W$	3, MI		4.	$(-G \lor H)$	1, Com
5.	$(--S \lor -G) \lor W$	4, DM		5.	$(-D \lor G)$	2, Com
6.	$(S \lor -G) \lor W$	5, DN		6.	$(G \rightarrow H)$	4, MI
7.	$(-G \lor S) \lor W$	6, Com		7.	$(D \rightarrow G)$	5, MI
8.	$-G \lor (S \lor W)$	7, As		8.	$(D \rightarrow H)$	6,7, HS
9.	$-(-G \lor -H)$	2, MI		9.	$-(-G \lor H)$	3, MI
10.	$(--G \cdot --H)$	9, DM		10.	$(--G \cdot -H)$	9, DM
11.	$--G$	10, Si		11.	G	10, Si, DN
12.	$(S \lor W)$	8,11, DS		12.	$-H$	10, Com, Si
				13.	$-G$	6,12, MT
				14.	$(G \lor W)$	11, Ad
				15.	W	13,14, DS

Something interesting is to be noted about the argument on the right just above, namely, lines 11 and 13 are contradictory. Line 13 directly denies what line 11 affirms. The last two lines of the proof show both that everything follows from a contradiction and also how this is accomplished in natural deduction. In the above proof, 'W' is derived; however, it could just as well have been 'R' or 'Q' or even '-(A → B).' We will encounter more instances of premises generating contradictions as we go along, especially in the section on *Reductio ad Absurdum*. If you ever encounter a contradiction in a proof, know that you can get the conclusion in just two moves, using Addition and Disjunctive Syllogism.

1.	$X \rightarrow (U \cdot W)$	
2.	$(-U \rightarrow Z) \rightarrow Y$ ⊢ $(Y \lor -X)$	
3.	$-X \lor (U \cdot W)$	1, MI
4.	$(-X \lor U) \cdot (-X \lor W)$	3, Di

5.	(-X v U)	4, Si
6.	(X → U)	5, MI
7.	-(-U → Z) v Y	2, MI
8.	-(--U v Z) v Y	7, MI
9.	-(U v Z) v Y	8, DN
10.	(-U • -Z) v Y	9, DM
11.	Y v (-U • -Z)	10, Com
12.	(Y v -U) • (Y v -Z)	11, Di
13.	(Y v -U)	12, Si
14.	(-U v Y)	13, Com
15.	(U → Y)	14, MI
16.	(X → Y)	6,15, HS
17.	(-Y → -X)	16, Cp
18.	(--Y v -X)	17, MI
19.	(Y v -X)	18, DN

1.	(N → -M)	
2.	(M ↔ N) ⊢ -(M v N)	
3.	(M • N) v (-M • -N)	2, ME
4.	(--M → -N)	1, Cp
5.	(M → -N)	4, DN
6.	(-M v -N)	5, MI
7.	-(M • N)	6, DM
8.	(-M • -N)	3,7, DS
9.	-(M v N)	8, DM

1.	-(-(E v Q) v -T) ⊢ E → (Q → T)	
2.	--(E v Q) • --T	1, DM
3.	--T • --(E v Q)	2, Com
4.	T • --(E v Q)	3, DN
5.	T	4, Si
6.	T v -(E • Q)	5, Ad
7.	-(E • Q) v T	6, Com
8.	(E • Q) → T	7, MI
9.	E → (Q → T)	8, Exp

1.	(P → Q) • (E → J)	
2.	(-Q v -J) ⊢ -(P • E)	
3.	(-Q → -P) • (E → J)	1, Cp
4.	(-Q → -P) • (-J → -E)	3, Cp
5.	(-P v -E)	2,4 CD
6.	-(P • E)	5, DM

Exercise: Ch. 7, Sect. 7.5.

A. Show the following arguments to be valid using any combination of the rules of inference and the axioms of replacement.

1. 1. (R • G) → Q
   2. -(S v -G)
   3. (Q → S) ⊢ -R

2. 1. L v -(B • N)
   2. -(B → V) → -L
   3. (-S • -Z)
   4. -(B • N) → S ⊢ V

3. 1. (P • Y)
      ⊢ P • (Y v T)

4. 1. [A v (-C v J)] → (J → -C)
   2. (C → A) v J ⊢ (-C v -J)

5.* 1. -(N → -R)
    2. (R → W) ⊢ (W v N)

6. 1. -I → (-O v U)
   2. -(I v U)
   3. (-U v -O) ⊢ -O

7. 1. (X → Z) • (Z → V)
   2. (Z → D) • (V → T)
   3. (X v Z)
      ⊢ (D v V) v -(V • D)

8. 1. (E → A) → [T v (G • K)]
   2. (T → A)
   3. (G → -E)
   4. -(-T • -G) ⊢ -(-T • -K)

9. 1. [C → (F → G)]
   2. (C • -G)
   3. [(-R v Y) v A]
   4. [-F → (R • -Y)] ⊢ A

10.*1. -[N v (M v O)] → E
    2. -(S v E) ⊢ -N → (-O → M)

11. 1. (F → -J) • (N → P)
    2. (P → T)
    3. (F v N) ⊢ (N v -J) v T

12. 1. (J → P) • [J → (J • O)]
    2. -(-J • -J) ⊢ (P v O)

13. 1. (I → J)
    2. (-F • S) v (D • -F)
    3. -(-Y v J) ⊢ (F ↔ I)

14. 1. (N → M) → -P
    2. (L v O) → P
    3. -N ⊢   -O

15.*1. (Aa ↔ Nn) ⊢ (Aa → Aa) • (Nn → Nn)

16. 1. (T → E)
    2. (-T → -I) • (P → G)
    3. -I → -(-I v G) ⊢   I

17. 1. -(-W → -X) → Y
    2. (-X → Z)
    3. (W v Y) → (-Z → A)
    4. -A ⊢   Z

18. 1. -[-R v (F → J)] → -R
    2. -R → (J • W)

19. 1. (A • C) v [A • (C ↔ D)]
    2. -D → (A → E)

3. -[L v (J → R)] → --R   3. -(B → C)   ⊦ (E v -A)
4. -J ⊦ {-F • [L v (J → R)]}

20.*1. (-R • T) v (Q v X)   21. 1. (D • Q) → E
   2. -(-R v L) ⊦ [T v (X v Q)]   2. (-R • D) ⊦ Q → (E v -D)

22. 1. -[-(S v -O) v B]   23. 1. (P v Q) v (Q • R)
   2. (B v O)   2. -(-Q → P) ⊦ (Q v P) v Q
   3. (O v O) → S ⊦ S

24. 1. -(-K → L)   25.*1. (E → S)
   2. (L • K) v (K • M)   2. -A ⊦ [E → (A → S)]
      ⊦ (K v L) v M

26. 1. (N v H) → (-H • -I)   27. 1. (B v Y) → O
   2. N v (H • J) ⊦ N v -(H v I)   2. Q → (Y • B) ⊦ (-Q v O)

28. 1. (D → -R) • (P → E)   29. 1. (F → H)
   2. (-E v O)   2. -(-H • F) → (J • -L)
   3. (-P → D)   3. (-L v J) → (T v I)
      ⊦ R → (O • O)   4. (T v C) ⊦ [T v (C • I)]

30.*1. -(Z → A) → -Y
   2. Y → (-B v A)
   3. -A ⊦ Y → -(B v Z)

7.6. The Rule of Conditional Proof

There is a convenient method sometimes used in natural deduction to obtain conditional statements in proofs. It is employed, in the main, when the conclusion of the argument is a conditional, but it may be used to obtain a conditional statement at any point in a proof, such as when a conditional is necessary to obtain the conclusion, which may or may not itself be a conditional.

One part of this method is what is known as *The Rule of Conditional Proof* (RCP). The rule itself can be stated in the following way: *When an assumption is made on a line in a proof, that assumption shall be designated as the antecedent to the conditional resulting from closing the scope of the assumption itself, the consequent to that conditional being the sentence that appears on the last line within the scope of the assumption.*

The method proceeds as follows: 1) assume the antecedent to the desired conditional, 2) derive the consequent, using some finite sequence of the rules of inference and/or the axioms of replacement, 3) close the scope of the assumption, and 4) write the conditional on the line directly succeeding the closure of the assumption. RCP is explicated schematically below:

Premise   The number of premises is of course
Premise   variable, even including the number
   φ   (A) Assumption   zero, as will be made clear in the
   •   section on proving logical truths,
   •   below. The scope of the assumption
   •   begins with 'φ' and ends with 'ψ.'
   ψ
(φ → ψ)

The scope of the assumption is designated visually by the indented sentences. The assumption will be the first indented sentence. All sentences thereafter will be indented until the desired conditional sentence is inferred. That sentence is *not* indented. All sentences inside the scope of an assumption are indented and no sentence outside the scope of an assumption is indented.

The following two proofs are examples of how RCP works. '(A)' is used in the justification line to indicate that the formula written is an assumption.

1.	(G → S)	
2.	G → (S → F) ⊢ (G → F)	
3. G	(A)	Assume the antecedent to the
4. S	1,3, MP	desired conditional; derive the
5. (S → F)	2,3, MP	consequent of the conditional;
6. F	4,5, MP	write the conditional; justify
7.	(G → F)	3-6, RCP	with '*RCP*.'

1.	(E v H) → -E ⊢ (E → H)	
2. E	(A)	
3. (E v H)	2, Ad	
4. -E	1,3, MP	
5.	(E → -E)	2-4, RCP	Here we have the desired
6.	(-E v -E)	5, MI	conditional well before the end
7.	-E	6, Re	of the proof. Lines 2, 3, and 4
8.	(-E v H)	7, Ad	constitute the scope of the
9.	(E → H)	8, MI	assumption in this proof.

In the first argument, the antecedent to the conclusion, 'G,' is assumed and, through a series of applications of the rule of inference *modus ponens*, 'F' is derived on line 6, after which the scope of the assumption is closed. Line 7 is the conclusion, and says merely that *if* 'G' is true, then 'F' is true.

In the second argument, unlike the first, the conclusion does not appear on the line directly after the closure of the assumption. Rather, to derive the conclusion itself requires deriving a preliminary conditional. As mentioned, RCP may be used *whenever* a conditional is needed.

It is vital that every assumption be, at some juncture, closed, and that the next line of the proof be a conditional statement, consisting in the assumed statement as the antecedent and the last statement within the scope of the assumption as the consequent. So, if '(p → q)' is the conditional we are looking to prove, then we assume 'p,' derive 'q' using the rules and axioms, then close the assumption with '(p → q).'

It is also essential to note that once an assumption is closed, one cannot use any formula in the assumption itself to obtain a further formula. The following proof contains two assumptions, and will make this point clear.

1.	(T v P) → (-T v K)		
2.	K → (-T → -K) ⊢ (T ↔ K)		
	3. T	(A)	Note that '(A)' and
	4. (T v P)	3, Ad	'RCP' can be used again
	5. (-T v K)	1,4, MP	and again in a proof, as
	6. --T	3, DN	can the axioms of
	7. K	5,6, DS	replacement and the
8.	(T → K)	3-7, RCP	rules of inference.
	9. K	(A)	
	10. (-T → -K)	2,9, MP	
	11. (K → T)	10, Cp	
	12. T	9,11, MP	
13.	(K → T)	9-12, RCP	
14.	(T → K) • (K → T)	8,13, Con	
15	(T ↔ K)	14, ME	

Notice that although 'K' appears on line 7 and is needed again to obtain the consequent ('(-T → -K)') in line 2 on a further line (10), which is outside the first closed assumption, since line 7 is within the scope of a closed assumption, 'K' must be obtained by opening a further assumption. Also note that line 8, which is outside the scope of any assumption, was used in line 14. Perfectly legitimate.

The following proof shows how two assumptions can be open at the same time. Lines 3 and 4 are assumptions.

1.	-C v (-J v L)		
2.	-(A → -J) ⊢ C → (U → L)		
	3. C	(A)	
	4. U	(A)	
	5. -(-A v -J)	2, MI	
	6. (--A • --J)	5, DM	
	7. C → (-J v L)	1, MI	
	8. (-J v L)	3,7, MP	
	9. (--J • --A)	6, Com	
	10. --J	9, Si	
	11. L	8,10, DS	
	12. (U → L)	4-11, RCP	
13.	C → (U → L)	3-12, RCP	

We can justify the use of RCP in general by noting the following considerations. By treating the antecedent to the conditional in the conclusion as a further premise in the argument (and that is what is being done, in effect, when one assumes the antecedent), one claims that the revised set of premises is sufficient to derive the consequent to the conditional in the conclusion. However, since the assumption is not actually a member of the original set of premises, it would be illegitimate merely to write it on a further line without using some specified rule or other. Hence, it is put forth as a hypothetical, a *what if?*, if you will, which conditions all the inferences drawn after its introduction. Now, since it is treated strictly as a hypothetical, when the scope of the assumption is terminated, the original assumption becomes that which conditions the immediate further statement. It is as though one said, "Given the truth of these premises, let's pretend that the following statement is also true." Whatever follows *from* the pretense, then, is conditioned *by* the pretense. Hence the conditional statement required when the assumption is closed.

The Rule of Conditional Proof can also be a helpful method for deriving a conclusion which is not itself a conditional but is equivalent to a conditional (i.e., where one derives a sentence from which the conclusion can be derived through a finite number of applications of the rules and axioms). In these sorts of cases it is not always obvious that RCP will be helpful. Consider the following proof:

1. $(B \rightarrow E)$
2. $(Y \leftrightarrow B) \vdash \quad (-Y \vee E)$
   3.   Y   (A)
   4. $(Y \rightarrow B) \cdot (B \rightarrow Y)$ 2, ME
   5. $(Y \rightarrow B)$ 4, Si
   6.   B   3,5, MP
   7.   E   1,6, MP
8. $(Y \rightarrow E)$ 3-7, RCP
9. $(-Y \vee E)$ 8, MI

The conclusion of the above argument can be changed into a conditional via Material Implication. So, also, the conditional could be changed into a disjunction. Recognizing this about a conclusion could suggest that RCP may be of assistance. This might in turn suggest that one examine the conclusion of the argument for which one is constructing a proof, to see whether RCP may be of some help. Keep in mind, then, that RCP can be used *whenever* you are trying to find a conditional, even if the conclusion is not itself a conditional. Examine once again the argument above with '$(T \leftrightarrow K)$' as the conclusion. In that instance, two conditionals were needed (lines 8 and 13) and therefore two assumptions were made, one for each conditional needed. There is, theoretically, no limit to the number of assumptions that can be made in any given proof.

Below are other examples of proofs using RCP.

1. (-Q → S)
2. -K v -(P v S) ⊢ (K → Q)
   3. K   (A)
   4. --K   3, DN
   5. -(P v S)   2,4, DS
   6. (-P • -S)   5, DM
   7. (-S • -P)   6, Com
   8. -S   7, Si
   9. --Q   1,8, MT
   10. Q   9, DN
11. (K → Q)   3-10, RCP

1. (-R v W)
2. [(-X v -R) → B]
3. (-P → -X) ⊢ [-B → (W v P)]
   4. -B   (A)
   5. -(-X v -R)   2,4, MT
   6. (--X • --R)   5, DM
   7. (X → P)   3, Cp
   8. (R → W)   1, MI
   9. [(X → P) • (R → W)]   7,8, Con
   10. --X   6, Si
   11. X   10, DN
   12. (X v R)   11, Ad
   13. (P v W)   9,12, CD
   14. (W v P)   13, Com
15. [-B → (W v P)]   4-14, RCP

1. [-(M v D) v (-M • I)] ⊢ D → (F → I)
   2. D   (A)
   3. [(-M • -D) v (-M • I)]   1, DM
   4. [-M • (-D v I)]   3, Di
   5. (-D v I)   4, Com, Si
   6. --D   2, DN
   7. I   5,6, DS
   8. (I v -F)   7, Ad
   9. (-F v I)   8, Com
   10. (F → I)   9, MI
11. D → (F → I)   2-10, RCP

1. {-(-T • R) → [G v (Z • K)]}
2. -(-G → E) ⊢ [(R → T) → (K → Z)]
   3. (R → T)   (A)
     4. K   (A)
     5. (-R v T)   3, MI

6.	--(-R v T)	5, DN
7.	-(--R • -T)	6, DM
8.	-(R • -T)	7, DN
9.	-(-T • R)	8, Com
10.	[G v (Z • K)]	1,9, MP
11.	[(G v Z) • (G v K)]	10, Di
12.	-(--G v E)	2, MI
13.	-(G v E)	12, DN
14.	(-G • -E)	13, DM
15.	-G	14, Si
16.	(G v Z)	11, Si
17.	Z	15,16, DS
18.	(K → Z)	4-17, RCP
19.	[(R → T) → (K → Z)]	3-18, RCP

1.	[M → (-N v O)]	
2.	[-(-O v P) → -N] ⊢ [-M v (N → P)]	
3.	M	(A)
4.	N	(A)
5.	(-N v O)	1,3, MP
6.	--N	4, DN
7.	O	5,6, DS
8.	--(-O v P)	2,6, MT
9.	(-O v P)	8, DN
10.	--O	7, DN
11.	P	9,10, DS
12.	(N → P)	4-11, RCP
13.	[M → (N → P)]	3-12, RCP
14	[-M v (N → P)]	13, MI

Exercise: Ch. 7, Sect. 7.6.

Use RCP, and the rules of inference and axioms of replacement, to show that the following arguments are valid.

1. 1.   -(-I → S) v -V   ⊢   (V → -S)

2. 1.   (R v T)
    2.   (O → -Q)
    3.   (-O → -T) ⊢ (Q → R)

3. 1.   -S
    2.   -(-H v S) → U
    3.   (W → -U) ⊢ (H → -W)

4. 1. (-V • -V) → -E
    2. (-R v -V)
    3. (-R → Q) ⊢ (-E v Q)

5.* 1. (A v -C)
    2. (-C v I)
    3. -(-N • A) ⊢ (N v -C)

6. 1. (G v -U) v -T
    2. (G → N) ⊢ -(T → J) → (U → N)

7. 1. [-(Q v -D) v P]
    2. {(-P v D) → (Q v -H)}
    3. [(P • P) → D] ⊢ [H → (D → Q)]

8. 1. [(J v L) v -C] → I
    2. (I v L) → E ⊢ (C → J) → E

9. 1. -V → (S • G)
    2. (S v G) → L
    3. (L → -X) ⊢ (V v -X)

10.*1. [(Z v E) → T] • (E → Y)
    2. -(-T → S) ⊢ Z → (K → Y)

7.7. Reductio ad Absurdum

The truth tree method for showing arguments to be valid or invalid required that we deny the conclusion of the argument and work for contradictions on each branch of the tree. We saw that if it was possible to hold the premises true and the conclusion false (this being the point of denying the conclusion) without generating a contradiction on each branch, then the argument was invalid.

A similar method in natural deduction, called *Reductio ad Absurdum*, uses RCP, the rules and axioms, and the denial of the conclusion as an assumption. The aim is to deny the conclusion, attempt to derive statements that contradict one another, *on separate lines*, and proceed then to obtain the conclusion on a further line, *outside the scope of the assumption*. Essentially, what one does here is "reduce to an absurdity" (with 'p' and '-p' on separate lines), and from this absurdity, via Addition and Disjunctive Syllogism, derive the conclusion. Consider the following proof:

    1. (-F v H)
    2. (F v S)
    3. (S → T) ⊢ (H v T)
        4. -(H v T)   (A, DC)

5.	(-H • -T)	4, DM
6.	(-T • -H)	5, Com
7.	-T	6, Si
8.	-S	3,7, MT
9.	(S v F)	2, Com
10.	F	8,9, DS
11.	--F	10, DN
12.	H	1,11, DS
13.	-H	5, Si
14.	H v (H v T)	12, Ad
15.	(H v T)	13,14, DS
16.	-(H v T) → (H v T)	4-15, RCP
17.	--(H v T) v (H v T)	16, MI
18.	(H v T) v (H v T)	17, DN
19.	(H v T)	18, Re

You will have noticed that there is something different about the line on which the assumption appears. It also contains 'DC,' which stands for "denial of the conclusion." This shows that the plan is to use *reductio ad absurdum* to derive the conclusion.

Some logicians use *reductio ad absurdum* differently from the way it is here used. The rule they cite is that "from a contradiction, the conclusion may be written on the line immediately following." In this way, one avoids the further steps of closing the assumption, applying the rules of Addition and Disjunctive Syllogism, and using RCP. However, when these steps are deleted, one may know *that* anything at all can be obtained from contradictory statements without the least idea *how* to show it. We will employ *Reductio ad Absurdum* here as a method rather than as a rule.

When using the *reductio* method, after getting 'p' and '-p' on separate lines, there is a fairly strict method for deriving the conclusion outside the scope of the assumption. The method is this: 1) Use the rule Addition to "Add" the conclusion to 'p' (line 14 above); 2) derive the conclusion via Disjunctive Syllogism (line 15), 3) close the scope of the assumption, 4) apply RCP to the closure of the assumption, yielding a conditional statement (line 16) made up of the statement that was assumed (the antecedent) and the conclusion (the consequent), 5) use Material Implication to derive '(--p v p)' (line 17), 6) get rid of the double negation, if there is one (as there is on line 17), and 7) use Replication to derive the conclusion of the argument itself, outside the scope of any assumption. Two further examples of the method of *reductio ad absurdum* follow:

1.	-(N v M) v (O • A)	
2.	-O ⊢ -N	
3.	--N	(A, DC)
4.	N	3, DN
5.	(N v M)	4, Ad

6.	$(N \lor M) \rightarrow (O \cdot A)$	1, MI
7.	$(O \cdot A)$	5,6, MP
8.	O	7, Si
9.	$(O \lor -N)$	8, Ad
10.	-N	2,9, DS
11.	$(N \rightarrow -N)$	3-10, RCP
12.	$(-N \lor -N)$	11, MI
13.	-N	12, Re

1.	$-X \rightarrow (-R \rightarrow -Z)$	
2.	$-(Z \cdot -X) \rightarrow -T \quad \vdash \quad (T \rightarrow R)$	
3.	$-(T \rightarrow R)$	(A, DC)
4.	$-(-T \lor R)$	3, MI
5.	$(--T \cdot -R)$	4, DM
6.	$--T$	5, SI
7.	$--(Z \cdot -X)$	2,6, MT
8.	$(Z \cdot -X)$	7, DN
9.	$-X$	8, Com, Si
10.	$(-R \rightarrow -Z)$	1,9, MP
11.	$-R$	5, Com, Si
12.	$-Z$	10,11, MP
13.	Z	8, Si
14.	$Z \lor (T \rightarrow R)$	13, Ad
15.	$(T \rightarrow R)$	12,14, DS
16.	$-(T \rightarrow R) \rightarrow (T \rightarrow R)$	3-15, RCP
17.	$--(T \rightarrow R) \lor (T \rightarrow R)$	16, MI
18.	$(T \rightarrow R) \lor (T \rightarrow R)$	17, DN
19.	$(T \rightarrow R)$	18, Re

The great majority of *reductio* proofs use Addition, Disjunctive Syllogism, RCP, Material Implication, Double Negation, and Replication, in that order, at the end. The proof before the one directly above is an example of a proof that doesn't use Double Negation toward the end.

Many times it is the assumption of the denial of the conclusion that will greatly facilitate obtaining contradictory formulas in a proof. However, if one can obtain a contradiction without making any assumption, then one can get absolutely any formula at all, including the conclusion of the argument. Consider the following argument.

$-(-E \rightarrow K)$
$(E \cdot R) \lor (E \lor K) \quad \vdash \quad H$

If this argument appears odd to you, perhaps it is because you are wondering how 'H' could follow from premises that do not contain 'H' as a component. *It is a valid argument, since the premises are contradictory.* Since they are contradictory, they cannot both be true at the same time. Hence, this argument cannot have all true premises as well as a false conclusion, which would prove invalidity. That the letter 'H' was chosen for the conclusion was completely arbitrary. It could just as well have been '-H' or '(H v Z),' or even '(I → O),' or any other statement (atomic or molecular) you can conceive. The reason for this is that all statements follow from a contradiction, including their negatives. The proofs below bear this out, since in the first, 'H' is the conclusion, and in the second, it is '-H.' Note that the premises in both arguments are exactly the same. Neither Rule of Conditional Proof nor *Reductio ad Absurdum* is used in either proof. You will see that both of the justification sets are exactly alike. The only difference in these proofs is the "Addition" of 'H' in the first and '-H' in the second. The most important thing to be learned from these proofs is that '-E' is asserted on line 8 and 'E' is asserted on line 9 in each proof. These are contradictory sentences.

1. -(-E → K)
2. (E • R) v (E v K) ⊢ H
3. -(--E v K)   1, MI
4. -(E v K)   3, DN
5. (-E • -K)   4, DM
6. (E v K) v (E • R)   2, Com
7. (E • R)   4,6, DS
8. -E   5, Si
9. E   7, Si
10. (E v H)   9, Ad
11. H   8,10, DS

1. -(-E → K)
2. (E • R) v (E v K) ⊢ -H
3. -(--E v K)   1, MI
4. -(E v K)   3, DN
5. (-E • -K)   4, DM
6. (E v K) v (E • R)   2, Com
7. (E • R)   4,6, DS
8. -E   5, Si
9. E   7, Si
10. (E v -H)   9, Ad
11. -H   8,10, DS

The following is a further example of RCP which is a bit more complicated, but only in terms of the rules and principles used to derive line 18. Note the same method of working with RCP is employed here.

1. (Q • T) → D
2. (Q • -T) → -D ⊢ {Q → [(T • D) v (-T • -D)]}

3.	Q	(A)
4.	-(Q • T) v D	1, MI
5.	(-Q v -T) v D	4, DM
6.	-Q v (-T v D)	5, As
7.	--Q	3, DN
8.	(-T v D)	6,7, DS
9.	-(Q • -T) v -D	2, MI
10.	-(Q • --T) v -D	9, DM
11.	(-Q v T) v -D	10, DN
12.	-Q v (T v -D)	11, As
13.	(T v -D)	7,12, DS
14.	(-T v D) • (T v -D)	8,13, Con
15.	(T → D) • (T v -D)	14, MI
16.	(T → D) • (-D v T)	15, Con
17.	(T → D) • (D → T)	16, MI
18.	(T ↔ D)	17, ME
19.	[(T • D) v (-T • -D)]	18, ME
20.	Q → [(T • D) v (-T • -D)]	3-19, RCP

Exercise: Ch. 7, Sect. 7.7.

Use RAA, and any combination of RCP, the rules and axioms to prove the following arguments to be valid.

1.   1. (T v -A) → B
     2. -(Q → B) ⊢ A

2.   1. S → (C v A)
     2. (-A • -C) ⊢ -S

3.   1. (W → K)
     2. (-I → -K) ⊢ (-I → -W)

4.   1. (-E → -V)
     2. (-X v T)
     3. (-T v -E) ⊢ -(V • X)

5* 1. (-N v -N) v U
     2. (N • U) → F   ⊢   (N • N) → F

6.   1. (Z v W) → A
     2. (-O • -W) → Z ⊢ O v (A v Z)

7.   1. H → (-S • -P)
     2. S → (H • -P)
     3. -(S → V) ⊢ (-H • -S)

8.   1. (M → -E)
     2. (K → -Q)
     3. (E v K) ⊢ (-M v -Q)

9.   1. -G
     2. (P v T) → (T → G)
     3. (G → T) • P ⊢ -T

10.*1. (I • J) v (-I • -J)
     2. -(-I → W) ⊢ -J

11. 1. (C v -W)
    2. (S → B)
    3. (B → -C) ⊢   (-W v -S)

12. 1. [-(-R • S) • -(S → R)]   ⊢   M

7.8. Logical Truths

Both Rule of Conditional Proof and *Reductio ad Absurdum* can be used to "prove logical truths" (that is, show sentences to be logically true). The method here is simply to proceed as though the sentence in question is a conclusion to some argument which has no premises. You will recall that this was precisely the method of proving logical truths with truth trees. With trees, we indicated that there were "zero premises" and we treated the sentence in question as a conclusion by denying it. We can adopt the same schema here, as so:

    1. Zero Premises ⊢ [Sentence to be proved]

Below is a proof showing the sentence '[P → (-P → P)]' to be L-true using RCP.

1. Zero Premises ⊢ [P → (-P → P)]
  2. P   (A)
  3. (P v P)   2, Ad
  4. (--P v P)   3, DN
  5. (-P → P)   4, MI
6. [P → (-P → P)]   2-5 RCP

Here is a proof, using *reductio*, showing '[-(P • P) → -P]' to be L-true.

1. Zero Premises ⊢ [-(P • P) → -P]
  2. -[-(P • P) → -P]   (A, DC)
  3. -[--(P • P) v -P]   2, MI
  4. [---(P • P) • --P]   3, DM
  5. ---(P • P)   4, Si
  6. --P   4, Com, Si
  7. -(P • P)   5, DN
  8. (-P v -P)   7, DM
  9. -P   6,8, DS
 10 -P v [-(P • P) → -P]   9, Ad
 11 [-(P • P) → -P]   6,10, DS
12 -[-(P • P) → -P] → [-(P • P) → -P]   2-11, RCP
13 --[-(P • P) → -P] v [-(P • P) → -P]   12, MI
14 [-(P • P) → -P] v [-(P • P) → -P]   13, DN

15   [-(P • P) → -P]   14, Re

Note that line 2 in both proofs above is an assumption. In proving logical truths, every "line 2" will be an assumption. When using RCP, line 2 will be the assumption of the antecedent to the conditional one is trying to derive, as in the above proof. When using *reductio ad absurdum*, line 2 will simply be the negation of the sentence to be proved.

Exercise: Ch. 7, Sect. 7.8.

Show that the sentences below are L-true.

1.   [F → (-T v F)]
2.   (T → F) ↔ (-F → -T)
3.   -(V • R) ↔ --(R → -V)
4.   [(H v -H) • (-H v H)]
5.* [(-N v D) v (N v -D)]
6.   -(E v R) → (-Q v -R)
7.   {[(I → Q) • I] → Q}
8.   -[(K → -L) ↔ (L • K)]
9.   -(F → G) v [-G → (F → -X)]
10.* [(-T → L) • -U] → (U → -L)
11. [-(C • D) • C] → -D
12. {-(B • W) v [B • (W v E)]}
13. -(A ↔ B) ↔ (-A ↔ B)
14. [Ee → (Ff → Gg)] → [(Ee → Ff) → (Ee → Gg)]
15.*{R → [(S • -S) v R]}

8. Predicate Logic

8.1. Preliminaries

The present chapter is an extension of Chapters 3, 4, 5 and 6. It deals again with translations and methods of proving various arguments to be valid or invalid. There are sections on both natural deduction and truth trees. But it goes beyond the simple sorts of sentences and arguments treated in those chapters. Adding a few symbols to our already existing set, we will be in a position to become extremely precise when translating sentences from natural language (in our case English) into symbolic notation.

Predicate logic will allow us to prove that many arguments which would be judged invalid in sentential logic are actually valid. For example:

(A) All physical objects are extended in space.
(B) Some physical objects are unobservable.
(C) Hence, some unobservable objects are extended in space.

This is a valid argument. In sentential logic, we would translate this argument as

A
B ⊢ C.

The translated argument is clearly invalid. Since the original argument is valid, there should be a way of showing this. We will be working in a system of logic that can handle arguments that cannot be handled within Sentential Logic. Predicate Logic goes beyond Sentential Logic.

8.2. Translations

Let us begin with a sentence that might be uttered by any teacher of United States geography.

Baltimore is a city with a population over one hundred thousand.

To translate this sentence with precision, we need to introduce new notation.

Since being a city with a population over one hundred thousand people is what is being said, or predicated, of Baltimore, we will call the phrase "is a city with a population over one hundred thousand people" a *Predicate*. (Note here that the word "predicate" does not have the exact meaning the grammarian gives to it.) Predicates will be symbolized by the upper case letters of the alphabet, called *Predicate Letters*. Since 'Baltimore' is the name of the object that is being referred to, we will call 'Baltimore' a *Name*. To denote names of objects, things, or individuals we will use lower case letters of the alphabet from 'a' through 't,' called *Name Letters*, also referred to as *Individual Constants*. Letting 'C' = 'is a city with a population over one hundred thousand people' and letting 'b' = 'Baltimore,' we symbolize the sentence above as: Cb.

Further examples of this sort of notation are:

Mind is a philosophical journal.	Jm
Charles Dickens was not a poet.	-Pd
Pink Floyd is a rock group.	Rp
Crazy Horse is a rock group.	Rc
Pink Floyd and Crazy Horse are rock groups.	(Rp • Rc)
Either Alaska or Siberia is coldest.	(Ca v Cs)
Rothko was a painter but Pepys wasn't.	(Pr • -Pp)
If *Bolero* is beautiful, so is *The Moldau.*	(Bb → Bm)

The importance of a translation dictionary should be obvious with the above sentences and their symbolic translations. For example, in the fifth sentence, 'R' = 'is a rock group,' 'p' = 'Pink Floyd,' and 'c' = 'Crazy Horse.' The sentence written in symbolic notation literally says, "Pink Floyd is a rock group and Crazy Horse is a rock group," which has the exact meaning as "Pink Floyd and Crazy Horse are rock groups." In the last example, 'B' = 'is beautiful,' 'b' = '*Bolero*,' 'm' = '*The Moldau.*'

When we begin to translate more complex sorts of sentences, we find the need to introduce new symbolism. Take, for example, the sentence,

All human adults have rights.

This is what is called a Universal Affirmative sentence. It is universal because the word "all" refers to every member of the class of human adults. It is affirmative because it makes a non-negative assertion. An informative way of representing what this sentence is saying is that if any being is a human adult, then it has a right. We might reword the sentence in the following ways:

If anything is a human adult, then that thing has rights.
If any object is a human adult, then that object has rights.

These sentences are about as precise as we can get, until we introduce the symbols of logic into the scheme. We can begin as follows:

Given any x, if x is a human adult, then x has rights.

The "x" you find occurring three times in the above sentence is called a *variable*. Variables may be thought of as place holders. The place they hold is for individual constants and name letters, such as 'k' in Lk, where 'L' = 'is lazy' and 'k' = 'Kathy.' (More will be said about variables as place holders in the section on proofs.) Variables are symbolized by lower case letters from the end of the alphabet: 'x,' 'y,' and 'z.' The phrase "Given any x," which in the original sentence is "All," corresponds to what we call the *Universal Quantifier*. (Other ways of referring to the Universal Quantifier in English are: "For any x," "For all x," "Given any z," and "No matter what x is.") In predicate logic, this quantifier is expressed as a single variable enclosed in parentheses: *(x)*. We can provide the following translation dictionary for the sentence "All adult humans have rights": 'Ax' = 'x is a human adult'; 'Rx' = 'x has rights.' Note that only the conditional indicator-phrase ("if . . . then") is not covered by either the quantifier or the dictionary. That logical component will be translated with the arrow, our symbol for the conditional. The translated symbolized sentence is:

$(x)(Ax \rightarrow Rx)$

It is very important to include the parentheses just as they are above. Each occurrence of a variable must be *bound* by a quantifier. A *free variable* is a variable that is not bound by, or within the scope of, any quantifier, as in *Ax*, which does not express any sentence in English. It is one thing for 'Ax' to represent some phrase in a translation dictionary, quite another for it to *mean* and *refer* to something.

The scope of any given quantifier extends from the proximate grouper to its matching grouper. For example, in the sentence $(x)[Rx \lor (Sx \cdot Tx)]$, the scope of the quantifier extends from the left bracket to the right bracket and all variables in 'Rx,' 'Sx,' and 'Tx' are bound by the quantifier. In the sentence $(x)Rx \rightarrow Ra$, however, the scope of the quantifier extends only over 'Rx.'

All Universal Affirmative sentences are translated in precisely the same way, though the content and hence the dictionaries vary. There are a variety of ways in which universal affirmative sentences can be expressed in English. Below are examples:

Every explorer is adventurous.	$(x)(Ex \rightarrow Ax)$
Members Congress are all U.S. citizens.	$(x)(Cx \rightarrow Ux)$
Each Hawaiian Island is beautiful.	$(x)(Hx \rightarrow Bx)$
Dolphins are mammals.	$(x)(Dx \rightarrow Mx)$
Only wolves hunt reindeer.	$(x)(-Wx \rightarrow -Rx)$

We can also translate the other Universal categorical sentence, i.e., the Universal Negative. We use the universal quantifier and an appropriate dictionary.

To translate 'No tigers are herbivorous,' let 'Tx' = 'x is a tiger' and let 'Hx' = 'x is herbivorous.' The translated sentence is:

$(x)(Tx \rightarrow -Hx)$

which reads: "Given any x, if x is a tiger, then x is not herbivorous." All Universal Negative sentences are translated in the same way. One can express these sentences in a variety of ways in English. Below are a number of examples.

There aren't any bald hairdressers.	$(x)(Bx \rightarrow -Hx)$
Left handed shortstops don't exist.	$(x)(Lx \rightarrow -Sx)$
Rainbow Trout are not mammals.	$(x)(Rx \rightarrow -Mx)$
No one is both rich and happy.	$(x)(Rx \rightarrow -Hx)$
Reptiles and mammals are mutually exclusive.	$(x)(Rx \rightarrow -Mx)$

To translate Particular Affirmative sentences and Particular Negative sentences, we need a way of symbolizing the *Existential Quantifier* "some." The symbolic form of the existential quantifier is $(\exists x)$. In predicate logic, we read '$(\exists x)$' as 'There exists an x such that.' Consider the following sentence:

Some jazz musicians also play blues.

What this sentence is saying is that there is at least one jazz musician who also plays the blues, or that there is a jazz musician *and* this musician also plays blues. We can begin to translate the sentence by inserting the variable, like so:

There is an x such that x is a jazz musician and x plays blues.

Note that the above sentence is a conjunction. The translation dictionary is as follows: 'Jx' = 'x is a jazz musician,' 'Px' = 'x plays blues.' The original sentence can now be fully symbolized, as

$(\exists x)(Jx \cdot Px)$

All Particular Affirmative sentences are translated in the same way. Examples of ways of expressing Particular Affirmative sentences are:

There are conservative Democrats.	$(\exists x)(Cx \cdot Dx)$
A lot of German cars are overpriced.	$(\exists x)(Gx \cdot Ox)$
At least one head of state is a woman.	$(\exists x)(Hx \cdot Wx)$
Sometimes parents are cranky.	$(\exists x)(Px \cdot Cx)$
Many people are afraid of snakes.	$(\exists x)(Px \cdot Ax)$

Particular Negative sentences are translated in the same way as Particular Affirmative sentences, that is, as conjunctions, but with the second conjunct denied. 'Some jazz musicians don't play blues' is translated as follows:

$(\exists x)(Jx \bullet -Px)$

The ways of expressing Particular Negative sentences in English are many. Some are:

Not all bees make honey.	$(\exists x)(Bx \bullet -Hx)$
Some calligraphers aren't graphic artists.	$(\exists x)(Cx \bullet -Gx)$
Many people are not afraid of snakes.	$(\exists x)(Px \bullet -Ax)$
There are mountains but not on Venus.	$(\exists x)(Mx \bullet -Vx)$
There is at least one philosopher who doesn't play chess.	
	$(\exists x)(Px \bullet -Cx)$

One can gain some insight into the translations of the categorical sentences above by seeing relationships that hold between them. For example, consider the following four sentences:

1.	2.
All surfers are athletic.	No surfers are athletic.
$(x)(Sx \rightarrow Ax)$	$(x)(Sx \rightarrow -Ax)$

3.	4.
Some surfers are not athletic.	Some surfers are athletic.
$(\exists x)(Sx \bullet -Ax)$	$(\exists x)(Sx \bullet Ax)$

Notice that 1 and 3 are contradictory, as are 2 and 4. Notice that 1 and 2 cannot both be true at the same time though they may both be false at the same time (e.g., if there were two surfers and one was athletic and one was not). Notice that 3 and 4 can both be true at the same time but cannot both be false at the same time (unless all the surfers were to disappear from the world).

Further Translations

There are, of course, many things we can say that do not fit exactly into the form of the four categories of sentences treated above. Some examples, and their translations, follow. Keep in mind that the translation dictionary is vital for proper translation of any sentence in predicate logic. For instance, in the fourth sentence below, let 'Cx' = 'x is a car,' 'Wx' = 'x is a work of art,' 'Wp' = 'Porsches are works of art.'

The president of the confederacy wasn't a Virginian. -Vp

There aren't any unicorns. -(∃x)Ux

Someone spilled the coffee and someone cleaned it up.
    (∃x)Sx • (∃x)Cx

Anyone drunk enough to fight is too drunk to fight well.
    (x)(Fx → Wx)

If any cars are works of art, Porsches are.
    (∃x)(Cx • Wx) → Wp

If every human is a person, then Willie Mays is.
    (x)(Hx → Px) → Pw

If ghosts exist, they're discontent but not evil.
    (x)[Gx → (-Cx • -Ex)]

Everything is observable. (x)Ox

Something is immovable. (∃x)-Mx

Not everything in nature is physical. -(x)Px

Nothing is immaterial. -(∃x)-Mx

Nobody eats eels for breakfast. -(∃x)Ex

Somebody bought the boat. (∃x)Bx

Somebody didn't clean up the mess. (∃x)-Cx

Everything is either observable or immaterial.
    (x)(Ox v -Mx)

Each player is either left handed or right handed.
    (x)[Px → (Lx v Rx)]

No player is both left handed and right handed.
    -(∃x)[Px • (Lx • Rx)]

All and only males are sons. (x)(Mx ↔ Sx)

No one is both a brother and a sister. -(∃x)(Bx • Sx)

Some daughters are not both mothers and grandmothers.
    (∃x)[Dx • -(Mx • Gx)]

Everyone is either a son or a daughter; and no one is both.
    [(x)(Sx v Dx) • -(∃x)(Sx • Dx)]

Some children, though certainly not all, are psychic.
    [(∃x)(Cx • Px) • (∃x)(Cx • -Px)]
    [(∃x)(Cx • Px) • -(x)(Cx → Px)]

Exercise: Ch. 8, Sect. 8.2.

A. Use the following translation dictionary to translate the sentences below into symbolic notation. [Ax = x is a master composer; Bx = x is beautiful; Cx = x is music written by Buddy Holly; Dx = x was born in Denver; Hx = x is music written by Rimsky-Korsakov; Lx = x is worth listening to; Mx = x is music written by George Gershwin; Px = x helped write *Porgy & Bess*; Rx = x wrote *Rhapsody in Blue*; Sx = x wrote *Scheherazade*; Ux = x is music; Wx = x could have written *Scheherazade*; b = Buddy Holly; g = George Gershwin; h = *Rhapsody in Blue*; p = *Porgy & Bess*; r = Rimsky-Korsakov; s = *Scheherazade*]

1. George Gershwin was not born in Denver.
2. Gershwin wrote *Rhapsody in Blue* and helped write *Porgy & Bess*.
3. Some of Gershwin's music is not beautiful.
4. Not all of the music written by Buddy Holly is beautiful.
5.* If any music written by George Gershwin was beautiful, *Rhapsody in Blue* certainly was.
6. *Scheherazade* is beautiful music that was written by Rimsky-Korsakov, though not all music written by Rimsky-Korsakov is beautiful or worth listening to.
7. Only a master composer could have written *Scheherazade*.
8. If Buddy Holly helped write *Porgy & Bess*, then some of Buddy Holly's music is beautiful.
9. Buddy Holly didn't write *Scheherazade* and neither did George
10.* All of George Gershwin's music is beautiful only if some of Buddy Holly's music is beautiful.

B. Translate the following symbolic sentences into normal English using the dictionary for exercise 8.A.

1. -(x)Bx
2. -(∃x)Bx
3. (∃x)Bx → Bp
4. (x)Bx → (x)(Cx → Bx)
5.* (x)[Ux → (Bx v -Lx)]
6. (Wb → Bs)
7. (∃x)(Rx • Sx)
8. (∃x)-(Rx v Sx)
9. (x){[(Hx v Cx) v Mx] → Lx}
10.*(x)[-(Px → Wx) • (Rx → Wx)]

C. Create dictionaries for the following sentences and translate them into the symbolic notation of predicate logic.

1. Some day-care providers are both beautiful and intelligent.
2. Not all paper-boys are honest as well as efficient.
3. There are people who neither vote nor care who runs for president.
4. If Socrates taught anyone, then he taught Plato.
5.* Only scientists use the scientific method.
6. Some people claim to be both scientists and creationists.
7. Affirmative Action advocates all commit *Argumentum ad Misericordiam*.
8. Any computer has intelligence only if the President has.
9. Some children don't know the value of a buck.
10.* Nothing has absolute and intrinsic value.
11. Not all people in Florida grow oranges.
12. One French Impressionist was either mentally ill or a nonconformist.
13. Every visitor to Tenerife misunderstood the guide's instructions.
14. It is false that all criminals are unhappy and genetic mutants.
15.*Children are innocent only if they have no moral awareness.
16. There are children who are neither innocent nor morally blameworthy.

17. Puerto Rico will become a state just in case its economy improves.
18. If all people are good, then some of my enemies are good.
19. Research on the genetic basis of criminal behavior is unscientific.
20.*It is false that no intelligent logicians write poetry.

8.3. Proofs

To work proofs in predicate logic, we retain all of the Rules of Inference and Axioms of Replacement found in Chapter 7.

Our method of proof will be *Reductio ad Absurdum*, but we will approach it in a somewhat different manner from the way we did in the last chapter. We will use *reductio ad absurdum* (RAA) as a rule now, rather than as a method. The rule for RAA will be: *Whenever a contradiction is explicitly found on a line of a proof, write the conclusion on the next line of the proof, which will then be the last line.* The starting point of a *reductio* proof is always the same, i.e., one assumes the denial, or negation, of the conclusion. In schematic form:

-Ca	(Assumption: denial of conclusion)
•	(A further line in the proof)
•	(A further line in the proof)
•	(A further line in the proof)
(Da • -Da)	(An explicit contradiction)
Ca	(The conclusion)

Using RAA as a rule is strictly a logician's short-cut. Using RAA as a rule, we are freed from having to make explicit use of the Rule of Conditional Proof. We know we *could*, in every case, go from contradictory sentences to any further sentence, using Addition, Disjunctive Syllogism, then closing the scope of the assumption and using RCP, Material Implication, Double Negation, and Replication. (Recall the method as outlined at the end of Chapter 7.) Those seven steps are avoided by simply making the contradiction explicit in the proof, and then drawing the conclusion itself. Let's try it out.

1.	(Ja → Ha)	
2.	-[Ja v (Fa v -Ja)]	⊢ (Fa → Ha)
3.	-(Fa → Ha)	(A, DC)
4.	-(-Fa v Ha)	3, MI
5.	(--Fa • -Ha)	4, DM
6.	-Ha	5, Com, Si
7.	-Ja	1,6, MT
8.	[-Ja • -(Fa v -Ja)]	2, DM
9.	-(Fa v -Ja)	8, Com, Si
10.	(-Fa • --Ja)	9, DM
11.	--Ja	10, Com, Si

12.	Ja	11, DN
13.	(Ja • -Ja)	7,12, Con
14.	(Fa → Ha)	3-13, RAA

Note that the scope of the assumption is not formally expressed, except in the justification of line #3 where 'A' indicates an assumed sentence. Line #13 expresses the contradiction outright. From there, we don' formally close the assumption, but rather simply write the conclusion on the next line (#14), indicating that we have used lines 3-13 and RAA.

8.3.1. Universal Instantiation

To work proofs in predicate logic using quantifiers requires a few further rules. We need a way of going from quantified sentences to unquantified sentences. We can begin with the universal quantifier. Take the following sentence and its translation, where 'Fx' = 'x is an FBI agent' and 'Cx' = 'x is cleared for viewing top secret papers.'

>Only FBI agents are cleared for viewing top secret papers.
>(x)(Cx → Fx)

Imagine this sentence as a premise in an argument on which we are doing a proof. Obviously, none of our existing rules of inference or replacement would apply to this sentence. It is only when it is unquantified that our rules will apply. To render this sentence unquantified, we simply pick out an individual, say, Perry, (where 'p' = 'Perry'), remove the quantifier and replace the occurrences of the bound variable with the individual constant. We derive the sentence "(Cp → Fp)," which says "If Perry is cleared for viewing top secret papers, then Perry is an FBI agent." What we have done here is pick out an individual instance (*instantiated*) to replace the variable, dropping the quantifier because the sentence no longer refers to just any individual or all individuals, but only to Perry (what is true of everyone must also be true of Perry). Dropping the quantifier and substituting an individual instance for every bound variable (every variable over which the quantifier ranges) is called *Universal Instantiation*. One is actually deriving one instance of the universal quantification. In other words, to instantiate is to replace a variable with an individual constant. The same variable is always to be replaced with the same individual constant in any given instantiation. The rule is called Universal Instantiation and is abbreviated as **UI** in the justification portion of the proof. Note that from the sentence above we can derive any individual instantiation. For example, letting 'j' = 'Jack Kennedy,' we derive "If Jack Kennedy is cleared for viewing top secret papers, then Jack Kennedy is an FBI agent." The sentence would then be instantiated with respect to 'j' and would appear as follows: (Cj → Fj). [It is standard practice to pick 'a,' 'b' and 'c' as individual constants when no translation dictionary is provided.]

Below is a proof using the rules we have so far.

1.   (x)(Fx → -Jx)
2.   (x)(Jx v -Gx)
3.   (x)Fx   ⊢ -(x)Gx
4.   --(x)Gx   (A,DC)
5.   (x)Gx   4, DN
6.   Ga   5, UI
7.   (Fa → -Ja)   1, UI
8.   (Ja v -Ga)   2, UI
9.   Fa   3, UI
10. -Ja   7,9, MP
11. -Ga   8,10, DS
12. (Ga • -Ga)   6,11, Con
13. -(x)Gx   3-12, RAA

To be able to work with the sentences appearing in lines 1, 2, 3, and 5, it required that the rule for Universal Instantiation be applied in each of those cases. The individual 'a' is not named, of course, since there is no translation dictionary. However, since each of those sentences applies universally, then each of those sentences can have 'a' as an instance, no matter who or what 'a' refers to. We *could* have picked 'b,' or 'c,' or 'd,' or *any* other individual constant. But, if we had instantiated with respect to 'a' in line #5, but with respect to 'b' in lines 1, 2, or 3, then we would not have been able to derive the desired contradiction in line #12. Instead, we would have derived the sentence "(Ga • -Gb)," which is not a contradiction.

8.3.2. Quantifier Exchange

Before proceeding to the instantiation of the existential quantifier, let us introduce four essential rules of predicate logic. They are commonly known as the *Quantifier Exchange Rules*. They are:

(x)Rx ⇔ -(∃x)-Rx
-(x)Rx ⇔ (∃x)-Rx
(∃x)Rx ⇔ -(x)-Rx
-(∃x)Rx ⇔ (x)-Rx

Each of these rules expresses a legitimate logical equivalence (note the hollow double arrows), and each is abbreviated as *QE*. The formula on the left side of the double arrow is equivalent to the formula on the right side of the double arrow. The one may be "exchanged" for the other whenever either occurs in a proof. To see the need for these rules, consider the formula "-(x)(Rx v Sx)." There is no rule of inference or principle of replacement that applies to this formula. In fact, UI does not apply either, since that formula is not a universal quantification, but rather a negated universal quantification. By turning the formula into an existential quantification, that is, '(∃x)-(Rx v Sx),' we are now free to use the existential instantiation rule.

To better understand the quantifier exchange rules as equivalence rules, it may be helpful to offer examples in English. Let 'Ex' = 'x is extended in space.' Each of the following pairs of sentences corresponds to one of the QE rules.

(x)Mx	Everything is extended in space.
-(∃x)-Mx	It is false that there exists a thing that is not extended in space.

-(x)Mx	Not all things are extended in space.
(∃x)-Mx	There is something that is not extended in space.

(∃x)Mx	Something is extended in space.
-(x)-Mx	Not all things are not extended in space.

-(∃x)	Mx Nothing is extended in space.
(x)-Mx	Everything is not extended in space.

8.3.3 Existential Instantiation

The second instantiation rule (there are only two since there are only two quantifiers) makes use of the existential quantifier '(∃x)' and is called *Existential Instantiation*. It is abbreviated as *EI* and allows us to pick an instance of an existential quantification. As a universal quantification is a formula beginning with a universal quantifier, so an existential quantification is a formula beginning with an existential quantifier. There is one very important restriction to the use of EI: When using the rule EI, one must *not* instantiate with respect to any individual constant that appears in a line of the proof (including the premises) prior to the existential instantiation itself. For example, if you are working a proof in which '(x)Rx v Ra' appears as one of the premises, then if some existential quantification, say, '(∃x)(Gx v Hx),' appears in one of the lines of the proof, it would be illegitimate to use EI to derive '(Ga v Ha)' as a further line, since 'a' appears prior to the instantiation of '(∃x)(Gx v Hx).' As a way of noting in a proof that some individual constant has been chosen via EI, we will adopt the practice of "flagging" a new letter introduced in an existential instantiation. We will write an asterisk followed by the letter as part of the justification of the instantiation. So, if 'c' has been used as part of an existential instantiation, we will write '*c' (without the quotes) to the far right. In this way we will indicate that 'c' has not appeared previously in the proof. There is, of course, no reason to flag any letter used as part of a universal instantiation, since there is no restriction on the use of individual constants in UI. Here is an example of flagging (line #3 below).

1. (∃x)(Gx v Lx)
2. (x)-Lx ⊢ Ga

3.	(Ga v La)	1, EI *a
4.	-Ga	(A, DC)
5.	-La	2, UI
6.	La	3,4 DS
7.	(La • -La)	5,6 Con
8.	Ga	4-7 RAA

Note that in the proof above, while 'a' appears in the conclusion (stated in line 2 directly after '⊢'), it is used in the instantiation in line 3. This is legitimate since the statement of the conclusion in line 2 is not part of the proof itself. Hence, the rule that a constant which appears in a line of a proof prior to an existential instantiation cannot be used in the instantiation is not violated.

Consider the following proof.

1.	(x)(Ax → Bx)	
2.	(x)-(Cx v Bx)	⊢ (x)-Ax
3.	-(x)-Ax	(A,DC)
4.	(∃x)--Ax	3, QE
5.	--Aa	4, EI *a
6.	(Aa → Ba)	1, UI
7.	-(Ca v Ba)	2, UI
8.	(-Ca • -Ba)	7, DM
9.	Aa	5, Si
10.	Ba	6,9, MP
11.	-Ba	8, Com, Si
12.	(Ba • -Ba)	10,11, Con
13.	(x)-Ax	3-12, RAA

If one were to have used UI before EI in this case, it would not have been possible to show that the argument is valid. This is so because using UI first would have put the occurrence of 'a' prior to the use of EI, in which case when EI was used, we would have had to instantiate with respect to another individual constant besides 'a.' It would have been impossible to derive the explicit contradiction in such a case. A rule to adopt: *Use EI before UI.*

The examples below use the rules introduced in this chapter. Note again that the system of predicate logic retains each of the rules of inference and the axioms of replacement. Recall, also, that we are using *reductio* a rule now, not as a method.

No being without a brain can think. Amoebae have no brains. Thus, amoebae cannot think. [Ax = x is an ameoba; Bx = x has a brain; Tx = x can think]

1.	(x)(-Bx → -Tx)	
2.	(x)(Ax → -Bx)	⊢ (x)(Ax → -Tx)
3.	-(x)(Ax → -Tx)	(A, DC)

4. (∃x)-(Ax → -Tx)   3, QE
5. -(Ar → -Tr)   4, EI *r
6. -(-Ar v -Tr)   5, MI
7. (--Ar • --Tr)   6, DM
8. Ar   7, Si, DN
9. --Tr   7, Com, Si
10. (Ar → -Br)   2, UI
11. -Br   8,10, MP
12. (-Br → -Tr)   1, UI
13. -Tr   11,12, MP
14. (-Tr • --Tr   9,13, Con
15. (x)(Ax → -Tx)   3-14, RAA

Nothing is both uncaused and finite. Hence, everything finite has a cause. [Fx = x is finite; Gx = x has a cause]

1. -(∃x)(-Gx • Fx)   ⊢   (x)(Fx → Gx)
2. -(x)(Fx → Gx)   (A,DC)
3. (∃x)-(Fx → Gx)   2, QE
4. -(Fa → Ga)   3, EI *a
5. (x)-(-Gx • Fx)   1, QE
6. -(-Ga • Fa)   5, UI
7. (--Ga v -Fa)   6, DM
8. (-Fa v Ga)   7, Com, DN
9. (Fa → Ga)   8, MI
10. [(Fa → Ga) • -(Fa → Ga)]   4,9, Con
11. (x)(Fx → Gx)   3-10, RAA

For the next argument, two ways are shown of proving validity, the first using RAA, the second not using RAA.

There is no logic teacher who does not use a book in class. Dale and Hannah are both logic teachers. So, both Dale and Hannah use books in class. [Bx = x uses a book in class; Tx = x teaches logic; d = Dale; h = Hannah].

1. -(∃x)(Tx • -Bx)
2. (Td • Th)   ⊢   (Bd • Bh)
3. -(Bd • Bh)   (A,DC)
4. (x)-(Tx • -Bx)   1, QE
5. -(Th • -Bh)   4, UI
6. (-Th v --Bh)   5, DM
7. Th   2, Com, Si
8. --Th   7, DN
9. --Bh   6,8, DS

10. Bh	9, DN
11. (-Bd v -Bh)	3, DM
12. -(Td • -Bd)	4, UI
13. (-Td v --Bd)	12, DM
14. --Td	2, Si, DN
15. --Bd	13,14, DS
16. -Bh	11,15, DS
17. (Bh • -Bh)	10,16, Con
18. (Bd • Bh)	3-17, RAA

1. -(∃x)(T • -Bx)	
2. (Td • Th) ⊢ (Bd • Bh)	
3. (x)-(Tx • -Bx)	1, QE
4. -(Td • -Bd)	3, UI
5. -(Th • -Bh)	3, UI
6. (-Td v --Bd)	4, DM
7. (-Th v --Bh)	5, DM
8. --Td	2, Si, DN
9. Th	2, Com, Si
10. --Th	9, DN
11. Bd	6,8, DS, DN
12. Bh	7,10, DS, DN
13. (Bd • Bh)	11,12, Con

Note: Although the number of steps is large in each of the proofs above, neither is very complicated. The key is to see why universal instantiation must be used twice in each proof. In the first proof, in line 4, the universal quantifier ranges over both 'Tx' and '-Bx.' It is improper to carry out more than one instantiation at a time, yielding '-(Td • -Bh)' line 4.

It is all right to kill nonhumans. If fetuses have no moral values, then they are not human. Fetuses do not have moral values. Hence, it is all right to kill fetuses. (Student's argument) [Fx = x is a fetus; Hx = x is human; Kx = it is all right to kill x; Mx = x has moral values]

1. (x)(-Hx → Kx)	
2. (x)[(Fx • -Mx) → -Hx]	
3. (x)(Fx → -Mx) ⊢ (x)(Fx → Kx)	
4. -(x)(Fx → Kx)	(A, DC)
5. (∃x)-(Fx → Kx)	4, QE
6. -(Fs → Ks)	5, EI *s
7. [(Fs • -Ms) → -Hs]	2, UI
8. (Fs → -Ms)	3, UI
9. -(-Fs v Ks)	6, MI

10.	(--Fs • -Ks)	9, DM
11.	Fs	10, Si, DN
12.	-Ms	8,11, MP
13.	(Fs • -Ms)	11,12, Con
14.	-Hs	7,13, MP
15.	(-Hs → Ks)	1, UI
16.	Ks	14,15, MP
17.	-Ks	10, Com, Si
18.	(Ks • -Ks)	16,17, Con
19.	(x)(Fx → Kx)	4-18, RAA

This is a good place to note that while 's' was used above in the existential instantiation, 's' is an arbitrary choice here. Any other constant could have been chosen. There is no restriction here.

Consider another translation and proof:

Some ethical dilemmas are avoidable. If there is any ethical dilemma that is avoidable, then either the dilemma is not a "life or death dilemma" or it is of minor importance. There is no such thing as a minor ethical dilemma. It follows that there is at least one ethical dilemma that is neither of minor importance nor is a life or death dilemma. [Ax = x is avoidable; Ex = x is an ethical dilemma; Lx = x is a life or death dilemma; Mx = x is of minor importance]

1.	(∃x)(Ex • Ax)	
2.	(x)[(Ex • Ax) → (-Lx v Mx)]	
3.	-(∃x)(Ex • Mx) ⊢ (∃x)[Ex • (-Mx v -Lx)]	
4.	-(∃x)[Ex • (-Mx v -Lx)]	(A, DC)
5.	(x)-[Ex • (-Mx v -Lx)]	4, QE
6.	(En • An)	1, EI *n
7.	-[En • (-Mn v -Ln)]	5, UI
8.	[(En • An) → (-Ln v Mn)]	2, UI
9.	(-Ln v Mn)	6,8, MP
10.	En	6, Si
11.	--En	10, DN
12.	(Mn v -Ln)	9, Com
13.	[-En v -(Mn v -Ln)]	7, DM
14.	-(Mn v -Ln)	11,13, DS
15.	[(Mn v -Ln) • -(Mn v -Ln)]	12,14, Con
16.	(∃x)[Ex • (Mx v -Lx)]	4-15, RAA

Note here that the third premise is not used in the proof of the validity of the argument. What this means is that the third premise is does not lend any support to the conclusion. It may be a persuasive premise and hence get the listener to lean toward accepting the argument, but, as can be seen, it does no logical work here.

There are many arguments that are easier to prove valid without using RAA. One such argument, along with the proofs, is:

No event is uncaused. Making the decision to have an abortion is an event. Rhoda made the decision to have an abortion. Hence Rhoda's decision was caused. [Cx = x is caused; Dx = x made the decision to have an abortion; Ex = x is an event; r = Rhoda]

1.	(x)(Ex → Cx)	
2.	(x)(Dx → Ex)	
3.	Dr ⊦ Cr	
4.	(Dr → Er)	2, UI
5.	(Er → Cr)	1, UI
6.	(Dr → Cr)	4,5, HS
7.	Cr	3,6, MP

1.	(x)(Ex → Cx)	
2.	(x)(Dx → Ex)	
3.	Dr ⊦ Cr	
4.	-Cr	(A, DC)
5.	(Er → Cr)	1, UI
6.	(Dr → Er)	2, UI
7.	-Er	4,5, MT
8.	Er	3,6, MP
9.	(Er • -Er)	7,8, Con
10.	Cr	4-9, RAA

While this proof is a mere 3 steps longer than the proof done without using RAA, still, if the point is proving validity, saving time can be important.

Exercise: Ch. 8, Sect. 8.3.

A. Fill in the blank spaces with either the appropriate proof line or the appropriate justification for the proof line.

1.
1.	(x)(Fx → Gx)	
2.	(x)-(Hx v Gx) ⊦ -Fe	
3.		(A, DC)
4.		1, UI
5.	-(He v Ge)	
6.		5, DM
7.	-Ge	

2.
1.	(x)[Px • (Qx • Rx)]	
2.	(x)[(Qx v Rx) → Sx] ⊦ Sf	
3.	-Sf	
4.		1, UI
5.		2, UI
6.	(Qf • Rf)	
7.		6, Si

8.	4,7, MT
9.	3,8, Con
10. -Fe	

8. (Qf v Rf)	
9.	8,5, MP
10.	3,9, Con
11. Sf	

3.
1. (x)Lx ⊢ (-Ld → Hs)		
2.	(A,DC)	
3. -(--Ld v Hs)		
4.	3, DM	
5. Ld		
6.	4, DN	
7.	6, Si	
8.	5,7, Con	
9. (-Ld → Hs)		

4.*
1. (x)[(Tx v Yx) • (-Ux v Yx)]		
2. (x)-(-Yx → -Ux) ⊢ Tn		
3. -Tn		
4.	1, UI	
5. -(-Yn → -Un)		
6.	5, MI	
7. (---Yn • --Un)		
8. [(Yn v Tn) • (Yn v -Un)]		
9.	8, Di	
10. -Yn		
11.	9,10, DS	
12. (Yn v Tn)		
13. Tn		
14.	3,13, Con	
15. Tn		

5.
1. (x)(Lx → Ix)	
2. -(Rc v -Lc)⊢ (∃y)(Ly • Iy)	
3. -(∃y)(Ly • Iy)	
4.	3, QE
5.	4, UI
6. (Lc → Ic)	
7.	2, DM
8. --Lc	
9. Lc	
10.	6,9 MP
11.	5, DM
12. -Ic	
13.	10,12 Con
14. (∃x)(Ly • Iy)	

This is a good place to bring up the use of different variables in a proof. Recall that variables are place-holders and can take any individual constant required by the proof. So, whether 'x' or 'y' is used, it should make no difference when one instantiates.

B. Fill in the missing lines and/or justifications in each proof.

1.
1. (x)(Dx v -Sx) ⊢ (x)-(Sx • -Dx)	
2.	(A, DC)
3.	2, QE
4.	3, EI *p
5.	4, DN
6.	1, UI
7.	5, Si, DN

8.		6, Com
9.		7,8, DS
10.		5, Com, Si
11.		9,10, Con
12.		2-11, RAA

2. 1. (x)[(-Ix → Rx) v -Lx]
    2. (x)Rx → Ra
    3. (x)-(Lx → Ix) ⊢ (x)Rx
    4.   (A, DC)
    5.   4, QE
    6.   5, EI *k
    7.   1, UI
    8.   3, UI
    9.   7, MI
    10.   9, DN, Com
    11.   10, As
    12.   6,11, DS
    13.   8, MI
    14.   13, DM
    15.   14, Si
    16.   12, Com
    17.   15,16, DS
    18.   14, Com, Si
    19.   17,18, Con
    20.   4-19, RAA

3. 1. (x)(Lx → Tx)
    2. (x)(Lx → Wx) ⊢ (x)[Lx → (Tx • Wx)]
    3.   (A, DC)
    4. (∃x)-[Lx → (Tx • Wx)]
    5.   4, EI *u
    6.   2, UI
    7. (Lu → Tu)
    8.   5, MI
    9. [--Lu • -(Tu • Wu)]
    10.   9, Si, DN
    11. Tu
    12.   6,10, MP
    13.   11,12, Con
    14.   9, Com, Si
    15.   13,14, Con
    16. (x)[Lx → (Tx • Wx)]

4. 1. (x)[-(Ax → Bx) → -Cx]
    2. (∃x)-Bx ⊢ (∃x)(-Cx v -Ax)
    3.   (A, DC)
    4.   3, QE
    5. -Ba
    6.   4, UI
    7.   1, UI
    8. [Ca → (Aa → Ba)]
    9.   8, Ex
    10. -(Ca • Aa)
    11. (--Ca • --Aa)
    12. (Ca • Aa)
    13.   10,12, Con
    14. (∃x)(-Cx v -Ax)

5.* 1. (x)Fx → (x)Gx   9. (Ha → Fa)
    2. (∃x)-Gx   10. -Ha
    3. (x)(Hx → Fx) ⊢ (∃x)-Hx   11. (x)--Hx
    4. -(∃x)-Hx   12. --Ha
    5. -(x)Gx   13. Ha
    6. -(x)Fx   14. (Ha • -Ha)
    7. (∃x)-Fx   15. (∃x)-Hx
    8. -Fa

6. 1. (x)(Lx → Rx) → (y)(Ty → -Ly)
    2. (∃x)-(Lx → Rx) → [(x)Cx • ((y)Ry • (z)Lz)]
    3. (∃y)-(Ty → Ly) ⊢ (y)Ry
    4. -(y)Ry   (A,DC)
    5.   3, QE
    6. -(x)(Lx → Rx)
    7.   6, QE
    8.   7,3, MP
    9. [((y)Ry • (z)Lz)) • (x)Cx]
    10.   9, As
    11. (y)Ry
    12. (y)Ry • -(y)Ry
    13. (y)Ry   4-12, RAA

C. Show that the following arguments are valid using natural deduction.

1. 1. (x)(Bx → Dx)   2. 1. (x)[Fx → (Sx → Mx)]
    2. (x)(Bx v Bx) ⊢ Dr   2. (x)Sx ⊢ (Mo v -Fo)

3. 1. (x)(Rx → Cx)
   2. -(-La → Ca) ⊢ -Ra

4. 1. (x)(Ox • Wx)
   2. (x)(Ox ↔ -Wx) ⊢ -(x)Wx

5.* 1. (x)[Kx v (Ax • Ix)]
   2. (x)-(Ix v -Ax) ⊢ -(x)-Kx

6. 1. (x)[Gx → (Px → Nx)]
   2. (x)(-Nx • Px) ⊢ -Gc

7. 1. (∃x)(Cx • Fx)
   2. (x)(Kx v -Cx) ⊢ (∃x)(Kx • Fx)

8. 1. (∃x)-Ix
   2. (x)(Gx → Ix) ⊢ (∃x)(-Gx v Hx)

9. 1. (Jc → Pc)
   2. -(∃x)Px ⊢ (∃x)-Jx

10.*1. (x)(Rx v Qx)
   2. (x)[Px v (-Qx • -Rx)] ⊢ (x)Px

11. 1. (∃x)(Fx → Hx) ⊢ (∃x)[(Hx v Lx) v -Fx]

12. 1. (x)-(Sx • -Lx)
   2. (x)(Rx • Sx)
   3. (x)[Lx → (Fx → -Rx)] ⊢ (x)-Fx

13. 1. -(∃x)-(-Ex v -Ax)
   2. (∃x)-(Mx → -Ex) ⊢ (∃x)-(Ax v -Mx)

14. 1. (x)[(Kx v Jx) v -Lx]
   2. (x)[-Mx → -(Nx v Kx)] ⊢ (x)[(-Lx v --Jx) v Mx]

15.*1. (x)[-(Bx → Cx) → -Ax]
   2. (x)[(Ax • Bx) v -(Bx v Ax)]
   3. (x)-(-Cx → -Dx) ⊢ (x)-Ax

16. 1. (x)(Zx v -Tx)
   2. (x)(Tx → Wx) ⊢ (x)[-(Wx • Zx) → -Tx]

17. 1. (x)Rx v (y)Ly
   2. (x)(Ox • Cx)
   3. (x)(Ax → Ox) → -(y)Ly ⊢ (x)Rx

18. 1. (x)(Gx → Ix)
   2. (x)[Gx v (Fx • Nx)]
   3. (x)(Fx → Jx) ⊢ (∃x)[(Lx → Ix) v Jx]

19. 1. (x)(Dx → Ix)
    2. (x)-(Dx → -Mx)
    3. -(∃x)Rx   ⊢ (x)[(Bx • Cx) v (-Rx • Ix)]

20.*1. (x)[-(Ux v Tx) v Xx]
    2. (∃x)(Ux • Dx)   ⊢ (∃x)Xx

D. Rewrite the following sentences using the quantifier exchange rules.

1. Nothing is unexplainable.
2. There is something that is precious.
3. Each thing is corporeal.
4. It is true that there are angels.
5.* Not everything is art.
6. It is false that everything is audible.
7. It is false that nothing is caused.
8. Not all things are humorous.
9. It is false that something is sacred.
10.*Everything is natural.
11. There aren't any unicorns.
12. Somebody murdered the butler.
13. Nobody saw the murder.
14. Everybody left the murder scene.
15.* Not everyone at the inn is innocent.

E. Translate the following arguments into symbolic notation and prove them to be valid using the method of natural deduction. A dictionary is provided.

1. If anyone gives a speech on animal rights at the rally, then someone will speak out in favor of experimentation on animals in medical research. If someone speaks in favor of animal experimentation in medical research, then either Abe will write to the editor of the newspaper, or Bonny will research the subject for her term paper. But Bonny is researching the habitat of wolves in the Yukon Territory for her term paper and not animal experimentation. So, if anyone speaks on animal rights, Abe will write to the editor. [Ax = x gives a speech on animal rights at the rally; a = Abe; b = Bonny; Ex = x speaks in favor of experimentation. . .; Tx = x researches the topic of experimentation on animals in medical research for a term paper; Wx = x writes to the newspaper editor; Yx = x is researching wolves' habitats in the Yukon]

2. Anybody who believes in the death penalty is guilty of a contradiction, from which it follows that if everybody believed in the death penalty, then everybody would be guilty of a contradiction. [Bx = x believes in the death penalty; Gx = x is guilty of a contradiction]

3. Combinations of atoms exist. Either everything is a combination of atoms or everything is a combination of monads. No combinations of atoms are combina-

tions of monads. Therefore, everything is a combination of atoms. [Ax = x is a combination of atoms; Mx = x is a combination of monads]

4. Everything is genetically controlled if and only if nothing is affected by its environment. So, either something is affected by its environment or everything is genetically controlled. [Ex = x is affected by its environment; Gx = x is genetically controlled]

5.* If Cory successfully evades paying his taxes this year, he will have enough money to buy the sailboat he's been wanting. If he gets that much money, he will surely contribute to the March of Dimes. Hence, if Cory successfully evades his taxes, then someone will contribute to the March of Dimes. [c = Cory; Ex = x successfully evades paying taxes; Mx = x contributes to the March of Dimes; Sx = x has enough money to buy the sailboat]

6. Some people aren't very good at handling money matters, but all Certified Public Accountants (CPA) are good at handling money matters. If any person isn't very good at handling money matters, then that person should hire a CPA. And whoever is good at handling money matters should offer her/his services to welfare recipients. So, some CPA's should offer their services to welfare recipients. [Cx = x is a CPA; Gx = x is good at handling money matters; Hx = x should hire a CPA; Ox = x should offer her/his services to welfare recipients; Px = x is a person]

7. Anyone who is thought of as dull either listens only to classical music or drinks nothing but sherry. Anyone who is thought of as hip either enjoys the Grateful Dead or drinks beer. Since everyone is thought of as either dull or hip, it follows that everyone either listens only to classical music or drinks sherry or enjoys the Grateful Dead or drinks beer. [Bx = x drinks beer; Dx = x is thought of as dull; Gx = x enjoys the Grateful Dead; Hx = x is thought of as hip; Lx = x listens only to classical music; Sx = x drinks nothing but sherry]

8. Every rapist is mentally ill and every sexist is ignorant, from which it follows that if everyone who is mentally ill is sexist, then every rapist is ignorant. [Ix = x is ignorant; Mx = x is mentally ill; Rx = x is a rapist; Sx = x is sexist]

9. Some people have been killed by bears. A bear will only kill a person if the bear feels threatened or is hungry. Bears never feel threatened, but they are always hungry. We can conclude that there are hungry bears. [Bx = x is a bear; Hx = x is hungry; Kx = x was killed by a bear; Px = x is a person; Tx = x feels threatened]

10.* The location of the lowest point in the continental United States is in Death Valley. The location of the highest point in the continental United States is on Mt. Whitney. Neither Death Valley nor Mt. Whitney is at sea level. Hence, neither the lowest nor the highest points is at sea level. [Dx = x is in Death Valley; Hx = x is the location of the highest point in the continental United States; Lx = x is the location of the lowest point in the continental United States; Mx = x is on Mt. Whitney; Sx = x is at sea level]

8.4. Truth Trees

Just as proofs in natural deduction can be worked in predicate logic, so too truth tree proofs are possible. Recall that one of the favorable aspects of truth trees in sentential logic is that one can show valid arguments to be valid *and* invalid arguments to be invalid whereas with natural deduction one cannot show invalid arguments to be invalid. This feature is retained with trees in predicate logic as well, except that now we will see that some invalid arguments yield *infinite trees*. An infinite tree is a tree that will never close, no matter how many different instantiations one performs.

The other aspect that was favored in trees over natural deduction is that the former are said to be mechanical. This, largely, is also retained, though there will be times when creativity will serve one very well when doing trees in predicate logic. This creativity will be needed when selecting individual constants in instantiations. More on this later.

The method of truth trees is the same in predicate logic as in sentential logic. That is, one sets up the argument in the same fashion, including the denial of the conclusion. The difference in procedure comes when there are quantified sentences in the argument. Then, at some point, one must instantiate with respect to the variables. Let's take a simple argument:

$$(x)(Px \rightarrow Qx)$$
$$-Qi \quad \vdash \quad (Pi \rightarrow Ri)$$

Now the first premise in this argument is not a conditional. Rather, it is a universal quantification. The primary logical symbol is the quantifier, which means that *Universal Instantiation* ("UI" in natural deduction) is the only rule one could apply here. The truth tree rule for UI, in schematic form, is:

$$(f)Af$$

$$A\alpha$$

where 'f' is any variable and 'α' is any individual constant. In English, we express this as follows: If a universal quantification falls on a branch of a tree, choose an individual constant, replace each occurrence of the variable with that constant, and write the sentence on the same branch. In this way, we can derive the following instantiations (among others):

$(x)Cx$	$(x)-Cx$	$(x)(Cx \lor Dx)$	$(x)[Cx \cdot (-Dx \leftrightarrow Ex)]$
Ca	$-Cf$	$(Cg \lor Dg)$	$[Cs \cdot (-Ds \leftrightarrow Es)]$

It is important to understand that, even though there is no justification line in truth trees, as there is in Natural Deduction, in trees each sentence that can be checked must be checked and numbered unless the branch on which the sentence appears closes without the sentence being checked. That is, if a branch closes and there remains any sentence unchecked that can be checked on that branch, the branch closing forestalls checking and numbering said sentence. So, the rule for checking and numbering of sentences applies to universal quantifications as much as to any other formula, whether it be a conditional, a disjunction, or whatever.

Again, trees in predicate logic work on the *reductio* method and it is imperative that one deny the conclusion. You may elect to deny the conclusion at any stage when doing a tree, generally. However, standard practice has it that it is the first "move" in constructing the tree.

Regarding the first argument in this section, the following tree shows it to be valid, as all branches close when the conclusion was denied.

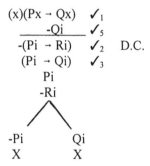

$(x)(Px \rightarrow Qx)$ ✓₁
$-Qi$ ✓₅
$-(Pi \rightarrow Ri)$ ✓₂ D.C.
$(Pi \rightarrow Qi)$ ✓₃
Pi
$-Ri$

$-Pi$ Qi
X   X

As we know, the first premise in this argument is known as a universal quantification. The rule for universal instantiation is applied to it directly after the denial of the conclusion. It would be well to understand why 'i' was chosen. If any other constant were chosen, say 'a,' the requisite contradictions would not be found, because 'i' is the individual constant found in both the second premise as well as the conclusion. Note that the first premise has been checked and numbered. All branches close; valid argument.

This is our first clue that truth trees in predicate logic are not wholly mechanical. That choosing 'i' was necessary to show the argument to be valid indicates that one cannot simply appeal to knowledge of the truth tree rules when constructing a tree. One must also use a certain amount of forward-looking creativity in judging how to construct the tree.

$(x)(Ix \rightarrow -Kx)$ ✓₃
$(x)(Kx \lor -Ex)$ ✓₄
$(x)Ix$ ✓₅
$--(x)Ex$ ✓₁ D.C.
$(x)Ex$ ✓₂
Ea
$(Ia \rightarrow -Ka)$ ✓₆

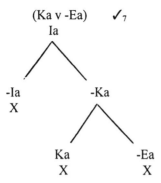

In the argument above, since the denied conclusion is a doubly negated universal quantification, the only truth tree rule that can be applied to it is the rule for double negation. When Double Negation has been applied, only then can the truth tree rule for universal instantiation be applied, as was done and indicated by "✓2."

The instantiation rules carry over from natural deduction to truth trees; quantifier exchange rules also carry over. Every quantifier exchange is checked and numbered in a truth tree.

$$-(\exists x)(Ax \lor Jx) \qquad ✓_1$$
$$\underline{(x)\text{-}Sx \to Jx)} \qquad ✓_2$$
$$-Sa \qquad \text{D.C.}$$
$$(x)\text{-}(Ax \lor Jx) \qquad ✓_3$$
$$(-Sa \to Ja) \qquad ✓_5$$
$$-(Aa \lor Ja) \qquad ✓_4$$
$$-Aa$$
$$-Ja$$

```
        /\
       /  \
    --Sa    Ja
     X      X
```

The first rule applied to a sentence in the above tree is a quantifier exchange, where "-(∃x)(Ax v Jx)' becomes "(x)-(Ax v Jx)." Though it is not necessary that this be the first step in the tree, it is a necessary step, as no rule other than quantifier exchange can be applied to the first premise.

The truth tree rule for *Existential Instantiation* can be presented in a schematic form as follows:

$$(\exists f)Af$$
$$\text{-------}$$
$$A\beta$$

where 'f' is any variable and where 'β' is any individual constant not appearing in any sentence prior to the instantiation. The schematic form of the rule is deceptive because it fails to take into account the condition that the individual constant one chooses cannot have appeared in any line of the tree prior to the existential instantiation itself (this proviso is unique to existential instantiation). It is very important to keep this in mind and, hence, as in natural deduction, we adopt the practice of "flagging" with an asterisk each and every existential instantiation, indicating the constant one has chosen. To prevent infinite trees, we will adopt the rule that an existential quantification be checked and numbered at most once. The following six examples will suffice to demonstrate these features.

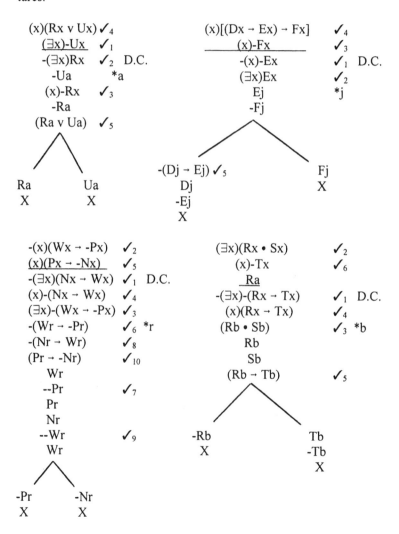

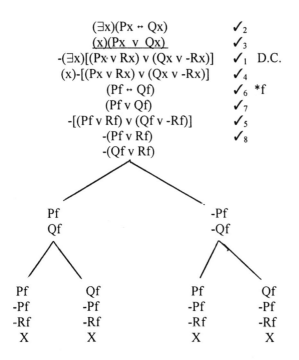

$$(\exists x)(Px \leftrightarrow Qx) \qquad \checkmark_2$$
$$\underline{(x)(Px \lor Qx)} \qquad \checkmark_3$$
$$-(\exists x)[(Px \lor Rx) \lor (Qx \lor -Rx)] \qquad \checkmark_1 \quad D.C.$$
$$(x)-[(Px \lor Rx) \lor (Qx \lor -Rx)] \qquad \checkmark_4$$
$$(Pf \leftrightarrow Qf) \qquad \checkmark_6 \ {}^*f$$
$$(Pf \lor Qf) \qquad \checkmark_7$$
$$-[(Pf \lor Rf) \lor (Qf \lor -Rf)] \qquad \checkmark_5$$
$$-(Pf \lor Rf) \qquad \checkmark_8$$
$$-(Qf \lor Rf)$$

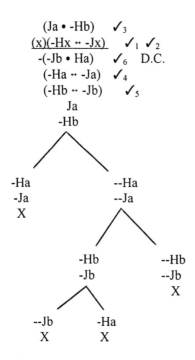

$$(Ja \bullet -Hb) \qquad \checkmark_3$$
$$\underline{(x)(-Hx \leftrightarrow -Jx)} \qquad \checkmark_1 \ \checkmark_2$$
$$-(-Jb \bullet Ha) \qquad \checkmark_6 \quad D.C.$$
$$(-Ha \leftrightarrow -Ja) \qquad \checkmark_4$$
$$(-Hb \leftrightarrow -Jb) \qquad \checkmark_5$$
$$Ja$$
$$-Hb$$

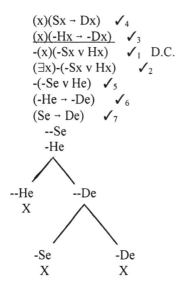

$(x)(Sx \rightarrow Dx)$ ✓₄
$(x)(-Hx \rightarrow -Dx)$ ✓₃
$-(x)(-Sx \lor Hx)$ ✓₁   D.C.
$(\exists x)-(-Sx \lor Hx)$ ✓₂
$-(-Se \lor He)$ ✓₅
$(-He \rightarrow -De)$ ✓₆
$(Se \rightarrow De)$ ✓₇
--Se
-He

--He   --De
X

-Se   -De
X   X

At this point we can introduce rather more complicated arguments. Consider the following argument, and especially the third premise, which is a conditional in which both antecedent and consequent are existential quantifications.

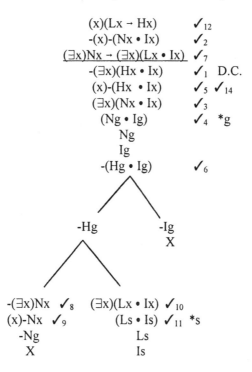

$(x)(Lx \rightarrow Hx)$ ✓₁₂
$-(x)-(Nx \cdot Ix)$ ✓₂
$(\exists x)Nx \rightarrow (\exists x)(Lx \cdot Ix)$ ✓₇
$-(\exists x)(Hx \cdot Ix)$ ✓₁   D.C.
$(x)-(Hx \cdot Ix)$ ✓₅ ✓₁₄
$(\exists x)(Nx \cdot Ix)$ ✓₃
$(Ng \cdot Ig)$ ✓₄   *g
Ng
Ig
$-(Hg \cdot Ig)$ ✓₆

-Hg   -Ig
           X

$-(\exists x)Nx$ ✓₈ $(\exists x)(Lx \cdot Ix)$ ✓₁₀
$(x)-Nx$ ✓₉ $(Ls \cdot Is)$ ✓₁₁ *s
-Ng   Ls
X   Is

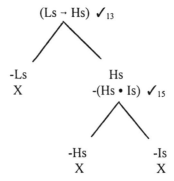

Notice again that the third premise is a conditional and hence that only the rule for the conditional can apply to it. When the rule *is* applied to it, the antecedent, '$(\exists x)Nx$,' is negated while the consequent is not. This is just as it should be on the truth tree rule for conditionals. When the rule has been applied to the third premise, the result is the appearance of two quantified sentences on two different branches. The quantified sentences are then treated as quantifications and only the rules for quantified sentences apply to them.

Also, you will see that one sentence has been checked twice. This is a major departure from truth trees in sentential logic where it was never necessary to check a sentence more than once. While it was not necessary to check the sentence twice, it serves as a good example for it being legitimate to do so. Recall that this is not allowed for existential quantifications.

One must take care to indicate, for every existential instantiation, which individual constant one has chosen. The two asterisks in the tree above show which constants were chosen at which junctures. Also note that "flagging" of the constants takes place on the sentence that is derived from the instantiation, not on the original sentence. This is merely a convention, and one we shall adopt here.

Further examples of trees are below.

$$\underline{(x)\text{-}(Mx \rightarrow \text{-}Tx)} \quad \checkmark_3$$
$$\text{-}(x)Tx \quad\quad\quad\; \checkmark_1 \quad \text{D.C.}$$
$$(\exists x)\text{-}Tx \quad\quad\; \checkmark_2$$
$$\text{-}To \quad\quad\quad\quad *o$$
$$\text{-}(Mo \rightarrow \text{-}To) \quad \checkmark_4$$
$$Mo$$
$$\text{--}To$$
$$X$$

Note here that '--To' has not been checked, though it could be. The reason for this is that '-To' contradicts '--To' and there is no need to extend the branch of the tree since it closes right there.

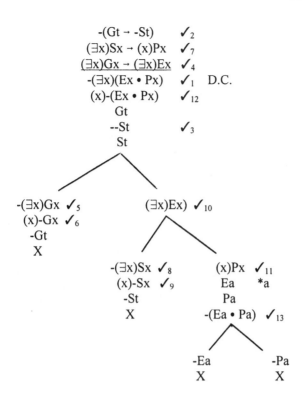

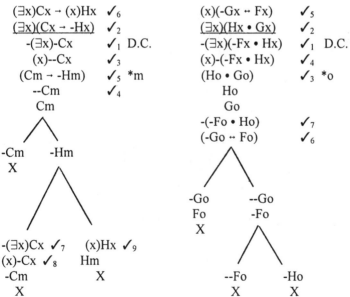

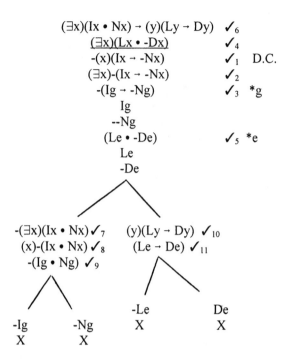

So far we have dealt only with valid arguments. It is time to consider the other side of the validity coin, i.e., invalid arguments. As an example, we can use what knowledge we have of inferences to see that '(x)(-Rx v -Bx)' does not follow from '(x)(Rx • Bx).' Letting 'Rx' = 'x is a raven' and 'Bx' = 'x is black,' we would have the following argument: "All ravens are black. Therefore, everything is either a non-raven or is not black." In the tree directly below, we see that the branch does not close after each of the sentences that can be checked has been checked. The problem is that it is always possible to instantiate with respect to another letter, say, 'b.' Though it is logically possible to use existential instantiation more than once on any existential quantification, if we were to do so, there would be no end to the tree we could construct; that is, we would have an infinite tree. To make the method of truth trees in predicate logic more mechanical, we adopt the convention of checking existential quantifications at most once. This violates no logical principle and gives more ease of proof.

$$\underline{(x)(Rx \cdot Bx)} \qquad \checkmark_6$$
$$-(x)(-Rx \ v \ -Bx) \qquad \checkmark_1 \quad \text{D.C.}$$
$$(\exists x)-(-Rx \ v \ -Bx) \qquad \checkmark_2$$
$$-(-Ra \ v \ -Ba) \qquad \checkmark_3 \quad *a$$
$$--Ra \qquad \checkmark_4$$
$$--Ba \qquad \checkmark_5$$
$$Ra$$
$$Ba$$

(Ra • Ba)   ✓₇
Ra
Ba
O

Recall that the ring located at the bottom of the branch indicates that no contradiction was found on that branch, and hence, that it is possible that the premises are true and the conclusion false. It is crucial all sentences that can be checked are checked prior to writing the ring. This is part of the rigor and completeness of the system we have adopted.

Respecting the above tree, if we were to instantiate with respect to 'b' in the above tree, we would still have at least one branch open; if 'c' were used, at least one branch would remain open, and so on. Hence, we judge the argument to be invalid.

On the following page is another tree for your consideration, showing that the argument is not valid:

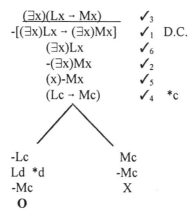

Note here that since 'c' has been used to instantiate the premise, 'c' cannot again be used for the instantiation on '(∃x)Lx.' Hence, some other constant must be chosen to instantiate with on the other existential quantification. Given that, we will be unable to close at least one of the branches. Precisely this occurs when 'd' is chosen at '✓6' leading to the left-hand branch remaining open. It should be clear that no matter which individual constant one chooses here, other than 'c,' the branch will remain open. Hence, the argument is invalid. Each of the following three truth trees is invalid:

(x)(Fx → Gx)   ✓₅
(∃x)Fx   ✓₄
-(x)(-Gx v Hx)   ✓₁   D.C.
(∃x)-(-Gx v Hx)   ✓₂
-(-Gw v Hw)   ✓₃   *w

--Gw
-Hw
Fn   *n
(Fn → Gn)   ✓₆

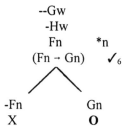

-Fn   Gn
X   **O**

(x)[Jx → (Tx v -Ox)] ✓₆
(x)[Hx v -(Ox → Tx)] ✓₅
(x)(-Hx → Kx) ✓₄
-(x)(Jx → Kx) ✓₁ D.C.
(∃x)-(Jx → Kx) ✓₂
-(Jd → Kd) ✓₃ *d
Jd
-Kd
(-Hd → Kd) ✓₈
[Hd v -(Od → Td)] ✓₉
[Jd → (Td v -Od)] ✓₇

-Jd   (Td v -Od) ✓₁₁
X

--Hd ✓₁₂   Kd
                   X

Hd   -(Od →Td) ✓₁₀
              Od
             -Td

Td   -Od
Hd   Hd
O   O   Td   -Od
                 X   X

$(x)Lx \cdot Li)$ ✓₁
$-[-(Rb \lor Br) \lor Lw])$ ✓₂   D.C.
$(x)Lx$ ✓₃
Li
$--(Rb \lor Br)$
$-Lw$
Lw
X

$(x)[-Sx \rightarrow (\exists y)(Ry \rightarrow Bx)]$ ✓₂
$(z)(-Rz \lor Sz)$ ✓₇
$-(\exists y)Sy$ ✓₁   D.C.
$(y)-Sy$ ✓₄
$[-Sa \rightarrow (\exists y)(Ry \rightarrow Ba)]$ ✓₃

$--Sa$ $(\exists y)-(Ry \rightarrow Ba)$ ✓₅
$-Sa$ $-Sa$
X $-(Rb \rightarrow Ba)$ ✓₆ *b
         Rb
         $-Ba$
         $(-Rb \lor -Sb)$ ✓₈

$-Rb$ $-Sb$
X   O

Exercise: Ch. 8, Sect. 8.4.

A. Determine which of the following arguments are valid and which are invalid using the method of truth trees.

1. $(\exists x)Cx \rightarrow (y)Cy$
   $(\exists x)(Cx \lor Hx)$
   $(\exists x)Hx$

2. $(x)(Ax \rightarrow Bx)$
   $(x)(-Cx \rightarrow -Bx)$
   $(x)(Cx \lor -Ax)$

3. $(x)[Rx \rightarrow (Sx \cdot Tx)]$
   $(x)(Rx \leftrightarrow Tx)$
   $(x)Sx$

4. $(x)Fx \lor (x)-Dx$
   $(Ds \rightarrow Ls)$
   $(x)(Lx \rightarrow -Fx)$

5.* $(\exists x)Wx \leftrightarrow (\exists x)Px$

6. $-[(\exists x)Hx \cdot (x)Jx]$

(∃x)(Wx → Px)

-(x)Jx → Cg
(x)(Cx → -Hx)
(∃x)-Hx

7. (x)[(Dx → Fx) v (Lx • -Fx)]
    (x)(-Fx → Lx)
    (x)(Dx • -Fx)
    -(x)(Lx • Ox)

8. (x)(Mx • Kx) → (∃y)Zy
    (x)-(-Kx v Zx)
    (∃x)(-Zx → -Mx)

9. (x)[Ax ↔ (Sx ↔ Ix)]
    (x)[(Sx ↔ Qx) ↔ -Vx]
    (∃x)Ax v (∃x)-Sx

10.*(∃x)Kx ↔ -(∃y)-Ky
    (x)Kx → (∃y)Ky
    (x)(Ax → -Kx)
    -(x)Kx

11. (x)[Rx v Ex) v Jx]
    (x)[Ex → (Gx ↔ -Lx)]
    (∃x)Rx → (∃x)Ex

12. (∃x)Px → -(∃y)-Hy
    (x)Jx v -(∃y)-Hy
    (x)(Hx • Px)
    (x)(Px • Jx)

13. (x)(-Tx → Mx)
    (x)Tx v Me
    (Me v -Te)

14. (∃x)Cx
    (x)(Cx → Gx)
    (x)[Cx → Gx) → Cx]

15.*(x)(Fx → Wx) v (∃x)Kx
    -(x)-(Wx v -Kx)
    -(x)-(Wx v Fx)

B. Translate the following arguments into symbolic notation. Then, determine whether each is valid using a truth tree.

1. If all theories are falsifiable, then Newton's theory is. If the correct theory is falsifiable, then Einstein's theory is. All theories are either correct or not falsifiable. Hence, either Newton's or Einstein's theory is falsifiable. [Cx = x is correct; Fx = x is falsifiable; Tx = x is a theory; e = Einstein's theory; n = Newton's theory]

2. Most, but not all, things are carbon based. Whatever is carbon based has a genetic code. There is nothing with a genetic code that is immortal. It follows that most things are not immortal. [Cx = x is carbon based; Gx = x has a genetic code; Mx = x is mortal]

3. Nothing is both a vampire and a saint, though there are saints who were killed by fire. It follows from these points that there existed a being who was not a vampire but was killed by fire. [Fx = x was killed by fire; Sx = x is a saint; Vx = x is a vampire]

4. If anybody has knowledge, then skepticism is false. Skepticism is false if, and only if, inductive inferences are acceptable. Inductive inferences being acceptable implies that somebody's having knowledge implies, and is implied by, skepticism being false. So, everyone has knowledge. [Ax = x is acceptable; Fx = x is false; Kx = x has knowledge; i = inductive inferences; s = skepticism]

5.* No sentence is both logically true as well as logically false. Any sentence that is logically true is also actually true. There are no actually true sentences that are meaningless. Hence, logically false sentences that are meaningful don't exist. [Ax = x is actually true; Lx = x is logically true; Mx = x is meaningful; Sx = x is a sentence]

C. Any argument appearing in the section on Natural Deduction may be treated with truth trees. You know that the arguments in that section are all valid, but it would still be excellent practice to construct trees using those arguments. Another way to practice is to create original arguments yourself, translate them into symbolic notation, and construct trees.

8.5. Relations

Up to this point we have considered only one-place predicates, represented with one predicate and one individual constant, such as 'Aa.' We now introduce two-place predicates, represented with one predicate and two individual constants, e.g., 'Aab.' A two-place predicate represents a relation between two individuals and is called a *Binary Relation*. An example of this is: "Galileo lived after Aristotle," translated as 'Lga.' (A *Ternary Relation* involves a three-place predicate, such as "Leon borrowed a pen from Jim.") Consider the relation "admires." If we want to say that Byron admires Clarice, we might stipulate the following dictionary: 'Axy' = 'x admires y'; 'b' = 'Byron'; 'c' = 'Clarice.' We would then represent the sentence "Byron admires Clarice" as "Abc." Simple enough. But if we want to represent the sentence "Everybody admires somebody," we need to add quantifiers to represent 'everybody' and 'somebody.' We can reword the sentence to say, "No matter what x is, there is a y such that x admires y." The translation is "(x)(∃y)Axy." "Everybody admires everybody" would be translated as "(x)(y)Axy." 'Byron admires everyone' would be translated as '(x)Abx.' Below are some of the many binary relations that can be represented in predicate logic:

loves	respects	cares for
sympathizes with	is the mother of	is greater than
is next to	is to the left of	is between
has the same color eyes as	is as tall as	is shorter than
wants to go out with	batted against	is angry at
took a class from	is a sister of	is bored by
believes in	fears	is jealous of

The translation dictionary will again prove essential to the adequate representation of sentences in symbolic notation. Take, for example, the sentence "All logicians are feared by their students," where 'Lx' = 'x is a logician'; 'Sxy' = 'x is a student of y'; 'Fxy' = 'x fears y.' We can translate the sentence as follows: (x)(y)[(Lx • Syx) → Fyx].

Another important concept to understand is that of a *Domain* (also known as the "Universe of Discourse"). A domain is a class of things or objects over which quantifiers and variables range. Another way to put it is to say that a domain is the class of things one is talking about in any given sentence. Up to this point, our domain has been everything. Sometimes, however, we will want to specify a domain smaller than the class of everything. Take the sentence "All Protestant Republicans fear God" [Fxy = x fears y; Px = x is a Protestant; Rx = x is a Republican; g = God]. If our domain is everything, the translation would be: (x)[(Px • Rx) → Fxg]. If, on the other hand, our domain is Republicans, the translation would be cut down to (x)(Px → Fxg); if our domain is Protestant Republicans, we get (x)Fxg. In what follows, unless otherwise specified, our domain will be everything. It is proper to express a domain within braces, as follows: {People}, which can be read as "the class of people." We will henceforth abbreviate 'domain' with 'Dom' and 'dictionary' with 'Dict.' Examples of translations with relations follow.

[Dom: {People}; Dict: d = Don; k = Karen; s = Sam; Wxy = x wrote y a letter]

Sam wrote a letter to Karen.	Wsk
Sam wrote letters to Karen and Don.	(Wsk • Wsd)
Someone wrote Karen a letter.	(∃x)Wxk
Karen wrote a letter to somebody.	(∃x)Wkx
Don wrote a letter to everyone.	(x)Wdx
Don wrote a letter to himself.	Wdd

[Dom: {People}; Dict: m = Mary; Lx = x looks tall; Rxy = x looks taller than y; Sxy = x stands next to y; Txy = x is taller than y]

Everyone is taller than Mary.	(x)Txm
Nothing is taller than itself.	-(∃x)Txx
No one is taller than everyone.	-(∃x)(y)Txy
Anyone who stands next to Mary looks tall.	(x)(Sxm → Lx)
Whoever looks taller than Mary is taller than Mary.	(x)(Rxm → Txm)

[Dom: {People}; Dict: Fxy = x is a friend to y (let 'Fxy' also be translated as 'x and y are friends'); Cx = x is drunk; Dx = x is a drunk; Exy = x envies y; Lxy = x lets y drive; Oxy = x is y's lover; Rxy = x respects y; Uxy = x understands y]

Everybody is somebody's friend.	(x)(∃y)Fxy
Friendship implies respect.	(x)(y)(Fxy → Rxy)

Friendship does not imply envy.	(x)(y)-(Fxy → Exy)
Some friends are lovers.	(∃x)(∃y)(Fxy • Oxy)
Friends don't let friends drive drunk.	(x)(y)[Fxy → (Cy → -Lxy)]
Only a drunk understands a drunk.	(x)(y)[Dx → (Uyx → Dy)]

[Dom: {Numbers}; Dict: a = two; b = ten; Ex = x is even; Dxy = x is divisible by y; Ixy = x is identical to y; Ox = x is odd; Px = x is prime]

Two is prime but ten is not.	(Pa • -Pb)
Two and ten are both even.	(Ea • Eb)
If two is even, so is ten.	(Ea → Eb)
If ten is divisible by 2, then ten is even.	(Dba → Eb)
Two is divisible by itself	Daa
Two is not divisible by ten.	-Dab
Every even number is divisible by two.	(x)(Ex → Dxa)
No odd number is even.	-(∃x)(Ox • Ex)
All even numbers are self-identical.	(x)(Ex → Ixx)
No prime is divisible by two.	-(∃x)(Px • Dxa)
No even number is prime.	-(∃x)(Ex • Px)
No number is both prime and non-prime.	-(∃x)(Px • -Px)
Two is the only even prime.	{(Ea • Pa) • (x)[(Ex • Px) → Ixa]}
There is just one even prime.	(∃x){(Ex • Px) • (y)[(Ey • Py) → Iyx]}

[Dom: {People}; Dict: Ax = x is an argument; a = Aristotle; Ex = x is acceptable; f = Frege; g = Gödel; Lx = x is a logician; q = Quine; Rxy = x respects y; r = Russell]

All logicians respect acceptable arguments.	(x){Lx → (y)[(Ay • Ey) → Rxy]}
Only logicians respect logicians.	(x)(y)[(Lx • Ryx) → Ly]
Some logicians don't respect anyone.	(∃x)(y)(Lx • -Rxy)

Every logician respects either Aristotle and Gödel, or Russell, Frege & Quine.
  (x){Lx → (Rxa • Rxg) v [Rxr • (Rxf • Rxq)]}

[Dom: {Sentences}; Dict: Ax = x is an argument; Cx = x is a conditional; c(xy) = the conjunction of x and y; Dx = x is a disjunction; d(xy) = the disjunction of x and y; Ex = x is acceptable; Ixy = x implies y; Sx = x is consistent; Tx = x is true]

An inconsistent sentence implies every sentence.	(x)(-Sx → (y)Ixy)
True sentences imply only true sentences.	(x)[Tx → (y)(Ixy → Ty)]
Each conditional implies some disjunction.	(x)[Cx → (∃y)(Dy • Ixy)]

The conjunction of any two true sentences is itself a true sentence.
  (x)(y)[(Tx • Ty) → Tc(xy)]
Sentences that imply one another imply exactly the same sentences.

$(x)(y)[(Ixy \cdot Iyx) \rightarrow (z)(Ixz \leftrightarrow Iyz)]$

Disjunctions are true only if one or both disjuncts are true.

$(x)(y)\{Td(xy) \rightarrow [(Tx \text{ v } Ty) \text{ v } (Tx \cdot Ty)]\}$

No false sentence implies, nor is implied by, any true sentence.

$(x)(y)[(-Tx \cdot Ty) \rightarrow (-Ixy \cdot -Iyx)]$

8.5.1. Relations: Natural Deduction

The methods of truth trees and natural deduction may be applied to relational arguments in predicate logic. All of the rules previously in force for those two systems remain in force here. Some examples will help.

1.	$(x)-Hxa$	
2.	$(x)(Fx \rightarrow (\exists y)Gyx)$	
3.	$(x)(-Gxa \text{ v } Hxa) \quad \vdash$	$-Fa$
4.	Fa	(A,DC)
5.	$(Fa \rightarrow (\exists y)Gya)$	2, UI
6.	$(\exists y)Gya$	4,5, MP
7.	Gba	6, EI *b
8.	$(-Gba \text{ v } Hba)$	2, UI
9.	$(Gba \rightarrow Hba)$	8, MI
10.	Hba	7,9, MP
11.	$-Hba$	1, UI
12.	$(Hba \cdot -Hba)$	10,11, Con
13.	$-Fa$	4-12, RAA

This is a fairly straight forward proof. Note that instead of writing '--Fa' as the denial of the conclusion, 'Fa' was written. Also note the flagging of 'b' in line 7. Since 'a' appears prior to the EI in 7, some letter besides 'a' had to be chosen. The following example is a bit more complicated.

1.	$(x)-Axx$	
2.	$(x)(y)(z)[(Axy \cdot Ayz) \rightarrow Axz] \quad \vdash$	$(x)(y)(Axy \rightarrow -Ayx)$
3.	$-(x)(y)(Axy \rightarrow -Ayx)$	(A, DC)
4.	$(\exists x)-(y)(Axy \rightarrow -Ayx)$	3, QE
5.	$-(y)(Aay \rightarrow -Aya)$	4, EI *a
6.	$(\exists y)-(Aay \rightarrow -Aya)$	5, QE
7.	$-(Aab \rightarrow -Aba)$	6, EI *b
8.	$-(-Aab \text{ v } -Aba)$	7, MI
9.	$(--Aab \cdot --Aba)$	8, DM
10.	$(Aab \cdot Aba)$	9, DN, DN
11.	$(y)(z)[(Aay \cdot Ayz) \rightarrow Aaz]$	2, UI
12.	$(z)[(Aab \cdot Abz) \rightarrow Aaz]$	11, UI
13.	$[(Aab \cdot Aba) \rightarrow Aaa]$	12, UI

14. Aaa	10,13, MP
15. -Aaa	1, UI
16. (Aaa • -Aaa)	14,15, Con
17. (x)(y)(Axy → -Ayx)	3-16, RAA

Some crucial points in the above proof are the following: (A) the existential instantiations in lines 5 and 7 are flagged, it being impossible to existentially instantiate with respect to 'a' in line 7 since 'a' appears in a prior line in the proof; (B) the quantifier exchanges in lines 3 and 5 were necessary before the existential instantiations in 5 and 7, because 3 and 5 are negative quantifications whereas 5 and 7 are quantifications; (C) the universal instantiations in lines 11, 12, and 13 are as they are to be able to apply *modus ponens* in line 14 and then the conjunction in line 16.

1.	(x)(y)(Lxy → Axy)	Instead of simply using
2.	(x)(y)[Axy → (Lxy → Cxy)]	a series of *modus ponens*
3.	(x)(y)Lxy ⊢ (x)(y)Cxy	in this proof, I chose to use
4.	-(x)(y)Cxy (A, DC)	Exportation and a few other
5.	(∃x)-(y)Cxy 4, QE	rules. It makes it a little more
6.	-(y)Cfy 5, EI *f	interesting and it is good practice.
7.	(∃y)-Cfy 6, QE	You might try doing this proof
8.	-Cfk 7, EI *k	using a third set of rules. Does it
9.	(y)(Lfy → Afy) 1, UI	turn out shorter?
10.	(Lfk → Afk) 9, UI	
11.	(y)[Afy → (Lfy → Cfy)] 2, UI	
12.	[Afk → (Lfk → Cfk)] 11, UI	
13.	[(Afk • Lfk) → Cfk] 12, Ex	
14.	-(Afk • Lfk) 8,13, MT	
15.	(-Afk v -Lfk) 14, DM	
16.	(-Lfk v -Afk) 15, Com	
17.	(y)Lfy 3, UI	
18.	Lfk 17, UI	
19.	--Lfk 18, DN	
20.	-Afk 16,19, DS	
21.	Afk 10,18, MP	
22.	(Afk • -Afk) 20,21, Con	
23.	(x)(y)Cxy 4-22, RAA	

1.	(∃x)[(y)(Cy → Wxy) • Mx] ⊢ (∃x)[(-Cn v Wxn) • Mx]	
2.	-(∃x)[(-Cn v Wxn) • Mx]	(A, DC)
3.	(x)-[(-Cn v Wxn) • Mx]	2, QE
4.	[(y)(Cy → Wry) • Mr]	1, EI *r
5.	-[(-Cn v Wrn) • Mr]	3, UI
6.	[-(-Cn v Wrn) v -Mr]	5, DM

7.	(--Cn • -Wrn) v -Mr]	6, DM
8.	[(Cn → Wrn) • Mr]	4, UI
9.	Mr	8, Com, Si
10.	--Mr	9, DN
11.	[-Mr v (--Cn • -Wrn)]	7, Com
12.	(--Cn • -Wrn)	10,11, DS
13.	Cn	12, Si, DN
14.	(Cn → Wrn)	8, Si
15.	Wrn	13,14, MP
16.	-Wrn	12, Com, Si
17.	(Wrn • -Wrn)	15,16, Con
18.	(∃x)[(Cn → Wxn) • Mx]	2-17, RAA

Exercise: Ch. 8, Sect. 8.5.1.

A. Translate the following sentences into symbolic notation, constructing your own domains and dictionaries.

1. Not everybody is afraid of the snakes, but Jeremy sure is.
2. Everyone admired Socrates, and Plato revered him.
3. If Strawson thought Russell was wrong, he didn't admire him.
4. Moore admired Russell only if both Wittgenstein and Ryle did.
5.* Somebody admires everybody; however, nobody is admired by everybody.
6. If any psychologist admired and respected Freud, then somebody thought Freud wasn't a madman.
7. All of Freud's patients feared, but loved, him.
8. If any judge believed Degas, he wouldn't have gone to Devil's Island.
9. If the skeptic is right, then no one is certain of anything.
10.*The tallest person in the world can see further than anybody.

B. Show the following arguments to be valid using the method of natural deduction.

1. 1. -(x)(y)-(-Tx → -Sxy)
    2. (x)(y)Sxy   ⊢   (∃x)Tx

2. 1. -(x)(∃y)(Uxy v Oxy)   ⊢   (∃x)-Oxx

3. 1. (x)(y)(∃z)-(-Nyx → Nxz)
    2. (∃x)(y)(Nxy ↔ Nyx)   ⊢   (∃x)-(y)Nxy

4. 1. (x)(y)Gxy → (x)(∃y)Hxy
    2. (x)Hx • (∃x)(y)-Hxy   ⊢   -(x)(y)Gxy

5.* 1. $(\exists x)(\exists y)Fxy$ $\vdash$ $(\exists x)(\exists y)Fyx$

6. 1. $(x)(y)(z)[(Cxy \cdot Cyz) \rightarrow Cxz]$
   2. $-(\exists x)Cxx$ $\vdash$ $(x)(y)(-Cxy \lor -Cyx)$

7. 1. $(x)(Exx \rightarrow M)$ $\vdash$ $(-M \rightarrow -(\exists x)Exx)$

8. 1. $(x)Wxx \rightarrow (\exists y)Qyy$
   2. $(x)Wxx \rightarrow -(\exists y)Qyy$ $\vdash$ $(x)-Wxx$

9. 1. $(x)(-Srx \lor Rxs)$
   2. $-(\exists x)Rxs \lor (\exists y)Rsy$ $\vdash$ $-(\exists x)Srx \lor (\exists y)Rsy$

10.*1. $(x)-Pxx$
   2. $(x)(y)(z)[(Pxy \rightarrow -Pyz) \rightarrow Pxz]$
   3. $(x)(y)(Pxy \rightarrow Pyx)$ $\vdash$ $(x)(y)-[Pxy \rightarrow (z)(Pzx \rightarrow Pzy)]$

C. Translate the following arguments into symbolic notation and prove them to be valid using the method of natural deduction.

1. Every mountaineer is either crazy or unafraid. If a mountaineer is crazy, then that person shouldn't handle sharp objects. On the other hand, if a mountaineer is simply unafraid, that person shouldn't use ropes. It follows that every mountaineer either shouldn't handle sharp objects or shouldn't use ropes. [Ax = x is afraid; Cx = x is crazy; Mx = x is a mountaineer; Oxy = x should use/handle y; r = rope; s = sharp object] [Dom: {Mountaineers}]

2. Some, though not all, psychologists are Jung scholars. No Jung scholars are interested in the writings of either Mary Hesse or Judith Jarvis Thomson; Whoever is not a Jung scholar is interested in the writings of Freud. Hence, someone is interested in the writings of Freud. [Ixy = x is interested in the writings of y; Jx = x is a Jung scholar; f = Freud; j = Judith Jarvis Thomson; m = Mary Hesse] [Dom: {Psychologists}]

3. Anyone who interviews an I.R.A. soldier and runs for Parliament in Northern Ireland will be elected, since, anyone who interviews an I.R.A. soldier will be breaking British law, and anyone who breaks British law and runs for Parliament in Northern Ireland will be elected. [Bx = x breaks British law; Ex = x is elected; Ixy = x interviews y; Rx = x runs for Parliament in Northern Ireland; s = I.R.A. soldier]

4. Some team wants each athlete who is both strong and dedicated, and since every athlete is strong and dedicated, any athlete who is strong is wanted by some team. [Ax = x is an athlete; Dx = x is dedicated; Sx = x is strong; Wxy = x wants y]

5* No honest person lies to somebody. But, everybody either admires or lies to everybody. So, all honest people admire somebody. [Axy = x admires y; Hx = x is honest; Lxy = x lies to y]

8.5.2 Relations: Truth Trees

Truth trees on arguments involving relations are not very different from trees on "nonrelational" arguments. The method and the procedure are the same. The main point to keep in mind has to do with the universal and existential instantiations. As in natural deduction, one must not instantiate with respect to more than one individual constant in any given instantiation. One must also take care to flag all existential instantiations, proceeding with the restriction on that rule in mind. A few examples will help.

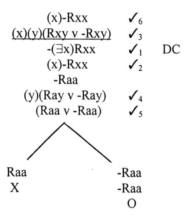

The first thing to notice here is that the argument is invalid. This is shown by the ring below the last occurrence of '-Raa' on the right hand branch. There are no contradictions on that branch and every formula that can be checked has been checked. The branch remains open. Second, there is no existential instantiation in this proof. Hence, no flags. Third, if one had chosen different letters to instantiate on, yielding, say 'Rab' and '-Rab,' still the tree wouldn't close. A second example:

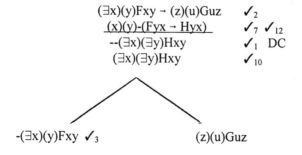

<pre>
(x)-(y)Fxy ✓₄   (y)-(Fyb → Hyb)
  -(y)Fay ✓₅   (∃y)Hay ✓₁₁ *a
  (∃y)-Fay ✓₆   Hac   *c
    -Fab *b   (y)-(Fyc → Hyc) ✓₁₃
(y)-(Fyb → Hyb) ✓₈   -(Fac → Hac) ✓₁₄
-(Fab → Hab) ✓₉   Fac
    Fab   -Hac
    -Hab   X
     X
</pre>

There are at least three interesting points to be made about this tree. First, on the right branch neither '(z)(u)Guz' nor '(y)-(Fyb → Hyb)' is checked. That is all right, since the branch on which those formulas occur closes without checking them. If the branch had remained open when all other formulas had been checked, then those formulas would also have had to be checked.

Second, note that 'a' is flagged on the right branch even though it occurs on the left branch. This is legitimate because we treat each branch as a separate entity, or, as in the rows of truth tables, as different interpretations. In short, the occurrences of 'a' on the left branch are not considered *prior* to the occurrences of 'a' on the right branch. Otherwise, the restriction which goes with the rule for existential instantiation would be violated.

Third, you will see that the second premise is checked twice. There is no restriction on universal instantiation. The second instantiation on the second premise was necessary for the closing of the right branch. The reason we could not use '(y)-(Fyb → Hyb)' is because we needed to use '(∃x)(∃y)Hxy' to close the branch and, since 'b' occurs prior to '(∃x)(∃y)Hxy' on that branch, i.e., in '(y)-(Fyb → Hyb),' we could not use 'b' on '(∃x)(∃y)Hxy.' Hence, we had to use some other individual constant; 'c' was chosen.

This third point brings up a matter regarding "double checking." You can double check both universal as well as existential quantifications. The restriction would be on the latter of these two, where you would have to instantiate with respect to a different constant on the second instantiation. For example, from '(∃x)(Rx v Bx)' you could derive both '(Ra v Ba)' as well as '(Rb v Bb).' The only restriction here would be that when you instantiate using 'a,' 'a' must not have appeared previously in the tree (or proof).

<pre>
(x)[Tx → (y)(-Sxy v -Hy)]   ✓₆
(∃x)[Tx • (y)(-Dy v Sxy)]   ✓₄ *j
    -(x)(-Hx v -Dx)   ✓₁ DC
    (∃x)-(-Hx v -Dx)   ✓₂ *i
    -(-Hi v -Di)   ✓₃
      --Hi
      --Di
   Tj • (y)(-Dy v Sjy)   ✓₅
</pre>

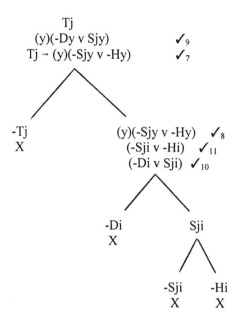

The crucial moves in the tree above are, once again, the instantiations. Since there are two existential sentences in the group (i.e., the second premise and the sentence derived from applying Quantifier Exchange to the denied conclusion), and since both of these sentences needed to be instantiated, two different constants were required. Once the letter 'i' was used, it could not be used again on the second premise. So, arbitrarily, the letter 'j' was used. Then, it was possible to instantiate using both 'i' and 'j' when the universal sentences were instantiated. It is important to remember that one cannot apply a truth tree rule to any quantified formula. For example, the first premise is a universal quantification, not a conditional. Hence, the tree rule for conditional does not apply to that sentence. One needs to instantiate the first premise before it becomes a conditional (to *make* it a conditional).

Exercise: Ch. 8, Sect. 8.5.2.

A. Determine whether the following arguments are valid or invalid using the method of truth trees.

1. (x)Dxx
    (x)Dxx → (y)Hyy
    (∃x)-Hxx

2. (x)(y)(Fxy v Gxy)
    (x)(∃y)-Gyx
    (∃x)(∃y)Fyx

3. [Srj ↔ (x)(y)Cxy]
    [Crj v (x)(y)-Eyx]
    [(x)(y)Cxy → -Erj]

4. (x)(y)(z)[(Rxy • Ryz) → Rxz]
    (x)-Rxx
    (x)(y)(Rxy → Ryx)

5.* -(x)-(y)Jxy → (z)Jzz
   (x)Jxx • (y)(z)-Jyz
   (y)Lyy

6. (x)(y)[Pxy → (z)Hzy]
   (x)(y)-(Pxy v -Hyx)
   (∃x)(y)-Hxy

7. -(x)(∃y)(Txy • -Wxy)
   (x)(y)(Wxx → Myy)
   (∃x)[(Txx ↔ Mxx) → -Wxx]

8. (x)(y)Dxy ↔ (∃x)-Ox
   (x)[Ox → (∃y)Ixy]
   (x)-Ox v (∃y)Oy

9. (x)(y)[Axy • (Gyx → Lyy)]
   (x)(y)-(-Lxy → Nxy)
   (x)(y)(Ayx → Nyy)
   (∃x)(∃y)(Gyx → Nxx)

10.*(x)(∃y)Kxy • (x)(y)Cyx
   (x)(y)-(Kxy • Jxy)
   (x)(y)[Cxy → (Jxy → Zxy)]
   (∃x)(∃y)(Zxy v Sxy)

B. Translate the following arguments into symbolic notation and determine the validity of each using truth trees.

1. All things bear some relation to each other. Whatever bears some relation to something else has something in common with that thing. Whatever has something in common with another thing is analogous to that thing. Hence, Jesus is analogous to Hitler. [Axy = x is analogous to y; Bxy = x bears some relation to y; Cxy = x has something in common with y; h = Hitler; j = Jesus]

2. So long as a person exists, he has not yet died, and once he has died, he no longer exists; so there seems to be no time when death, if it is a misfortune, can be ascribed to its unfortunate subject. (Thomas Nagel, "Death") [Do: Everything; Dict: Dx = x has died; d = death; Ex = x exists; Mx = x is a misfortune; Mxy = x is a misfortune for y]

3. Some, but not all, scientists are inductivists. No inductivist ever won a Nobel Prize. Some inductivists think they're the greatest. Hence, some scientists who have never won a Nobel prize think they are the greatest.
[Do: Scientists; Dict: Gxy = x thinks y is the greatest; Ix = x is an inductivist; Wxy = x won y; p = the Nobel Prize]

4. If any professional thief can open any bank safe, then since every metropolitan city has at least one professional thief, no bank is impenetrable. But, not every bank is penetrable. Therefore, not every thief can open every bank safe. [Bx = x is a bank; Cx = x is a metropolitan city; Hxy = x has y; Oxy = x can open y; Px = x is penetrable; Sx = x is a bank safe; Tx = x is a professional thief]

5.* If Folk Psychology can explain desires, then anything can. Every dualist system can explain desire and Folk Psychology is a dualist system. Now, Sociobiology is a materialist system. It follows that some materialist systems can explain desires. [Dx = x is dualist system; d = desires; Exy = x can explain y; f = Folk Psychology; Mx = x is a materialist system; s = Sociobiology]

C. Which of the following sentences are true and which are false?

1. 'Alice resembles Linda.' expresses a binary relation.
2. 'Alice walked up the hill with Everett.' expresses a ternary relation.
3. Translations can be made simpler, in some cases, by specifying a domain.
4. In predicate logic with relations, it is always necessary to work a quantifier exchange prior to either an existential or universal instantiation.
5.* A domain is a set of objects over which quantifiers and variables range.
6. It is never proper to specify "everything" as the domain.
7. '-(x)(y)Rxy' is a negated universal quantification.
8. '(x)-(y)Ryx' is a negated universal quantification.
9. If 'Fxy' = 'x fears y,' then '(x)(y)Fxy' and '(x)(y)Fyx' express the same sentence.
10.* Both (a) and (b) below follow from '(∃x)(y)Rxy':
    a. (Rcc v Rcd)
    b. [(Rcc v Rcd) • (Rdc v Rdd)]

8.6. Identity

Consider the following argument:

> Caleb and Faith both have brown eyes.
> Caleb and Faith are the only people in the cave.
> Hence, everyone in the cave has blue eyes.

Translating this argument into symbolic notation using only the symbols we have up to this point, we can see that the symbolic argument would be invalid. On our present system, where 'Bx' = 'x has brown eyes,' 'Cx' = 'x is in the cave,' 'Ixy' = 'x is identical with y,' 'c' = 'Caleb,' 'f' = 'Faith,' with {People} as the domain, we would translate the argument thus:

(Bc • Bf)
(x)[Cx → (Ixc v Ixf)]   ⊢   (x)(Cx → Bx)

The following counterexample will show that the *symbolized* argument is invalid. Domain: {0,1,2, . . .}; Dictionary: 'c' = '0'; 'f' = '0'; 'Bx' = 'x is even'; 'Cx' = 'x is odd'; 'Ixy' = 'x is greater than y.' However, since we know the original argument is valid, our translation must be inadequate. We can show the argument to be valid by adding one further symbol to our set, viz., the identity symbol ('=').

We need to be clear about what function the identity symbol is to have in our system. To that end, note that the verb "to be" is ambiguous. In the sentence "Bryon is shy," the 'is' is the "is of predication." That is, shyness is being predicated of Bryon and the proper translation would be "Sb." However, in the sentence "Michael Caine is Maurice Micklewhite," the 'is' is the "is of identity" since it *identifies* Michael Cain with Maurice Micklewhite. The proper translation of that sentence is "c = m."

Consider now the following argument and translation; let 'a' = 'Woody Allen'; 'Dxy' = 'x directed y'; 'w' = "*Whatever Works*"; 'k' = 'Allen Konigsberg.'

Woody Allen directed *Whatever Works*	Daw
Woody Allen is Allen Konigsberg.	a = k
Hence, Allen Konigsberg directed *Whatever Works*.	Dkw

To show this argument to be valid, we need to stipulate the appropriate rules for dealing with formulas/sentences such as "a = k." One such rule we will call the *Rule of Identity (ID)*, the schematic form of which is:

(. . . x . . .)
x = y ⊢ (. . . y . . .)

Another rule to be adopted now, the *Rule of Self-Identity (SID)*, says that the formula "(x)(x = x)" may be introduced as a new line of a proof in natural deduction, or may be introduced on a branch of a tree, at *any* time. The formula in question may be read as "everything is identical with itself."

The third rule we include here is the *Rule of Identity Symmetry (IS)*. This rule can be schematized with the following formula:

(x)(y)(x = y → y = x).

As with the Rule of Self-Identity, the formula for Identity Symmetry can be introduced as a new line of a proof, or on a branch of a tree, at any time.

We can now translate the argument about Caleb and Faith more precisely and hence show it to be valid, the proof of which follows.

1.	(Bc • Bf)	
2.	(x)[Cx → (x = c v x = f)] ⊢ (x)(Cx → Bx)	
3.	-(x)(Cx → Bx)	(A, DC)
4.	(∃x)-(Cx → Bx)	3, QE
5.	-(Ca → Ba)	4, EI *a
6.	[Ca → (a = c v a = f)]	2, UI
7.	-(-Ca v Ba)	5, MI
8.	(--Ca • -Ba)	7, DM
9.	Ca	8, Si, DN
10.	(a = c v a = f)	6,9, MP
11.	-Ba	8, Com, Si
12.	(-Bc v -Bf)	10,11, ID
13.	--Bc	1, Si, DN
14.	-Bf	12,13, DS
15.	Bf	1, Com, Si
16.	(Bf • -Bf)	14,15, Con
17.	(x)(Cx → Bx)	3-16, RAA

The Rule of Identity applied in line 12 is the crucial step allowing us to derive the contradiction. The tree below shows how the rule applies in truth trees.

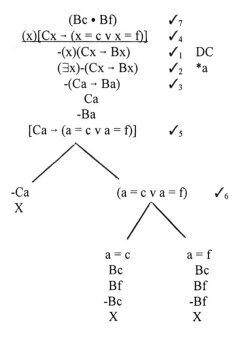

The sentences '-Bc' and '-Bf' at the very bottom of the branches of the tree are the result of applying the Rule of Identity using '-Ba' which resulted from '✓₃,' and 'a = c' on the left-hand branch, and 'a = f' on the right-hand branch. Note that neither 'a = c' nor 'a = f' are checked.

8.6.1. Translations With Identity

With the inclusion of the identity sign, we can translate many sentences that were closed to us before. Examples are below. A note is in order on the symbolization of *nonidentity*. There are two acceptable ways of indicating nonidentity symbolically: (x ≠ y) and -(x = y). The former of these will be used throughout the rest of the chapter.

Dictionary: Ax = x is/was an astronomer; Axy = x admired y; a = Aristotle; Bx = x is a biologist in this class; Cx = x is a chemist in this class; e = Einstein; g = Galileo; Lxy = x liked y; Nx = x is a novelist in this class; Px = x is/was a philosopher; p = Plato; Sxy = x was a student of y; s = Socrates.

There were at least two philosophers Aristotle admired.
$$(\exists x)(\exists y)[(Aax \bullet Aay) \bullet x \neq y]$$

There are at least three biologists in this class.

$(\exists x)(\exists y)(\exists z)\{[(Bx \bullet By) \bullet Bz] \bullet [(x \neq y \bullet x \neq z) \bullet y \neq z]\}$

There is at most one chemist in this class.

$(\exists x)[Cx \bullet (y)(Cy \rightarrow x = y)]$

There are at most two novelists in this class.

$(\exists x)(\exists y)\{(Nx \bullet Ny) \bullet (z)[Nz \rightarrow (z = x \vee z = y)]\}$

There was exactly one philosopher that Einstein admired.

$(\exists x)[(Px \bullet Aex) \bullet (y)(Aey \vee Py) \rightarrow x = y)]$

Galileo admired exactly two astronomers.

$(\exists x)(\exists y)\{[Ax \bullet Agx) \bullet (Ay \bullet Agy)] \bullet (z)[(Az \bullet Agz) \rightarrow (z = x \vee z = y)]\}$

Every philosopher except Plato admired Aristotle.

$(Pp \bullet -Apa) \bullet (x)[(Px \bullet x \neq p) \rightarrow Axa\}]$

Domain: {natural numbers}; Dictionary: Dxy = x is divisible by y; Ex = x is even; Gxy = x is greater than y; Ixy = x implies y; Lxy = x is less than y; Ox = x is odd; o = one; Px = x is prime; s = seven; t = two; z = zero.

All numbers are self-identical. $(x)x = x$

No two numbers are identical. $-(\exists x)-(\exists y)(x \neq y \bullet x = y)$

There is exactly one even prime.

$(\exists x)\{(Ex \bullet Px) \bullet (y)[(Ey \bullet Py) \rightarrow x = y]\}$

Two is less than every other prime. $(x)[(Px \bullet x \neq t) \rightarrow Ltx]$

Two is the only even prime. $\{(Et \bullet Pt) \bullet (x)[(Ex \bullet Px) \rightarrow x = t]\}$

Every number except zero is greater than zero. $(x)(x \neq z \rightarrow Gxz)$

One is divisible only by itself. $\{Doo \bullet (x)(x \neq o \rightarrow -Dox)]$

Zero, one, and two are different numbers. $[(z \neq o \bullet z \neq t) \bullet o \neq t]$

Two numbers are identical only if they imply one another.

$(x)(y)[x = y \rightarrow (Ixy \bullet Iyx)]$

If two is odd and seven is even, there are two numbers that are not identical.

$(Ot \bullet Es) \rightarrow (\exists x)(\exists y)x \neq y$

Numbers divisible by the same numbers are themselves the same.

$(x)(y)[(z)(Dxz \leftrightarrow Dyz) \rightarrow x = y]$

A number is prime if, and only if, it is divisible only by one and itself.

$(x)\{Px \leftrightarrow (y)[Dxy \rightarrow (y = x \vee y = o)]\}$

Domain: {Human Beings}; Dict: Axy = x admires y; Cx = x is clever; Dxy = x is more admired than y; Ex = x is an elf; Fxy = x fears y; Hxy = x hates y; Jxy = x is more jolly than y; Mxy = x is more famous than y; Nx = x was born in North Carolina; Px = x was the eleventh U.S. President; p = Plato; Rxy = x is more ruthless than y; Sxy = x was the student of y; Txy = x was the teacher of y.

The eleventh U.S. President was born in North Carolina.

$(\exists x)\{[Px \bullet (y)(Py \rightarrow (x = y))] \bullet Nx\}$

Everybody fears the most ruthless person in the world.

(∃x)[(y)(x ≠ y → Rxy) • (z)Fzx]

The most ruthless person fears every clever person.

(∃x)[(y)(x ≠ y → Rxy) • (z)(Cz → Fxz)]

If the most ruthless person is clever, that person fears her/himself.

(∃x){[(y)(x ≠ y → Rxy) • Cx] → Fxx}

No one hates the jolliest elf.

-(∃x){(y){(z)[((Ey • Ez) • y ≠ z) → Jyz] • Hxy}}

Plato's most famous student did not admire Plato's teacher.

(∃x){(y)[[(Sxp • Syp) • x ≠ y] → Mxy] • (∃z)[(u)(Tzp • (u = z)] → -Axz)}

The most famous of Plato's students is also the most admired.

(∃x)(∃y){(z)[(Sxp • Szp) • (x ≠ z → Mxz)] • (u)[y ≠ u → Dyu] • (x = y)}

Exercise: Ch. 8, Sect. 8.6.

A.   Show that the following arguments are valid using natural deduction.

1.   1.   (x)(Dx → Rx)
     2.   (x)(y)(Rx → x = y)
     3.   (∃x)(∃y)-(x = y) ⊢ (∃x)-Dx

2.   1.   (x)Fxj • -(∃y)Fyg
     2.   (x)(Fjx → x = g) ⊢ (y)Fyg

3.   1.   (∃x)(y)(y = x ↔ Ny)   ⊢ (x)Nx → (y)(∃z)y = z

4.   1.   (x)(∃y)(x = y)   ⊢ (x)(∃y)[(Jxy v Jxx) → Jyy]

5.* 1.   (x)(∃y)(Sxy v Syx)   ⊢ (x)(∃y)(x = y → Sxy)

6.   1.   (x)(y)(z)[(Rxy v Ryz) → Rxz]
     2.   (∃x)(y)Ryx   ⊢ (x)(y)(Rxy v x ≠ y)

7.   1.   (x)(y)(Fxy → Lxy)
     2.   (x)(y)[x = x → (-Gxy • -Lxy)] ⊢ (x)(∃y)[Fxy → (∃z)Gzy]
8.   1. (∃x)(y)[(x ≠ y → Hxy) • Wx]   ⊢ (x)[Wx v (∃y)(Hyx • x ≠ y)]

9.   1. (∃x)(y)(y = x ↔ Ky)   ⊢ (x)Kx → (y)(z)y = z

10.* 1. (x)(y)[(Axy • Ayx) → x = y]
     2. (x)(y)-(-Ayx • Axy)   ⊢ (x)[(∃y)(Ayx v Axy) → Axx]

B. Determine the validity of the following arguments via truth trees.

1. (∃x)(∃y)x ≠ y
    (x)(x ≠ f) → -Mx)
    (∃x)-Mx

2. (x)(y)(z)[(Qxy • Qyz) → Qxz]
    (∃x)(∃y)x = y
    (∃x)Qxx

3. (x)(y)(Exy v -Exy)
    (x)(y)(x ≠ y • -Eyx)
    (y)-Eyy

4. (x)Pxx • (y)(z)Pyz
    (x)(∃y)(x ≠ y → -Pyy)
    (∃x)(y)(Pxy → Kyx)

5.* (x)(∃y)(∃z)(x = y v x = z)
    (x)(y)(Sxy → -Gxy)
    (∃x)(∃y)(-Gyx → Sxy)

6. r = j
    (x)(y)(Ixy → Iyx)
    -(Ije • -Iej)

7. (x)[-Gx v -(y)-(Fxy • Ey)]
    (Gs • s = t)
    (x)(y)(Fxy → Fyx)
    (∃x)(Ex • Fxt)

8. (x)(y)(z)(Nyx → Nxz)
    (∃x)x = d
    (∃x)Nxx

9. a = b v a = c
    (x)(y)[Cy → (-Pxa → Kc)]
    (x)(y)(-Kx v -Pay)
    (∃x)Pxx

10.*(x)(y)[(-Rx • x = y) → Ry]
    (∃x)(∃y)x = y
    (∃x)(∃y)(Lxy → Rx)

11. (x)(∃y)Gyx ≠ Gxy
    (y)(∃x)Gxy = Gyy

12. [(a = b • b = c) → a = c]
    (x)(y)(z)(y = x • x = z)
    (c = b • a ≠ c)

Solutions to Selected Exercises

Chapter 1.

1.A.   5. False; 10. False; 15. True; 20. False

1.B.
5. *Premise:* I have not said anything that would rule out the possibility of someone's treating considerations as authoritative that would ordinarily be regarded as amoral, or morally eccentric, or even immoral.

Conclusion: A complementary objection would be that I have exaggerated the degree to which a fine-grained naturalistic view can accommadate traditional ideas about the authority of morality and it might be said that I have not given any reason to think that the considerations that are authoritative for an individual will always be moral considerations, in any plausible sense of that term.

10. *Premise #1:* Individuals of the same variety or sub-variety of our older cultivated plants and animals differ more from each other than do the individuals of any species or variety of the same nature.

Premise #2: There is a vast diversity of the plants and animals which have been cultivated, and which have varied during all ages under the most different climates and treatment.

Conclusion: This great variability is due to our domestic productions having been raised under conditions of life so uniform as, and somewhat different from, those which parent species had been exposed under nature.

15. *Premise #1:* Heat is a secondary quality, unlike solidity.
Premise #2: Secondary qualities are not in the objects themselves.
Conclusion Fire is not hot.

1.C.
5. There are two arguments in this passage:
   A. *Premise #1:* There are no pictures or conversations in the book.
   Premise #2: There is no use to a book without pictures or conversations.
   Conclusion: There is no use to the book.

230

B. *Premise #1:* There are no pictures or conversations in the book.
Premise #2: A book without pictures or conversations is boring.
Conclusion: Alice is bored.

10. There are two arguments in this passage.

A. *Premise #1:* The self presents itself as an organized whole, and integrated structure.

Premise #2: Experiences are related to one another not through but within the whole.

Conclusion: When the structure is modified the nature of the experiences and relationships between them are also modified.

B. *Premise:* The different experiential groups of the self are interdependent.

Conclusion: The self is a structure which is organized and makes sense" and each member occupies its proper place within the structure.

15. *Premise #1:* There are seven windows given to animals in the domicile of the head, through which air is admitted...

Premise #2: In the heavens, as in a macrocosmus, there are two favorable stars, two unpropitious, two luminaries, and Mercury undecided and indifferent.

Conclusion: The number of planets is necessarily seven.

20. There are two arguments in this passage.

A. *Premise #1:* Color is surface spectral reflectance (along with other objective wavelength phenomena).

Premise #2: These physical properties have certain additional characteristics only in relation to human perceptual apparatuses.

Premise #3: The color at a point (or small area) is a proportion of incident energy of each wavelength that is reflected at that point (or in that small area).

Premise #4: No point (or small area) can have two different colors simultaneously.

Premise #5: No point can simultaneously reflect different proportions of incident energy of a given wavelength.

Conclusion: Nothing can be (seen as) red and green all over at the same time.

B. *Premise:* No point (or small area) can have two different colors simultaneously.

Conclusion: No point can simultaneously reflect different proportions of incident energy of a given wavelength.

25. *Premise:* All societies of the Near East are now defunct.
Conclusion: All societies of the Near East had anthropologists.

1.D.

The following two arguments are counterexamples to the arguments presented in the exercise set.

5. Sting is either a singer or a bass guitarist.
   Sting is a singer.
   So, he isn't a bass guitarist..

10. No goats are Venusians.
    No mammals are Venusians.
    So, no goats are mammals.

Chapter 2.

5. Implied ad Baculum.
11. ad Populum.
18. ad Hominem Circumstantial.
25. ad Hominem *Tu Quoque.*
30. No Fallacy. This is a *conditional* sentence. Not an argument.
35. Deontic Fallacy, *if* the first sentence in this passage is offered as support for the second sentence. There is no conclusion indicator here and it is, therefore, it may be difficult for some people to judge.
40. Straw Person. This arguer has misrepresented Descartes' argument.

Descartes argued that we cannot *wholly* trust our senses. What this means, in Cartesian terms, is that knowledge gained through our senses does not afford us *absolute certainty.*

Chapter 3.

3.A.

5. $[(S \cdot -E) \to O]$

[E = England sees a threat to its own economy; O = The Orkney Islands will become an independent state; S = Scotland is willing to grant independence to the Orkney Islands]

10. $[-J \cdot (A \cdot -B)]$

[A = Janet apologizes profusely to Carla; B = Janet will borrow Carla's notes again; J = Janet will remember to return Carla's notes]

15. $[R \to (H v L)]$

[H = a high pressure front moves in with the jet stream tonight; L = a low pressure front moves in with the jet streasm tonight; R = It will rain tomorrow]

20. $\{(P \to E) v [(B \to P) \cdot -(B \to E)]\}$

[B = one understands Bohr; E = one understands Einstein; P = one obtains a Ph.D. in physics]

3.B.

5. Brahe rejected the Copernican theory only if he (Brahe) was not admired by Kepler.

10. If Copernicus was the father of astronomy, then if he held a heliocentric theory, then neither was Ptolemy the father of astronomy nor did Kepler admire Brahe.

15. If Brahe's rejecting the Copernican theory implies that Copernicus held a heliocentric theory, then Copernicus didn't contradict Ptolemy.

3.C.   5. True; 10. False; 15. True.

3.D.

Dictionary: C = the leaders are creative; I = production is increased; L = there are good students; R = there is such a thing as good teaching; W = the workers are satisfied.

5. If good teaching implies and is implied by the existence of good students, then there is such a thing as good teaching.

10. If creative leadership implies increased production, then that implication itself implies and is implied by satisfied workers.

Chapter 4.

4.2.A.

5. Disjunction; 10. Biconditional; 15. Conditional;
20. Negated Biconditional.

4.2.B.   10 & 20 are True; 5 & 15 are False.

4.3.A.   5 & 15 are L-true; 10 is L-false; 20 is L-Indeterminate.

4.3.B.   5, 10 & 20 are Incompatible; 15 is Contradictory.

4.3.C.   5 & 10 are True.

Chapter 5.

5.1.A.   5, 10, 15 & 20 are True.

5.1.B.   5, 10, 15 & 20 are Valid.

5.1.C.

5. Invalid
$[-O \rightarrow (G \bullet C)]$ $[O \bullet H) \rightarrow P]$ $(O \bullet J)$ $\vdash$ S
[C = we should concentrate on more down to earth matters than searching for truth; G = we should give up the search for truth; H = securing the truth would

help us solve many "down to earth"   matters; J = it is the job of the philosopher to seek the truth; O = it is possible to obtain/secure the truth; P =   we
should pay people to search for the truth; S = we should pay philosophers to
search for the truth]

    10. Invalid

        [(-C • B) → O] [-O → (C → E)] (-E v H) -H ⊢ O

    [B = the Britrail pass is good for eleven days; C = the cost of the London hotel is too expensive; E = we will stay in Edinburgh; H = we will visit Hume's birthplace; O = we will take our vacation in October]

    15. Valid

        (S v -T) (-P • --T) ⊢ S

    [P = no reputable publisher of a logic book would let the truth table for the conditional be correct; S = a conditional sentence is true when the consequent is true; T = the truth table is correct]

5.2. 5 & 20 are Valid; 10 & 15 are Invalid.

Chapter 6.

6.A.

    5 & 10 are Valid; 15 and 20 are Invalid.

6.B.

    5 is L-true; 10 is L-false; 15, 20 & 30 are L-indeterminate.

6.C.

    5. {[P • (Lo • Lr) v (-T • -L)}

       [T → (C • P)]

       [(-Rp • -Rl) → (-T • -L)]

       Rp   ⊢   M   Invalid

    10. [(R v L) → (F → B)]

       {-(F v S) → [R → (M v C)]}

       (F v R)

       -F   ⊢   [L • (M v C)]   Invalid

    15. [(-D • B) v W]

       [W → (B → R)]

       [-C → (D • B)]

       -C ⊢ R   Valid

    20. [R → (Ra • F)]

       [(-R → -P) → -M] ⊢ (-M → -R)   Invalid

Chapter 7.

7.4.A.

5.   3.   S
     4.   (S v Q)

10.   5.   -R
      6.   [H v (G ↔ L)]
      7.   (I → R)
      8.   -I

7.4.B.

5.   4.   3, Si
     5.   2,4 DS
     6.   1,5 MP

7.4.C.

5.   3.   (-L • J)   1, Si
     4.   -L   3, Si
     5.   --(S → I)   2,4 MP

10.   4.   R   3, Si
      5.   (S • T)   1,4 MP
      6.   S   5, Si
      7.   (U • V)   2,6 MP
      8.   [(S • T) • (U • V)]   5,7 Con

15.   4.   {(R → C) • [(R → C) → (B → K)]}   1,3 Con
      5.   [C v (B → K)]   2,4 CD

20.   4.   [D → (G ↔ S)]   1, Si
      5.   -D   3,4 MT
      6.   S   2,5 DS
      7.   (S v R)   6, Ad

7.5.A.

5.   3.   -(-N v -R)   1, MI
     4.   (--N • --R)   3, DM
     5.   --R   4, Com, Si
     6.   R   5, DN
     7.   W   2,6 MP
     8.   (W v N)   7, Ad

10.   3.   (-S • -E)   2, DM
      4.   -E   3, Com, Si
      5.   --[N v (M v O)]   1,4 MT
      6.   [N v (M v O)]   5, DN

7. [N v (O v M)]   6, Com
8. [--N v (--O v M)]   7, DN, DN
9. [-N → (--O v M)]   8, MI
10. [-N → (-O → M)]   9, MI

15. 2. [(Aa → Nn) • (Nn → Aa)]   1, ME
    3. (Aa → Nn)   2, Si
    4. (Nn → Aa)   2, Com, Si
    5. (Nn → Nn)   3,4 HS
    6. (Aa → Aa)   3,4 HS
    7. [(Aa → Aa) • (Nn → Nn)]   5,6 Con

20. 3. (--R • -L)   2, DM
    4. --R   3, Si
    5. (--R v -T)   4, Ad
    6. -(-R • T)   5, DM
    7. (Q v X)   1,6 DS
    8. [(Q v X) v T]   7, Ad
    9. [T v (X v O)]   8, Com, Com

25. 3. (-E v S)   1, MI
    4. [(-E v S) v -A]   3, Ad
    5. [-A v (-E v S)]   4, Com
    6. [(-A v -E) v S]   5, As
    7. [(-E v -A) v S]   6, Com
    8. [-E v (-A v S)]   7, As
    9. [E → (-A v S)]   8, MI
    10. [E → (A → S)]   9, MI

30. 4. --Y → --(Z → A)   1, Cp
    5. Y → --(Z → A)   4, DN
    6. Y → (Z → A)   5, DN
    7. -Y v (-B v A)   2, MI
    8. -Y v (Z → A)   6, MI
    9. -Y v (-Z v A)   8, MI
    10. (-Y v -Z) v A   9, As
    11. (-Y v -B) v A   7, As
    12. A v (-Y v -Z)   10, Com
    13. A v (-Y v -B)   11, Com
    14. [A v (-Y v -B)] • [A v (-Y v -Z)]   12,13 Con
    15. A v [(-Y v -B) • (-Y v -Z)]   14, Di
    16. (-Y v -B) • (-Y v -Z)   3,15 DS
    17. -Y v (-B • -Z)   16, Di
    18. Y → (-B • -Z)   17, MI
    19. Y → -(B v Z)   18, DM

7.6.

5.

4.	-N	(A)
5.	(--N v -A)	3, DM
6.	(N v -A)	5, DN
7.	-A	4,6, DS
8.	-C	1,7, DS
9.	(-N → -C)	4-8, RCP
10.	(--N v -C)	9, MI
11.	(N v -C)	10, DN

10.

3.	Z	(A)
4.	K	(A)
5.	(Z v -E) → T	1, Si
6.	(E → Y)	1, Com, Si
7.	-(--T v S)	2, MI
8.	(---T • -S)	7, DM
9.	-T	8, Si, DN
10.	-(Z v -E)	5,9 MT
11.	(-Z • --E)	10, DM
12.	--E	11, Com, Si
13.	E	12, DN
14.	Y	6,13 MP
15.	(K → Y)	4-14, RCP
16.	Z → (K → Y)	3-15, RCP

7.7.

5.

3.	-[(N • N) → F]	(A, DC)
4.	-[-(N • N) v F]	3, MI
5.	--(N • N) • -F	4, DM
6.	(N • N)	5, Si, DN
7.	-F	5, Com. Si
8.	-(N • U)	2,7, MT
9.	(-N v -U)	8, DM
10.	N	6, Re
11.	--N	10, DN
12.	-U	9,11, DS
13.	U v (-N v -N)	1, Com
14.	(-N v -N)	12, 13, DS
15.	-N	14, Re
16.	N v [(N • N) → U]	10, Ad
17.	[(N • N) → U]	15,16, DS
18.	-[(N • N) → U] → [(N • N) → U]	3-17, RCP

19. --[(N • N) → U] v [(N • N) → U]   18, MI
20. [(N • N) → U] v [(N • N) → U]   19, DN
21. [(N • N) → U]   20, Re

10.

3.	J	(A, DC)
4.	(I ↔ J)	1, ME
5.	(I → J) • (J → I)	4, ME
6.	(J → I) • (I → J)	5, Com
7.	(J → I)	6, Si
8.	-(--I v W)	2, MI
9.	-(I v W)	8, DN
10.	(-I • -W)	9, DM
11.	-I	10, Si
12.	I	3,7, MP
13.	(I v -J)	12, Ad
14.	-J	11,13, DS
15.	(J → -J)	3-14, RCP
16.	(-J v -J)	15, MI
17.	-J	16, Re

7.8.

5. 1. Zero Premises ⊢ (-N v D) v (N v -D)
    2. -[(-N v D) v (N v -D)]   (A, DC)
    3. -(-N v D) • -(N v -D)   2, DM
    4. -(-N v D)   3, Si
    5. (--N • -D)   4, DM
    6. -(N v -D)   3, Com, Si
    7. (-N • --D)   6, DM
    8. -N   7, Si
    9. N   5, Si, DN
    10. N v [(-N v D) v (N v -D)]   9, Ad
    11. (-N v D) v (N v -D)   8,10 DS
    12. -[(-N v D) v (N v -D)] → [(-N v D) v (N v -D)]   2-11, RCP
    13. --[(-N v D) v (N v -D)] v [(-N v D) v (N v -D)]   12, MI
    14. [(-N v D) v (N v -D)] v [(-N v D) v (N v -D)]   13, DN
    15. (-N v D) v (N v -D)   14, Re

10. 1. Zero Premises ⊢ [(-T → L) • -U] → (U → -L)
    2. -{[(-T → L) • -U] → (U → -L)}   (A, DC)
    3. -{-[(-T → L) • -U] v (U → -L)}   2, MI
    4. --[(-T → L) • -U] • -(U → -L)   3, DM
    5. [(-T → L) • -U] • -(U → -L)   4, DN
    6. (-T → L) • -U   5, Si
    7. -(U → -L)   5, Com, Si

8.	-(-U v -L)	7, MI
9.	(--U • --L)	8, DM
10.	U	9, Si, DN
11.	-U	6, Com, Si
12.	U v [(-T → L) • -U] → (U → -L)	10, Ad
13.	[(-T → L) • -U] → (U → -L)	11,12 DS
14.	-{[(-T → L) • -U] → (U → -L)} → {[(-T → L) • -U] → (U → -L)}	
		2-13 RCP
15.	--{[(-T → L) • -U] → (U → -L)} v {[(-T → L) • -U] → (U → -L)}	
		14, MI
16.	{[(-T → L) • -U] → (U → -L)} v -{[(-T → L) • -U] → (U → -L)}	
		15, DN
17.	[(-T → L) • -U] → (U → -L)	16, Re

15.	1.	Zero Premises ⊢ {R → [(S • -S) v R]}	
	2.	-{R → [(S • -S) v R]}	(A, DC)
	3.	-{-R v [(S • -S) v R]}	2, MI
	4.	--R • -[(S • -S) v R]	3, DM
	5.	--R	4, Si
	6.	-[(S • -S) v R] • --R	4, Com
	7.	-[(S • -S) v R]	6, Si
	8.	-(S • -S) • -R	7, DM
	9.	-R • -(S • -S)	8, Com
	10.	-R	9. Si
	11.	-R v {R → [(S • -S) v R]}	10, Ad
	12.	{R → [(S • -S) v R]}	5,11, DS
	13.	-{R → [(S • -S) v R]} → {R → [(S • -S) v R]}	2-12, RCP
	14.	--{R → [(S • -S) v R]} v {R → [(S • -S) v R]}	13, MI
	15.	{R → [(S • -S) v R]} v {R → [(S • -S) v R]}	14, DN
	16.	{R → [(S • -S) v R]}	15, Re

Chapter 8

8.2.A.

5. (∃x)(Mx • Bx) → Bh
10. (x)(Mx → Bx) → (∃x)(Cx • Bx)

8.2.B.

5. Music is either beautiful or not worth listening to.

10. It is false that whoever helped write *Porgy & Bess* could have written *Scheherazade*, but whoever wrote *Rhapsody in Blue* could have written *Scheherazade*.

8.2.C.

5. (x)(Mx → Sx)   15. (x)[(Cx • Ix) → -Mx]
10 -(∃x)(Ax • Ix)   20. -(x)[(Ix • Lx) → -Wx]

8.3.A.

4. 1.   (x)](Tx v Yx) • (-Ux v Yx)]
    2.   (x)-(-Yx → Ux)   ⊢ Tn
    3.   -Tn   (A,DC)
    4.   (Tn v Yn) • (-Un v Yn)   1, UI
    5.   -(-Yn → -Un)   2, UI
    6.   -(--Yn v -Un)   5, MI
    7.   (---Yn • --Un)   6, DM
    8.   (Yn v Tn) • (Yn v -Un)   4, Com,Com
    9.   [Yn v (Tn • -Un)]   8, Di
    10. -Yn   7, Si,DN
    11. (Tn • -Un)   9,10, DS
    12. Tn   11, Si
    13. (-Tn • Tn)   3,12, Con
    14. Tn   3-13, RAA

8.3.B.

5. 1.   (x)Fx → (x)Gx
    2.   (∃x)-Gx
    3.   (x)(Hx → Fx)   ⊢ (∃x)-Hx
    4.   -(∃x)-Hx   (A, DC)
    5.   -(x)Gx   2, QE
    6.   -(x)Fx   1,5, MT
    7.   (∃x)-Fx   6, QE
    8.   -Fa   7, EI *a
    9.   (Ha → Fa)   3, UI
    10. -Ha   8,9, MT
    11. (x)--Hx   4, QE
    12. --Ha   11, UI
    13. Ha   12, DN
    14. (Ha • -Ha)   10,12, Con
    15. (∃x)-Hx   4-14, RAA

8.3. C.

5. 1.   (x)[Kx v (Ax • Ix)]
    2.   (x)-(Ix v -Ax)   ⊣ -(x)-Kx
    3.   --(x)-Kx   (A, DC)
    4.   (x)-Kx   3, DN
    5.   -(Ie v -Ae)   2, UI
    6.   (-Ie • --Ae)   5, DM
    7.   [Ke v (Ae • Ie)]   1, UI
    8.   -Ke   4, UI

9. (Ae • Ie)   7,8, DS
10. Ie   9, Com, Si
11. -Ie   6, Si
12. (Ie • -Ie)   10,11, Con
13. -(x)-Kx   3-12, RAA

10. 1. (x)(Rx v Qx)
    2. (x)[Px v (-Qx • -Rx)] ⊣ (x)Px
    3. -(x)Px   (A, DC)
    4. (∃x)-Px   3, QE
    5. -Pn   4, EI *n
    6. [Pn v (-Qn • -Rn)]   2, UI
    7. (-Qn • -Rn)   5,6, DS
    8. (Rn v Qn)   1, UI
    9. -Rn   7, Com, Si
    10. Qn   8,9, DS
    11. -Qn   7, Si
    12. (Qn • -Qn)   10,11, Con
    13. (x)Px   3-12, RAA

15. 1. (x)[-(Bx → Cx) → -Ax]
    2. (x)[(Ax • Bx) v -(Bx v Ax)]
    3. (x)-(-Cx → -Dx)   ⊣   (x)-Ax
    4. -(x)-Ax   (A, DC)
    5. (∃x)Ax   4, QE
    6. Ag   5, EI *g
    7. -(-Cg → -Dg)   3, UI
    8. -(--Cg v -Dg)   7, MI
    9. -(Cg v -Dg)   8, DN
    10. (-Cg • --Dg)   9, DM
    11. (-Cg • Dg)   10, DN
    12. (Ag • Bg) v -(Bg v Ag)   2, UI
    13. -(Bg → Cg) → -Ag   1, UI
    14. (Ag • Bg) v -(-Bg v Ag) 12, MI
    15. (Ag • Bg) v (- -Bg • -Ag) 14, DM
    16. (Ag • Bg) v (Bg • -Ag)   15, DN
    17. [(Ag • Bg) v Bg] • [(Ag • Bg) v -Ag]   16, Di
    18. (Ag • Bg) v -Ag   17, Com, Si
    19. -Ag v (Ag • Bg)   18, Com
    20. --Ag   6, DN
    21. (Ag • Bg)   19,20, DS
    22. Bg   21, Com, Si
    23. -Cg   11, Si
    24. (Bg • -Cg)   22,23, Con

25.	-(-Bg v Cg) → -Ag	13, MI
26.	(--Bg • -Cg) → -Ag	25, DM
27.	(Bg • -Cg) → -Ag	26, DN
28.	-Ag	24,27, MP
29.	(Ag • -Ag)	6,28, Con
30.	(x)-Ax	4-29, RAA

20.
1.	(x)[-(Ux v Tx) v Xx]	
2.	(∃x)(Ux • Dx)	⊢ (∃x)Xx
3.	-(∃x)Xx	(A, DC)
4.	(x)-Xx	3, QE
5.	(Ua • Da)	2, EI *a
6.	-Xa	4, UI
7.	-(Ua v Ta) v Xa	1, UI
8.	(-Ua • -Ta) v Xa	7, DM
9.	Xa v (-Ua • -Ta)	8, Com
10.	(-Ua • -Ta)	6,9, DS
11.	-Ua	10, Si
12.	Ua	5, Si
13.	(Ua • -Ua)	11,12, Con
14.	(∃x)Xx	3-13, RAA

8.3.D.
5. Something is not art.
10. Nothing is non-natural.
15. Someone at the inn is not innocent.

8.3.E.
5.
1.	(Ec → Sc)	
2.	(Sc → Mc)	⊢ Ec → (∃x)Mx
3.	-[Ec → (∃x)Mx]	(A, DC)
4.	-[-Ec v (∃x)Mx]	3, MI
5.	[--Ec • -(∃x)Mx]	4, DM
6.	-(∃x)Mx	5, Com, Si
7.	(x)-Mx	6, QE
8.	(Ec → Mc)	1,2, HS
9.	-Mc	7, UI
10.	-Ec	8,9, MT
11.	Ec	5, Si, DN
12.	(Ec • -Ec)	10,11, Con
13.	Ec → (∃x)Mx	3-13, RAA

10
1.	(x)(Lx → Dx)
2.	(x)(Hx → Mx)
3.	(x)[Sx → (-Dx • -Mx)] ⊢ (x)[Sx → (-Lx • -Hx)]

4.	-(x)[Sx → (-Lx • -Hx)]	(A, DC)
5.	(∃x)-[Sx → (-Lx • -Hx)]	4, QE
6.	-[Sa → (-La • -Ha)]	5, EI *a
7.	-[-Sa v (-La • -Ha)]	6, MI
8.	--Sa • -(-La • -Ha)	7, DM
9.	Sa	8, Si, DN
10.	Sa → (-Da • -Ma)	3, UI
11.	(-Da • -Ma)	9,10, MP
12.	(La → Da)	1, UI
13.	(Ha → Ma)	2, UI
14.	(La → Da) • (Ha → Ma)	12,13, Con
15.	-(-La • -Ha)	8, Com, Si
16.	(--La v --Ha)	15, DM
17.	(La v Ha)	16, DN, DN
18.	(Da v Ma)	14,17, CD
19.	-(Da v Ma)	11, DM
20.	(Da v Ma) • -(Da v Ma)	18,19, Con
21.	(x)[Sx → (-Lx • -Hx)]	4-20, RAA

8.4.A.

5 is Valid; 10 & 15 are Invalid.

8.4.B.

5. Invalid
    (x)[Sx → -(Lx • -Lx)]
    (x)[(Sx • Lx) → Ax]
    -(∃x)[(Sx • Ax) • -Mx]
    -(∃x)[(Sx • -Lx) • Mx]

8.5.1.A.

5. (∃x)(y)Axy • -(∃x)(y)Ayx
10. (x)(y){[(Px • Py) • Txy] → (z)Sxz}

8.5.1.B.

5. 1. (∃x)(∃y)Fxy ⊢ (∃x)(∃y)Fyx
    2. -(∃x)(∃y)Fyx   (A, DC)
    3. (∃y)Fmy   1, EI *m
    4. Fmp   3, EI *p
    5. (x)-(∃y)Fyx   2, QE
    6. -(∃y)Fyp   5, UI
    7. (y)-Fyp   6, QE
    8. -Fmp   7, UI
    9. (Fmp • -Fmp)   4,8, Con

10. (∃x)(∃y)Fyx   2-9, RAA

10. 1. (x)-Pxx
    2. (x)(y)(Pxy → Pyx)
    3. (x)(y)(z)[(Pxy → -Pyz) → Pxz] ⊢ (x)(y)-[Pxy → (z)(Pzx → Pzy)]
    4. -(x)(y)-[Pxy → (z)(Pzx → Pzy)]   (A, DC)
    5. (∃x)-(y)-[Pxy → (z)(Pzx → Pzy)]   4, QE
    6. -(y)-[Pay → (z)(Pza → Pzy)]   5, EI *a
    7. (∃y)[Pay → (z)(Pza → Pzy)]   6, QE
    8. [Pab → (z)(Pza → Pzb)]   7, EI *b
    9. (y)(z)[(Pay → -Pyz) → Paz]   3, UI
    10. (z)[(Pab → -Pbz) → Paz]   9, UI
    11. (Pab → -Pba) → Paa   10, UI
    12. -Paa   1, UI
    13. -(Pab → -Pba)   11,12, MT
    14. -(-Pab v -Pba)   13, MI
    15. (--Pab • --Pba)   14, DM
    16. Pab   15, Si, DN
    17. (z)(Pza → Pzb)   9,16, MP
    18. (Pba → Pbb)   17, UI
    19. --Pba   15, Com, Si
    20. Pba   19, DN
    21. Pbb   18,20, MP
    22. -Pbb   1, UI
    23. (Pbb • -Pbb)   21,22, Con
    24. (x)(y)-[Pxy → (z)(Pzx → Pzy)]   4-24, RAA

8.5.1.C.
    5. 1. (x)(∃y)(Hx → -Lxy)
    2. (x)(y)(Axy v Lxy)   ⊢   (x)(∃y)(Hx → Axy)
    3. -(x)(∃y)(Hx → Axy)   (A, DC)
    4. (∃x)-(∃y)(Hx → Axy)   3, QE
    5. -(∃y)(Hr → Ary)   4, EI   *r
    6. (y)-(Hr → Ary)   5, QE
    7. (∃y)(Hr → -Lry)   1, UI
    8. (Hr → -Lrt)   7, EI   *t
    9. -(Hr → Art)   6, UI
    10. -(-Hr v Art)   9, MI
    11. (--Hr • -Art)   10, DM
    12. Hr   11, Si, DN
    13. -Art   11, Com, Si
    14. -Lrt   8,12, MP
    15. (y)(Ary v Lry)   2, UI
    16. (Art v Lrt)   15, UI

17. Lrt	13,16, DS
18. (Lrt • -Lrt)	14,17, Con
19. (x)(∃y)(Hx → Axy)	3-18, RAA

8.5.2.A.

5 & 10 are Valid.

8.5.2.B.

5. Efd → (x)Exd
    (x)(Dx → Exd) • Df   Valid
    <u>Ms</u>
    (∃x)(Mx • Exd)

8.5.2.C.

5 is true; 10 is false.

8.6.A.

5.
1. (x)(∃y)(Sxy v Syx) ⊢ (x)(∃y)(x = y → Sxy)	
2. -(x)(∃y)(x = y → Sxy)	(A, DC)
3. (∃x)-(∃y)(x = y → Sxy)	2, QE
4. -(∃y)(r = y → Sry)	3, EI *r
5. (y)-(r = y → Sry)	4, QE
6. (∃y)(Sry v Syr)	1, UI
7. (Src v Scr)	6, EI *c
8. -(r = c → Src)	5, UI
9. -(r ≠ c v Src)	8, MI
10. --(r = c) • -Src	9, DM
11. r = c	10, Si, DN
12. -Src	10, Com, Si
13. Scr	7,12, DS
14. Scc	11,13, ID
15. Src	11,14, ID
16. (Src • -Src)	12,15, Con
17. (x)(∃y)(x = y → Sxy)	2-16, RAA

10
1. (x)(y)[(Axy • Ayx) → x = y]	
2. (x)(y)-(-Ayx • Axy) ⊢ (x)[(∃y)(Ayx v Axy) → Axx]	
3. -(x)[(∃y)(Ayx v Axy) → Axx]	(A, DC)
4. (∃x)-[(∃y)(Ayx v Axy) → Axx]	3, QE
5. -[(∃y)(Ayc v Acy) → Acc]	4, EI *c
6. -[-(∃y)(Ayc v Acy) v Acc]	5, MI
7. --(∃y)(Ayc v Acy) • -Acc	6, DM
8. (∃y)(Ayc v Acy)	7, Si, DN
9. -Acc	7, Com, Si
10. (Awc v Acw)	8, EI *w

11. (y)[(Awy • Ayw) → w = y]	1, UI
12. (Awc • Acw) → w = c	11, UI
13. (y)-(-Ayw • Awy)	2, UI
14. -(-Acw • Awc)	13, UI
15. (--Acw v -Awc)	14, DM
16. (-Acw → -Awc)	15, MI
17. (--Awc v Acw)	10, DN
18. (-Awc → Acw)	17, MI
19. (-Acw → Acw)	16,18, HS
20. (--Acw v Acw)	19, MI
21. (Acw v Acw)	20, DN
22. Acw	21, Re
23. (y)-(-Ayc • Acy)	2, UI
24. -(-Awc • Acw)	23, UI
25. (--Awc v -Acw)	24, DM
26. (-Acw v Awc)	25, Com, DN
27. --Acw	22, DN
28. Awc	26,27, DS
29. (Awc • Acw)	22,28, Con
30. w = c	12,29, MP
31. Acc	28,30, ID
32. (Acc • -Acc)	9,31, Con
33. (x)[(∃y)(Ayx v Axy) → Axx]	3-33, RAA

8.6.B.

5 is Invalid; 10 is Valid.

GLOSSARY

This glossary is designed to give the reader partial understanding of how certain terms are used throughout the text. It is not designed to give either very detailed or complete information. For that, it is requisite that the reader consult the appropriate chapter(s), designated by the numbers in parentheses.

Acceptable argument: An argument that is taken to have true premises which lead to a conclusion either conclusively or with a high degree of probably. An argument that could lead one to action. (1)

Accident: An informal fallacy occurring when one applies a general rule incorrectly to a specific case or in a specific situation. (2)

Antecedent: The component in conditional sentences that implied the consequent. Example: 'A' is the antecedent in '(A → B)'. (1, 3)

Argument: A series of sentences, one of which (the conclusion) is intended to follow from the other(s) (premises) either conclusively or with a high degree of probability. (1)

Argumentum ad Baculum: An informal fallacy occurring when one person threatens another person in order to persuade the second person to accept some conclusion. (2)

Argumentum ad Hominem/Abusive: An argument directed toward a person in which the arguer attacks the character of the person in an abusive manner. An informal fallacy. (2)

Argumentum ad Hominem/Circumstantial: An argument directed toward a person in which the arguer attacks the person by pointing out the special situation the person is in. An informal fallacy. (2)

Argumentum ad Hominem/Tu Quoque: An argument directed toward a person in which the arguer accuses the person of having said or done something similar to what the arguer allegedly said or did. An informal fallacy. (2)

Argumentum ad Ignorantiam: An informal fallacy occurring when one states that nothing is or can be known about some object and then states something that is known about the object. (2)

Argumentum ad Misericordiam: An informal fallacy occurring when one appeals to a listener's feeling of pity for some person(s) in order to get the listener to accept some conclusion or other. (2)

Argumentum ad Populum: An informal fallacy occurring when one appeals to a listener's desire or need to be 'one of the group' to get the listener to accept some conclusion or other. (2)

Argumentum ad Vericundiam: An informal fallacy occurring when one appeals exclusively to the authority of a person to get some conclusion or other accepted. (2)

Arrow: Logical symbol ('$\rightarrow$') used to designate conditional sentences. Example: $(A \rightarrow B)$. (3,4,5,6,7,8)

Bar: Logical symbol ('-') used to designate negative sentences. Examples: -A, $-(A \vee B)$. (3,4,5,6,7,8)

Begging the question: See Petitio Principii

Biconditional sentence: A compound sentence in which the components are said to imply one another. Example: The Yankees will win if, and only if, they play the Orioles. In symbolic terms, the biconditional is expressed as follows: $(A \leftrightarrow B)$. (3,4,5,6,7,8)

Checked formula/sentence: In truth trees, a sentence to which a rule has been applied. (6,8)

Closed branch: In truth trees, a closed branch is a branch on which there exists an explicit contradiction. (6,8)

Composition: An informal fallacy occurring when one argues that because something is true of the parts of some whole it is therefore also true of the whole itself. (2)

Compound sentence: A sentence consisting in two or more simple sentences. Example, where 'John plays ball' and 'Julie plays chess' are each simple sentences, then 'John plays ball and Julie plays chess' is a compound sentence. (3)

Conclusion: The sentence in an argument that follows, or is supposed or intended to follow, from a number of other sentences, called the premises. (1)

Conclusion indicator: A word or phrase, e.g., 'hence', 'therefore', etc., marking the presence of the conclusion in an argument. (1)

Conditional sentence: A conditional sentence in which one sentence is said to imply or entail another sentence. (All)

Conjunct: A component sentence in a conjunction. Example: 'A' and 'B' are conjuncts in '(A • B)'. (3)

Conjunction: (Conjunctive Sentence) A compound sentence in which it is asserted that both components are true. Conjunctions contain one or more occurrences of conjunctive terms such as 'and', 'but', 'yet', 'however', etc. Example: The Giants won the game and Mays hit two home runs. (3)

Consequent: The component in conditional sentences that is implied by the antecedent. Examples: 'it will rain' is the consequent in 'if the wind blows from the north, then it will rain'; 'B' is the consequent in '(A → B)'. (1)

Contradictory sentences: Two sentences are contradictory if and only if they have opposite truth values under all interpretations. Contradictory sentences cannot both be true at the same time and cannot both be false at the same time. Example: 'All musicians listen to the Beatles' and 'Some musicians do not listen to the Beatles'. (4,5,6,7,8)

Contradiction: A contradiction is committed either when one asserts a logically false sentence or when one asserts any sentence and its negation as both true or both false. (4,5,6,7,8)

Contraposition: A method of inference in Aristotelian Logic holding for certain sentences whereby the subject term is replaced by the negation of the predicate term and the predicate term is replaced by the negation of the subject term. Also, an Axiom of Replacement in Natural Deduction whereby the antecedent in a conditional is replaced by the negation of the consequent and the consequent is replaced by the negation of the antecedent. (7,8)

Counterexample: An argument designed to show the invalidity of a different argument by having the precise form of the other argument, but which has true premises and a false conclusion. (1)

Deontic fallacy: An informal fallacy occurring when one draws a conclusion which is prescriptive in nature based only on descriptive statements as premises. (2)

Disjunct: The component sentences in disjunctions. Example: 'A' and 'B' are disjuncts in '(A v B)'. (3)

Disjunction: (Disjunctive sentence) A sentence in which it is asserted that one or the other of two sentences is true. Disjunctions contain one or more occurrences of disjunctive terms such as 'or', 'neither/nor', 'unless', etc. Example: 'Either the Braves will win or the owners will be mad'. (3)

Division: An informal fallacy occurring when one argues that because something is true of the whole of some object it is also true of the parts of the whole. (2)

Dot: Logical symbol ('•') used to designate conjunctions. Example: (A • B). (3,4,5,6,7,8)

Double arrow: Logical symbol ('↔') used to designate biconditionals. Example: (A ↔ B). (3,4,5,6,7,8)

Double hollow arrow: Logical symbol ('⇔') used to designate sentences which are logically equivalent. Example: '(A v B) ⇔ (B v A)' indicates a logical equivalence between '(A v B)' and '(B v A)'. (7,8)

Equivalent sentences: Two sentences are said to be equivalent if and only if they are true under the same interpretations *and* false under the same interpretations. Example: (A → B) and (-A v B) are equivalent. (4)

Equivocation: An informal fallacy occurring when one uses a word or phrase in two or more senses (meanings) within the same sentence or paragraph (in the same context). (2)

Existential quantifier: The logical symbol designated by words and phrases such as 'some' and 'a few'. The logician takes its literal meaning to be 'there exists at least one'. The symbolic representation for 'there exists at least one x' is '($\exists$x)'. (8)

False cause: An informal fallacy occurring when one draws a conclusion on the basis of an erroneous causal relationship. (2)

Hasty generalization: An informal fallacy occurring when one argues to a generalization on the basis either of atypical cases or an insufficient number of cases. (2)

Incompatible sentences: Sentences that have the same truth values under some interpretations and different truth values under other interpretations. Example: '(A v B)' and '(A ↔ B)' are incompatible sentences. (4)

Individual constant: See Name Letter.

Inductive argument: An argument in which the conclusion follows from the premises with *some* degree of probability above 0.0 and below 1.0. (1)

Infinite tree: A truth tree that will never close, no matter how many instantiations are made. (8)

Instantiation: The process of replacing instances of variables with individual constants. Example: '(Ai v Bi)' is an instantiation of the quantified sentence "(x)(Ax v Bx)". (8)

Interpretation: Each row in a truth table, each branch in a truth tree, and each instantiation, is considered an interpretation. (6,8)

Invalid argument: An argument in which it is possible for the premises to be true and the conclusion false. (All)

Law of Excluded Middle: The 'law of thought' expressing the fact that every sentence is either true or false and that no sentence is both true and false. (4)

Limited alternative: An informal fallacy occurring when an arguer suggests/presents a lesser number of [obvious] alternatives than there actually are. (2)

Logic: The study of correct and incorrect reasoning. The study of techniques used to distinguish valid from invalid arguments. (All)

Logically false sentence: A sentence that is true under no interpretations. A logically false sentence is self-contradictory. Example: '(A • -A)'. (4)

Logically indeterminate sentence: A sentence that is true under some but not all interpretations. A sentence which is neither logically true nor logically false. Example: '(A → B)'. (4)

Logically true sentence: A sentence that is true under all interpretations. Example: '(A v -A)'. (6)

Name letter: The logical symbol (a lower case letter from 'a' to 'o') representing an individual or constant, e.g., 'a' in 'Ra'. (8)

Necessary Condition: In a conditional sentence, the necessary condition is represented by the consequent. Example: In '(A → B)', 'B' is the consequent, and is, hence, a necessary condition for 'A'. (3)

Open branch: In truth trees, an open branch is a branch that does not contain a contradiction when all formulas on the branch that can be checked have been checked. (6,8)

Petitio Principii: A fallacy occurring when one assumes the very conclusion for which one is arguing. Alternatively, also occurring when one fails to make explicit a premise that is at the heart (usually very controversial) of the issue/point about which one is arguing. (2)

Predicate: In symbolic logic, 'R' in 'Ra' is the predicate. In natural language, the predicate indicates what is said about an individual or object, e.g., in 'Catheline is an architect', ''is an architect' is the predicate. (8)

Predicate letter: In symbolic logic, the symbol (an upper case letter) which represents the predicate, e.g., 'R' in 'Ra'. (8)

Premise(s): The sentence(s) in an argument designed to provide support for a further sentence, called the conclusion. (1)

Premise indicator: A word or phrase, e.g., since, marking the presence of a premise in an argument. (1)

Primary connective: In a symbolized sentence the primary connective is the connective with the widest scope, i.e., ranges over all other symbols in the sentence. Example: In '[(A • B) → C]' the arrow is the primary connective. (6)

Proof: A formal demonstration of the validity of an argument in Natural Deduction. (7,8)

Quantifier: A word, phrase, or logical symbol in a sentence that indicates the quantity of class membership. Example: In 'Some plums are red', the term "some" is the quantifier term. In symbolic terms, in '(x)Lx', '(x)' is the quantifier. '(x)' can be read as "given any x". (8)

Quantifier Exchange: The process of replacing one quantifier form with another, equivalent, quantifier form. Example: '-(x)Rx' can replace or be replaced by '(∃x)-Rx' at all occurrences. (8)

RAA: Abbreviation, in proofs, for '*Reductio ad Absurdum*'. (7,8)

RCP: Abbreviation, in proofs, for 'Rule of Conditional Proof'. (7)

Reductio ad Absurdum: A method of determining validity in which one assumes the conclusion to be false and attempts to derive a contradiction using the premises in conjunction with the denied conclusion. Alternatively, a rule stating that if the conclusion of a given argument is assumed to be false and a contradiction results, then the original argument is valid. (6,7,8)

Rule of Conditional Proof: In Natural Deduction, the use of a rule whereby one assumes any sentence (φ), derives another sentence (ψ) through a finite number of applications of the rules of inference and/or axioms of replacement, then closes the scope of the assumption, after which a further sentence (χ) is derived, in the form of a conditional in which 'φ' is the antecedent and 'ψ' is the consequent. (7)

Self-contradiction: A logically false sentence. (4,5,6,7,8)

Simple sentence: A sentence expressing essentially one idea. (5)

Sound argument: Any argument that is valid and has true premises. (1)

Subordinate connective: Any connective in a symbolized sentence that is not the primary connective. Example: In '[(A • B) → -C]' both the dot and the bar are subordinate connectives. The arrow is the primary connective. (6)

Sufficient condition: In a conditional sentence, the sufficient is represented by the antecedent. In '(A → B)', 'A' is the sufficient condition for 'B'. (3)

Tautology: A logically true sentence. Examples: (A v -A), (A → A). (1,3)

Translation: A replacement of a sentence in natural language, e.g., English, with a sentence in symbolic notation. (3,4,5,6,7,8)

Translation dictionary: A dictionary for sentence letters used in translating sentences from natural to artificial language. (3.4.5,6,7,8)

Truth functional connective: The words or phrases, e.g., and/or/if and only if, connecting the simple sentences in conjunctions, conditionals, disjunctions, and biconditionals. In symbolic form, the truth functional connectives are represented by the arrow, dot wedge, bar and double arrow. (3,4,5,6)

Truth table: A method by which arguments are shown to be valid or invalid and by which sentences are shown to be logically true, logically false, or logically indeterminate. (4,5)

Truth tree: A method by which arguments are shown to be valid or invalid and by which sentences are shown to be logically true, logically false, or logically indeterminate. (6,8)

Truth value: In truth functional logic (sentential logic), which is a two-valued system, the values are 'truth' and 'falsehood'. In truth tables, we assign 't' for true (truth) and 'f' for false (falsehood). A sentence has the truth value 'true' if the sentence is true and has the value 'false' if it is false. (4,5)

Universal quantifier: The universal quantifier is designated by words and phrases such as 'all', 'every', 'each', 'no', 'none', 'not any'. The symbolic representation is '(x)', which can be read as 'for all x' or 'given any x'. (2,8)

Valid argument: Any argument in which it is impossible for the premises to be true while the conclusion is false. (All)

Variable: In symbolic logic, a letter (e.g., x, y, z) used as a placeholder for individual constants. Example: (x)Ax. (8)

Wedge: Also known as the 'vee' or the '*vel*'. Logical symbol used to designate disjunctions. Example: '(A v B)'. (3,4,5,6,7,8)

Truth Tables

(p • q)	(p v q)	(p → q)	(p ↔ q)	-p
t t t	t t t	t t t	t t t	f t
t f f	t t f	t f f	t f f	t f
f f t	f t t	f t t	f f t	
f f f	f f f	f t f	f t f	

Truth Tree Rules

Conjunction
(p • q)
  p
  q

Negated Conjunction
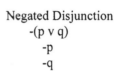
-(p • q)

Disjunction

(p v q)

Negated Disjunction
-(p v q)
  -p
  -q

Conditional

(p → q)

Negated Conditional
-(p → q)
  p
  -q

Biconditional

(p ↔ q)

Negated Biconditional
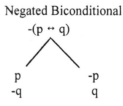
-(p ↔ q)

Double Negation
--p
p

Rules of Inference

Modus Ponens
(p → q)
p ⊢ q

Modus Tollens
(p → q)
-q ⊢ -p

Disjunctive Syllogism
(p v q)
-p ⊢ q

Simplification
(p • q) ⊢ p

Hypothetical Syllogism
(p → q)
(q → r) ⊢ (p → r)

Addition
p ⊢ (p v q)

Constructive Dilemma
[(p → q) • (r → s)]
(p v r) ⊢ (q v s)

Conjunction
p
q ⊢ (p • q)

Axioms of Replacement

DeMorgan's Theorems
-(p v q) ⇔ (-p • -q)
-(p • q) ⇔ (-p v -q)

Commutation
(p • q) ⇔ (q • p)
(p v q) ⇔ (q v p)

Material Implication
(p → q) ⇔ (-p v q)

Contraposition
(p → q) ⇔ (-q → -p)

Material Equivalence
(p ⇔ q) ⇔ [(p → q) • (q → p)]
(p ⇔ q) ⇔ [(p • q) v (-p • -q)]

Replication
p ⇔ (p • p)
p ⇔ (p v p)

Association
[p • (q • r)] ⇔ [(p • q) • r]
[p v (q v r)] ⇔ [(p v q) v r]

Double Negation
p ⇔ --p

Distribution
[p v (q • r)] ⇔ [(p v q) • (p v r)]
[p • (q v r)] ⇔ [(p • q) v (p • r)]

Exportation
[(p • q) → r)] ⇔ [(p → (q → r)]

Rule of Conditional Proof

α   assumption
·
·
·
β
$(α → β)$

Reductio ad Absurdum (Ch. 8)

-α   assumption (denial of conclusion)
·
·
·
$(β · -β)$ explicit contradiction
α   conclusion

Rules for Quantifier Exchange

$(x)fx ⇔ -(∃x)-fx$ $-(x)fx ⇔ (∃x)-fx$

$(∃x)fx ⇔ -(x)-fx$ $-(∃x)fx ⇔ (x)-fx$

Rules for Instantiation

Universal Instantiation: $\dfrac{(x)fx}{fa}$

Existential Instantiation*: $\dfrac{(∃x)fx}{fa}$ *Restriction: 'a' must not have occurred prior to the line of instantiation.